Koufax

KOUFAX

D# 22071

by Sandy Koufax

with Ed Linn

New York | The Viking Press

First published in 1966 by The Viking Press, Inc.
625 Madison Avenue, New York, N.Y. 10022

Published simultaneously in Canada by
The Macmillan Company of Canada Limited

Library of Congress catalog card number: 66-19162
Printed in U.S.A.

Frontispiece photograph courtesy Wide World Photos, Inc.

Second Printing October 1966

Contents

Koufax

1

Will I Ever Play the Violin Again?

I have nothing against myths. But there is one myth that has been building through the years that I would just as soon bury without any particular honors: the myth of Sandy Koufax, the anti-athlete. The way this fantasy goes, I am really a sort of dreamy intellectual who was lured out of college by a bonus in the flush of my youth and have forever after regretted—and even resented—the life of fame and fortune that has been forced upon me. Since I have never done a thing to indicate that I don't like being a ballplayer, the myth also has to say that I am mightily concerned about projecting a sparkling All-American image—presumably so that nobody will suspect how much I really dislike what I am doing. Look, if I could act that good I'd have signed with 20th Century-Fox instead of Brooklyn, and I'd be able to resent a life of fame and fortune on the Silver Screen.

If I don't want to be a ballplayer, what *do* I want to be? According to the myth, I have always burned to be an architect. To prove how intellectual I am, I am supposed to read Aldous Huxley and Thomas Wolfe, and listen to Beethoven, Bach, and Mendelssohn. In the ten or so years I have been seeing this nonsense the names have never changed. I have never seen any writers listed except Huxley and Wolfe, or any composers except Beethoven, Bach, and Mendelssohn. Poor Brahms apparently couldn't make the squad.

Actually I *have* read enough books to know that there are

themes that appeal to writers. There's the one about the sensitive man longing to lead the monkish, contemplative life for which he is best suited by nature—enjoying good music, reading the masters—who is doomed by a freakish physical ability to suffer through life as a national hero amidst the howling mobs, winning a success which he despises but cannot somehow give up. Because where else, after all, could he earn that kind of money?

It's a wonderful theme, all right. Somebody should write a play about it. And somebody, of course, has. Clifford Odets. The hero-victim of Odets's play, *Golden Boy,* wanted to be a violinist rather than an architect, and was tricked into becoming a fighter rather than a ballplayer. But those are only technicalities. Having a fighter in the lead role makes things considerably easier dramatically, because all Odets had to do was have his fighter break his hand in the ring, thereby ending the career as a fighter and the dream of becoming a great violinist all in one great blow.

If this *Golden Boy* theme has been imposed upon me more and more these last few years, it may well be that my troubles with my finger and my elbow have reminded some people—consciously or subconsciously—of the poor doomed fighter.

Give it to me straight, Doc, will I ever be able to build a glass skyscraper on Fifth Avenue?

Just between you and me, I think I'd enjoy being a doomed, tragic figure as much as anybody. The only trouble with this tale of one man's struggle against his inner nature is that none of it is true. I wish my reading tastes were classier, but they happen to run to the best-seller list and the book-club selections.

We always did have music around the house when I was growing up, and I enjoy all music, from classical to pop. I have built a hi-fi unit in my own home and there is almost always music playing in the background. If you dropped in unexpectedly, however, there'd probably be a show tune or a Sinatra album on the turntable rather than either Mendelssohn, Beethoven, or Bach.

But far from being a non-athlete before I signed with the Dodgers, I had no interest as a boy in anything *except* sports. The conversation at our house usually ran:

"Where are you going, Sandy?"

"Out."

"What are you going to do?"

"Play."

As a student, I was—to give myself all the best of it—indifferent. Throughout most of my school years I was one of those kids who was just bright enough to be able to get by without bringing any books home. The only time I ever buckled down to anything like serious studying came when my mother threatened to cut me off from all sports unless my grades improved.

I never had any overwhelming ambition, then, to be an architect, or, for that matter, to be a doctor, a lawyer, or an Indian chief. What did I want to be? I don't know. In all high-school class books the prospective graduates list their goals in life. Alongside my picture—to make me wince—it says only: "To be successful and make my family proud of me," a line which I cite here not to show what a good and dutiful boy I was but to indicate that I didn't have the slightest idea what I wanted to be.

The only honor you will find for me is that I was voted the Boy Athlete of the Year.

The story about my thirst to become an architect came about because my uncle is an architect, and I had worked one summer in his office, performing such stimulating tasks as operating the blueprint machine and sharpening pencils. And so I knew that if I left college with a degree in architecture there was somebody in this world who *had* to hire me.

Even then, I enrolled at the University of Cincinnati, which I was attending on a basketball scholarship, as a liberal-arts major rather than an architecture major—although I did intend to move over to the architectural school before I was through. And I did study architecture at Columbia University for one semester at the end of my first year with the Dodgers.

I was at Cincinnati, I was aware, only to play basketball, and so when, to my utter astonishment, I began to get offers to play baseball in the major leagues I felt I owed it to myself to find out whether I could really do it.

All I did in leaving college was to swap basketball, which had been my first love, for baseball.

What offends me about the myth, aside from its sheer falsehood, is that it makes me sound as if I feel I'm above what I'm doing, which is an insult not to me but to all ballplayers. I *like* what I'm doing. I find that pitching, both as an art and a craft, is endlessly demanding and endlessly fascinating. There were times in the early years when I wondered whether I was ever going to make it. At one period of my career I was so discouraged that I was ready to give it all up. But never for a moment did I regret having given myself the chance.

Wake me up in the middle of the night, ask me what I am, and I will tell you rather proudly, "I am a big-league pitcher."

Following the 1965 World Series, *Time* magazine managed to gather together all the myths into one great orgy of mythmaking, which speaks very well for their research files if not for their overwhelming passion for accuracy.

Just to give you the flavor of it, they inserted me into their story with the rather provocative line, "Just because a man does his job better than anybody else doesn't mean that he has to take it seriously—or even like it."

That is a statement which is almost too absurd to answer. But I will. There are those who are kind enough to say that I am the best pitcher in baseball. I may not sing and dance and yell "Whoopee," but does anybody really think that anybody could do anything well if he didn't enjoy doing it? What is there in life, when you come right down to it, except the chance to try to do whatever you do better than anybody else can do it?

Having opened with a flat statement of their own, they closed by proving their point out of my own mouth. In answer to a question about whether I wasn't thrilled and excited, I had apparently said, "I'm just glad it's over and I don't have to do this again for four whole months."

4

It should have been perfectly obvious—to anybody not pushing the *Golden Boy* theme—that I was saying I was almost too tired to be excited. Since I had not missed a turn since April and had just finished a tough game, after only two days of rest, I was perhaps entitled to make that much of a show at being weary.

Anybody at the game could see how I leaped up at the final out, throwing my arms out in pure boredom, beaming in sheer distaste. . . .

Nor did they neglect my intellectual background. My parents, they decided, were "a little taken aback when Sandy decided to spend his life throwing a ball around." "To this day," they said, "baseball is never discussed in the Koufax household."

To this day, little else is discussed in the Koufax household. When I first signed with Brooklyn, those many years ago, I told the writers quite frankly that I had never thought of playing baseball professionally, because I was primarily a basketball player. No, I said in answer to the questions, baseball wasn't discussed around the house. In going through the files, somebody apparently decided that what was true when I had no thought of becoming a baseball player was still true after I had been playing big-league baseball for eleven years.

I can assure you that, although my mother had never seen a baseball game before I became a Dodger, she became a red-hot fan practically overnight. I assure you that my mother and father take the same pleasure in my success that your mother and father take in yours.

And I can assure you that one of my own great joys out of that somewhat belated success has been the pleasure it has given my parents and everyone else who knew me in the old days or helped me along the way.

But *Time* magazine knows that I am an anti-athlete "who suffers so little from pride that he does not even possess a photograph of himself."

If you walk into my den you are overwhelmed by a huge, immodest action painting (it's reproduced on the jacket of this book) showing me in four successive positions of my delivery. It was given to me by friends, I like it, and I do not hide it away in the closet.

On the side wall are the MVP Award and the two Cy Young Awards.

I have stacks of postcard-size pictures of myself to send out to the kids who write in for autographs.

I'd invite the writer from *Time* down to see it all, but I'm sure he'd get the wrong address too.

I'm used to that kind of nonsense by now, of course—in fact, I sometimes feel that I should have said originally that I wanted to be a doctor so they could use all the jokes. What griped me about their story was that they painted me as a stranger in my own clubhouse. The writer did not seem to understand that when John Roseboro says I'm "cool" he does not mean that I'm cold and aloof. If I were running a mass-circulation magazine, I'd be tempted to lay down a flat edict that any editor not familiar with the current usage of the word "cool" should be encouraged to find some other way of earning a living.

And so what was meant, in all probability, as a compliment, came out as a sort of bewildered disapproval, not only by John —who happens to be one of my best friends—but by the whole ball club.

To tie it all up, Fresco Thompson, one of the Dodger vice presidents, was quoted by *Time* as saying, "What kind of a line is he drawing anyway—between himself and the world, between himself and the team?"

Fresco told me he never said anything like that, and, since he is a vice president and I am a hired hand, he has no particular reason to lie to me. *What line?* I go home after the game, like everybody else. I live in a five-room ranch house instead of an apartment because I have found that I'd rather live in a house than in an apartment.

For as long as I can remember, I have been playing sports, and for as long as I can remember, my best friends have been my teammates. The camaraderie of the locker room is one of the greatest pleasures you get out of the life of a ballplayer.

Belonging to a baseball club is like being a member of a social club such as the Rotary Club or the Knights of Columbus. Only more so. Instead of dropping in every Wednesday night to listen to the minutes of the last meeting and shoot some pool, you are out with the boys every night.

In other ways, however, a ball club is nothing at all like a social club. We are from widely differing backgrounds and we have widely differing outside interests. If it were not for this one common bond, an ability to play baseball better than almost anybody else in the country, it is rather unlikely that any two of us would ever have met. But the difference means nothing. There is among us all a far closer relationship than the purely social one of a fraternal organization because we are bound together not only by a single interest but by a common goal: to win! Nothing else matters, and nothing else will do. A winning clubhouse after the game is one of the rare places where you will find thirty people smiling happily.

And there's even more to it than that. What we have is something of the *esprit* of the members of an infantry platoon that has been through the battles and has known what it is to bury its dead. No matter how successful any individual player may be at any moment, we all know there are days of grief for him ahead. We all know that if you play this game long enough, it —just rr—is going to humble you.

In baseball there is no politics, no jockeying for position. Not because we are a superior breed of cat but only because politicking and jockeying are irrelevant to our success. No publicity man can add one point to your batting average, and no friendly critic can take away one loss from your pitching record. We have an absolute democracy—or maybe it's an aristocracy—of ability. You either make your contribution to the over-all effort, or you can go home.

Even the player who isn't getting the chance he thinks he deserves knows very well that it is only because the manager, in his honest opinion, doesn't believe he can do the job. Because the manager's job, even more than the players', hangs upon whether he wins or loses.

A baseball career is temporary, yes. But that does not mean that the baseball world is an unrealistic world. Quite the contrary. In many ways it is the most realistic world of all.

In baseball you have to accept your defeats, not rationalize them. You cannot turn your losses into victories. When you haven't got it, you know you haven't got it because there is, unhappily, no earthly way to rationalize a curve ball that doesn't break.

Nor are there any handy little face-saving devices for the pitcher who has allowed five hits and two walks in two-thirds of an inning. You can go back to the locker room and hope that your teammates get you off the hook, but the record is there in the box score for all the world to see. When you win, there is a W before your name. When you lose, there is that big black L, and not all the perfume in the world can wash it away. Of all the sad words of tongue or pen, the saddest to me are these: *Losing pitcher, Koufax*.

There is simply no way that you can look at that box score and work things around so you can convince yourself that you won even a moral victory. There *are* no moral victories in the statistics. If your record at the end of the year is 18–12, you cannot separate a 1–0 loss from a first-inning shelling. You cannot even cop out by blaming a teammate for making an error, because the same teammate has quite probably saved you a game a couple of starts earlier by making a sparkling play on a ball he had no right to get close to.

And that's what makes baseball so fascinating too. It is a game played by human beings. Baseball is exciting because what happens in the next minute is not only in your own hands but in the laps of the gods. I won a 10-inning, 1–0 ball game last year when Roberto Clemente, one of the very best defensive outfielders in the league, dropped a fly ball. *Roberto Clemente*. If I waited for that to happen again, I'd have the rest of my life mapped out for me.

But that's the beauty of the game. If you knew what every hitter could hit and what every fielder could field, this game would be easy. If every player were that consistent, you could feed the information into a computer and find out who was going to win the pennant before the season began. Instead, the only rule of life in the National League seems to be that the team that's picked to win the pennant won't. The Dodgers could be picked to win the pennant in 1964 and finish in the second division, and then be picked to finish in the second division in 1965 and come back to win the pennant.

The same ball can be hit by the same batter to the same person on consecutive days, and on one day he will make the play and the next day he won't. In the second game of the 1965 World Series, Versalles hit a ground ball that went off Junior Gilliam's glove and into left field, and I was in trouble. In the final game Gilliam made a great play on a ground ball hit by Versalles—a far more difficult chance—and I was out of trouble.

What is true of hitters and fielders is even more true of pitchers. On one day the ball seems light, and your rhythm is so perfect that the baseball almost seems to be an extension of your body. Not only can you feel yourself at work, you seem to be able to observe yourself at work. The next start, you come up absolutely empty, and every pitch seems to be thrown against the grain. Why? I wish I knew.

I don't want to leave the impression that I enjoy everything about the life of a baseball player. I could very easily do without the endless traveling and the suitcase living, I don't enjoy spending three days out of four *not* playing ball, and I am not particularly thrilled about finding myself working on what has become a night job. In my first year in baseball the Dodgers set a league record by playing twenty-nine night games at home. In 1965 we played fifty-six night games in Los Angeles.

Most clubs play double-headers on Sunday and have Mondays off, not because of any labor-management agreement, but only because most clubs cannot draw enough people on a Monday night to make expenses. Los Angeles fans have been so great that we have been able to fill the park with a single game on Sunday and draw quite adequately on Monday night.

You can pray for rain, of course, but it doesn't do you any good. We never get rained out in Los Angeles, as the Chamber of Commerce will happily attest. As the season progresses, Sunday night—the one night you can call your own—takes on an enormous importance in your life.

But these are only the irritations, the occupational hazards of our particular profession. The game itself is something else again. If it were only the baseball, I'd enjoy playing for the rest of my life. The actual pitching—I love it. I love it when it's going good, when the rhythm is with you and you're doing everything you want out there. And I love it when I've got nothing and I'm struggling to survive. Because that's exactly what it becomes—survival. It's scuffling and sweating and trying a little of this and a little of that to hang in there until the rhythm comes back to you. When you have your stuff, you *should* win. But when you can end up winning, not on the strength of your arm, which is after all a gift from the heavens, but on the strength of your brains and your experience and your knowledge, it is a victory that you feel belongs peculiarly to yourself.

And that brings me to the final point. The whole meaning of the anti-athlete myth I've been talking about here is that I do not like baseball because it is an essentially adolescent game that does not satisfy some kind of intellectual curiosity I'm supposed to possess. Let me make a couple of points about that.

1. Baseball is not a game to professionals. Baseball is only a game when you can wake up on a Sunday morning, lie back comfortably, and decide whether or not you feel like going down to the park. A professional doesn't even think in terms of "a game of baseball," he thinks in terms of a day's work of baseball.

When I get into a taxicab to go to the park, the driver and I are working men together. If either of us has a bad day we're going to have that much more trouble making a living. When a pitcher says, "I hate all hitters, they're trying to take the bread and butter out of my mouth," he is not just playing with clichés. He means it.

2. I now have to add very quickly that you are not really playing for money any more than a writer writes for money or an artist paints for money. Pitching to me is an art in the sense that the driving force, the original motivation, is the pride you have in yourself. When an artist paints a portrait, he does it for himself. Once the canvas is complete, he tries to get the best price he can, just as a ballplayer lays his record on the table at the end of the season and tries to negotiate the best contract he can. But that comes after the fact and is as completely divorced from the actual performance as the act of painting is from the showing in the museum.

If a man walked up to the plate thinking, "If I get two hits I'll make more money," or went to the mound thinking, "If I win this game, it's worth an extra thousand to me," he would not get the hits or win the game. I don't know why that should be so, but I am convinced that it is. The batter must want to get the hits because his pride pushes him to show how good he is—the same motivation that pushed him on the playgrounds. The pitcher must want to win every ball game because the central point of his life is his conviction that he is a good pitcher.

Branch Rickey's dictum about "the hungry player" being the best player may have been true once, but it is not true today. Any player who has been around for five or six years is making a pretty good salary. He has the degree of security that is possible in this line of work. He goes on and he stays to the end, because—well, because of the same image of himself that sends marathoners running twenty-six miles for a bowl of porridge. Because this is what he does best.

These are men who have always dreamed of being big-leaguers. They are men who are in that most fortunate of all positions: they are doing the one thing in life they would rather do than anything else. *That's* what pushes them.

3. Baseball is not the simple game so many people seem to

think it is. There is a misconception—and for some reason a growing one—that there is nothing happening on the field that is not visible to the naked eye. That isn't so. The subtleties of positioning on each batter are observed by very few fans; the pitcher's success or failure in getting the batter to hit according to the positioning of his fielders, by even fewer.

If baseball becomes boring to a fan, it isn't because he can see everything that's going on; it is because you have almost had to play big-league ball yourself to have an understanding of what is taking place beneath the surface.

Consider this situation: I am locked in a pitching battle, there are two outs, nobody on base, and the number eight hitter is at bat. The number eight hitter is hardly one of the most fearsome hitters in the lineup, and, even if he should get on base, the pitcher is coming up. It is a lazy part of the game for the fan. Even the most rabid Dodger rooter would be relaxed.

But not from where I'm standing. I want this batter, and I want him bad. I don't want to have to face the pitcher this inning; I want him leading off the next inning, because if we can get the first man out we have taken a lot of things away from the other team. We have taken away the bunt and gone a good way toward taking away the hit-and-run. We have made it far less likely, certainly, that they can get a man on third with less than two outs, from where he can score on a fly or a ground ball.

We have also completely removed the possibility that they can score on a double play. (I lost my first World Series start, 1–0, precisely that way.)

But I want the pitcher leading off the inning for another reason, too. I'm not thinking of just the next inning now; I'm thinking two innings ahead. If I can retire the side in order in the next inning, I will have their number three hitter—their best hitter—leading off the following inning, and that is precisely where I want him.

Now that may seem like a complete contradiction of everything I have been saying. Since I have just finished explaining how important it is to get the first man, why would I want, say,

Willie Mays, leading off an inning? Not only does Willie have the best possible chance of getting on, he is a dangerous man on the base paths.

But something else is involved here now that is just as important in the over-all swing of the game as getting the lead-off man. Dangerous as Mays is leading off, he is even more dangerous with men on base. Willie Mays, Hank Aaron, and Roberto Clemente hit their .300 year in and year out because— well, because they can hit. That means they are going to get their share of hits off me too. I know that not only from the statistics but from experience. If they are up at bat with men on base often enough, those hits are going to drive in runs. In point of fact, they become even better hitters with the game on the bases, because great hitters have a way of rising to the occasion. They become better hitters with men on base for another, purely technical reason, too. When hitters of this caliber are up with nobody on base, they might tend to go for the long ball. The harder the batter swings, the better the chance of getting him out. With men on base, they will be trying to make sure they get a piece of the ball, since it only takes a single to drive in a run.

Anyone who observes baseball with any regularity is aware that the rhythm of most ball games swings on how many men are on base when the big hitters come up. If you can get the Mayses, Aarons, Clementes, and Robinsons up there time and again with nobody on, the other team's offense is not nearly as potent.

Ideally, I'd like Mays up there with nobody on and two men out. But that means the inning would have to start with the lead-off man, which happens to be the situation the opposing manager has selected as the best possible way for *him* to start an inning. No, I'm much better off getting the pitcher up there in front of the lead-off man at the start of an inning, which—all things being equal—is tantamount to giving the other team only two outs in the first inning of the game. Especially if its a pitcher who hits like I do.

So for two very good reasons that number eight hitter, who

looks so meaningless from the stands, has become for me one of the key batters in what might be called the management of the ball game.

I think I've made it fairly clear by now that I don't like to see my profession degraded unnecessarily. I don't want to exalt it unduly either. I do not think the ballplayer is of any extraordinary importance in our national life. We do not heal the sick or bring peace and comfort to a troubled world. All we do is provide a few hours of diversion to the people who want to come to the park, and a sort of continuing interest in a harmless sort of conflict to those who identify their fortunes with ours through the season.

And yet, though the game of baseball itself is an entertainment, I don't think ballplayers are really entertainers. An entertainer works directly with his audience, adjusting his performance to its reactions. The audience is the second party. We are in a contest—every one guaranteed to be a bit different—and we adjust ourselves not to the reactions of the spectators but to the actions and reactions of the opposing team. The spectators are a third party.

The difference, I would suppose, is found somewhere in those two words: audience and spectators. The customers come to hear the entertainer perform; they come to watch us live a part of our lives.

By its nature, it is a brief, self-liquidating life. It is a temporary life, really, a period between the time of our youth and the beginning of a lifetime career. If there are those who think it is a frivolous life, an essentially meaningless life, I cannot agree with them. All I can say to anybody who finds himself in a position similar to the one I was in back in 1954 is, "Come on aboard. You'll have a helluva time."

2

Where the Games Were

I always had a strong arm. When I was a little kid I was aware that any time I got into a snowball fight I could retreat back to where I could pepper the other kids and they couldn't come close to reaching me. Very useful. Playing baseball on the sandlots, I could make long throws from the outfield. That wasn't very useful because I didn't particularly like to play the outfield. In high-school basketball we had a play where I would take the ball out of bounds after the other team had scored and rifle a length-of-the-court pass to a forward who had broken for the other hoop. (I drove the coach crazy by sometimes rifling the ball over the kid's head and off the wall or backboard.)

I'm not boasting about it because there's nothing to boast about. It wasn't anything I *accomplished;* it was just something I could do.

But, as you can see, I always associated the strength of my arm with distance, never with speed. If you had asked me if I could throw farther than any other kid on the block, I'd have said, "I sure can." If you had asked me whether I could throw faster, I'd have just scratched my head and looked bewildered.

I didn't pitch a game of baseball until I was fifteen years old, and that was purely accidental and quickly forgotten. I didn't become a pitcher on anything like a regular basis until I was seventeen. I didn't think for a moment about pitching professionally until a big-league scout told me, somewhat to my amazement, that I could get a bonus.

I was born in the Borough Park section of Brooklyn on December 30, 1935, the son of Jack and Evelyn Braun. My parents were divorced when I was three, and my mother married Irving Koufax when I was nine. When I speak of my father, I speak of Irving Koufax, for he has been to me everything a father could be.

My childhood was divided into three parts: the period before my mother remarried, a brief stay on Long Island, and my high-school years after we moved back to Brooklyn. To me the difference in geography was only a difference in the games we played. I was a street kid—"street," in this sense, meaning the schoolyard, the playground, the parks, the beaches, the community centers. I went where the games were.

Most people seem to have a wholly false impression of Brooklyn. The Brooklyn of my youth, it seems to me, was a collection of small middle-class neighborhoods, each with its own very distinctive tone and style. You traveled five blocks in any direction and you were, in a manner of speaking, in another small town.

My mother, who is an accountant, had to go out to work, and so when I was very young we lived with my grandparents. My grandfather, Max Lichtenstein, was a plumber who had managed to buy some real estate and was, it seems to me, relatively comfortable. He was a remarkable man. He loved good music and the theater and the movies. His great boast was that he had spotted Paul Muni as a young boy named Muni Weisenfreund in his first appearance in the Yiddish theater and had immediately predicted that he was going to be a great star.

I spent most of my time really with my grandparents. On Saturday morning I'd be up almost with the dawn, so that I could go to the beach for a swim before breakfast. Then we'd set out for the day, my grandfather and I, for the theater or the movies or a concert.

When I wasn't with my grandparents, I was out on the

streets. The buildings were privately owned single- and double-story wooden houses, with what we called "stoops" in Brooklyn, although they seem to be called porches every place else. Leading up to the stoops were three or four steps on which the younger kids would play stoop ball—throwing the ball against the steps until somebody's mother came out and kicked you away.

The rules were very strict. The official ball, the only ball ever used, was a small hard pink rubber ball that would really fly if you could catch the edge of the step. Although it had the name "Spalding" plainly printed across its middle, it was known without fail—any group of kids, any neighborhood—as "a Spal-*deen*," with the last syllable hit as hard as possible. The pronunciation was important; it gave the game its special flavor and gave us players a special status. By hitting the last syllable so hard, we made it seem—kids being great fancifiers—as if we were hard guys playing with a hard ball.

Besides, the special pronunciation made it *our* ball. Little kids are always getting pushed around, and this was one thing that belonged to us and us alone.

I still see small pink balls in variety stores and drugstores, and I always wonder whether the kids still call them spal-*deens*. If they don't, they're not really playing the same game we played. They are just throwing a ball against some steps.

From stoopball you graduated into stickball and punchball. In punchball you stuck to the spal-*deen*; in stickball you used an old tennis ball because the seams let you pretend it was really a baseball. Stickball and punchball, for the outlanders, are almost the same game except that in punchball you hit the ball from out of your own hand with your fist, while in stickball (when it is played in the street) the ball is served up to you on the bounce and you hit it with a small bat or broomstick.

In both games you had full teams if you had enough kids around. If you didn't you just did the best you could. The bases were probably the fender of a car on one side of the street and a hydrant on the other, with a sewer cover for second base.

17

The ball, being fairly soft, could not be hit for any great distance, and if you hit one that covered two sewers you were a man of distinction among your peers.

Mothers left you pretty much alone. You were now battling automobiles and cops.

In my neighborhood we had our own special stadium for our own special brand of stickball, the schoolyard of PS 103 (my first alma mater). At the far end of the school building there was a sort of open court. Painted onto the wall behind it was a rectangular strike zone of rather arbitrary size. The batter stood in front of the strike zone, and the pitcher whipped the ball in on the fly and was entitled to put as much stuff on it as he could.

The strike zone would become faded and weatherbeaten, but just as it seemed as if it were about to fade completely away we would come to the playground and find it painted over freshly. In my entire career at PS 103 neither I nor any of my friends ever saw anyone actually paint it, and we could only assume that it was done by the bigger kids. It didn't seem possible that the school janitor could be doing it, because it was an article of our faith—to say nothing of our enjoyment— that our game was frowned upon by the school authorities, a belief to which we were most certainly entitled, since on rare occasions a ball would hit the protective screening in front of the windows at just the right angle so that it would pop through the screen and break a pane.

But who knows? I suppose it is possible that the school authorities, aware that the spice would go out of the game if we did not believe we were defying authority, had it painted over secretly in the dark of night.

There was one very important rule in the game. If you hit the ball onto the roof you were out. The reason it was so important was that if the ball didn't come back down, the game was over. Unless, of course, one of the bigger kids, in a fit of big-brotherhood, could be persuaded to shinny up the drainpipe and get it for us. The first great heroes in my life were the kids who could go scooting up and down the drainpipe like monkeys. Most of the time, though, the bigger kids were our enemy, and a far tougher enemy than mothers or cars. Any time they wanted the court for themselves, they just swept us away.

One of the older kids was my next-door neighbor, Butch, whose sister was my babysitter. He is known these days as Buddy Hackett, and he just might be the funniest man alive.

I never played with Buddy, of course, because he was four or five years older than I was. When he had nothing else to do, though, he'd clown around with us kids on the stoop. Even in those days, when he was perhaps thirteen or fourteen years old, he was always performing. To get right down to it, he was the "nutty kid" of the neighborhood. To my grandmother, who never could quite appreciate his talents, he was known as "the meshugana," as in "get off my stoop and go bother someone else, you meshugana." That approach proving ineffective, she took to simply opening the window and pouring water down on him whenever he made an appearance. After that kind of basic training, I'm sure he was ready for the hecklers in the Catskills.

Shortly after my mother remarried, we moved. My uncle, Sam Lichtenstein, had been doing some architectural work out in Rockville Centre, and he ended up by buying a two-story home. He and his family moved into the second floor, and we moved into the first.

Rockville Centre is only nineteen miles from Manhattan, which makes it, by today's standards, practically on the outskirts of the city. In those days, with the postwar building boom just getting under way, it was considered to be way "out on the Island." And it really was open territory with a fresh, countrified atmosphere.

We lived right across the street from the high school, which meant that the games moved from the streets to the high-school field. The games became baseball in the summer and football in the fall. No leagues. No supervision. Just fun and bruises. As far as baseball was concerned, I suppose I played every position except pitcher.

Whatever the season, I would lose myself completely in the games and get home late for supper. Since my mother was rushing home from work to prepare a hot supper, she would become understandably annoyed. But I had an ally. When my mother remarried I had got myself not only a father but a sister, Edith, a few years older than I.

Edie would try to keep me out of trouble by touring the playgrounds for me. She didn't always find me. I'd come running in, sweaty and dirty, after everybody else was at the table and I'd be saying, "I'm sorry . . . I'm sorry . . . I'm sorry. . . ." It finally got to the point where as soon as I'd come through the door they would all look up from the table and begin to chant, "I'm sorry . . . I'm sorry . . . I'm sorry. . . ."

The great moment of my life in Rockville Centre came when my grandparents presented me with a bicycle, a maroon Rollfast, for my tenth birthday. It is the only bike I have ever owned, and it was to me a thing of incredible beauty. I've had cars and I've won a couple of Corvettes for my World Series performances, and I can say without boasting that there are few cars I cannot afford to buy today. But there will never be another vehicle in my life like my maroon Rollfast. An automobile is only a means of transportation. A bike to a ten-year-old boy is a magic carpet and a status symbol and a gift of love.

It can also be hazard to life and limb. I was riding my magic carpet to a Halloween party at twilight, and I apparently rode into a cross-section just as the light was turning yellow. All of a sudden there was an automobile bearing down on me. I swerved, the car caught me on the knee, and down I went. When I tried to get up I found I couldn't walk. A crowd had collected and somebody—probably the woman who had hit me—-drove me home.

My folks had gone out for the evening themselves by then, so my uncle drove me a couple of blocks to a doctor's office. Once the doctor had determined that there were no bones broken, he bandaged the leg up and instructed me to stay in bed for three or four days.

By the time I got home again, I was pretty shook up. I

asked my sister to tell my folks what had happened and immediately went to sleep.

Edie apparently wasn't too eager to break the news.

The next morning my mother came into my room as usual to get me up for school.

"Didn't Edie tell you?" I asked.

"Tell me what?"

"That I got hit by a car and—"

Down went my mother in a dead faint.

The bad knee ruined the whole football season for me and was hardly an aid and comfort in the compulsory physical training–hygiene class in school. There were all kinds of physical tests that had to be passed before you could get your credit, and I was so anxious to pass with flying colors that I kept trying to take them before the knee had healed, which only served to keep it from getting better.

I persevered, though, and eventually made up all the tests I had originally failed or missed. Then the report cards came out and I found I had been flunked anyway. I had been so concerned about passing all the physical tests that I had forgotten to bring in my dental completion note.

I may have a couple of diamond belts from Hickok to prove that I was voted the Athlete of the Year of 1963 and 1965, but I'm sure the Morris School in Rockville Centre is unimpressed. And why not? They can look right in their records and see that I couldn't pass an elementary course in physical training.

There is one other vivid memory that remains from my days in Rockville Centre, an even more unpleasant one than the bicycle accident. My parents both worked in Manhattan and took the same commuter train home. One winter evening I came running in, late as usual, but for once there was nobody at the table waiting for me. Edie, looking worried, was standing by the radio. There had been a terrible accident in the Rockville Centre station, she told me. The commuter train my folks almost always came home on had gone through a stop signal and collided head-on with an empty train traveling in the other direction.

We huddled by the radio, really frightened, listening to the bulletins about the crash. Dead bodies were being carted away. Welders were cutting through the wreckage to rescue the people still trapped inside. The known dead already numbered in the twenties, and the toll was still going up. Blood plasma was being rushed to the scene. The injured, already over a hundred, were overtaxing the facilities of the hospital.

When the phone finally rang, I'm sure we thought it was the hospital or worse. It was, thank God, my mother telling us that they had just barely missed the train at Penn Station. The wreck had quite naturally stopped all the through traffic behind it, and the passengers had been taken back to New York.

The same thing had happened to them two months earlier when a couple of empty trains had collided, killing some railroad men. Commuting on the Long Island Railroad seemed to be becoming rather hazardous.

We moved to the Bensonhurst section of Brooklyn on the day I graduated from the ninth grade of school. Actually, the rest of the family moved in the morning. I had stayed on to finish out the day, and when my last class ended I went right to the station, boarded a train, and went looking for my new home.

We had moved into what was known as a 608 project, a sort of housing development alongside the Belt Parkway. The buildings were three-story red brick garden apartments.

In Brooklyn the games changed again, which is a way of saying that basketball, which had been practically nonexistent in Rockville Centre, became my main sport. I suppose it gets down to a matter of space. In Brooklyn every square foot of recreational area has to be used—and that's about all the space you need to set up a basket.

Still, I can't remember playing very much basketball until I went to Lafayette High. I had entered Lafayette in the fall of 1949, just in time to catch a complete blackout in high-school sports. The teachers in the New York school system were refusing to supervise any extracurricular activity unless they got paid in money instead of leave time. Extracurricular activity included sports, the teachers included all the coaches, and that took care of my sophomore year.

We did have a regular gym class, though. Gym, I discovered, meant basketball. I was already beginning to grow. I had suddenly developed outsize hands and feet. The hands were a great help for basketball, and the feet didn't particularly hinder me. While I never had a really good shot, I could—believe it or not—run very well and, most of all, I could jump. I could jump through the roof. I could jump as naturally as I could throw. I just *could.*

Some of the kids from my gym class suggested that I come down to the Jewish Community House on Bay Parkway to play for their team in the JCH league. The J was set up pretty much like any YMCA or community house, with a basketball court, weight room, handball court, swimming pool, steam bath, and so on. The heart of the place, though, was the basketball court.

For the next year, the J became my second home. In the seasons when there were overlapping sports, life could get a little hectic. In the early spring I'd get into a baseball game after school and then stop off for a three-man game of basketball in some playground. By that time it would be too late to go home for supper and still be able to get to the J in time for my league game, so I'd stop off at a luncheonette and gulp down a tuna-fish-salad sandwich on white toast, with a Coke, a diet on which I somehow managed to thrive.

I usually carried a little airline bag around with me to hold my sneakers and shorts, and I'm afraid there were times when I and my little bag had all the charm and pungency of a locker room.

Over the weekend I'd play a league game on Saturday night and be back on Sunday morning, waiting for someone to come along and open the door. While other kids spent their time practicing their shooting, I'd be practicing my timing off the backboards. I wasn't exactly Elgin Baylor, but I could hang up there in the air and control my body very well. I keep emphasizing my rebounding ability because of all those stories that were written upon my supposed lack of coordination in my early years with the Dodgers. The one thing I did have, above everything else, was coordination. The only sport I didn't participate in was track, and that was only because neither the school nor the JCH had a track team.

Actually, you could be playing basketball most of the time, because wherever there was room—in the schoolyards, in the little brick parks—there would be a basket, and wherever there was a basket there would be a three-man game in progress. Even where there were full courts, you would more often than not find three-man games going on at both ends. That was the great virtue of the game; it kept every basket in use.

The rules of the game are simple. Ten points are needed to win, but you have to win by four points; that is, by two baskets or the equivalent.

If the defensive team gets the rebound, they have to retreat back behind the foul line before they can start a play. If the offensive team gets it, they can keep the ball in play as they choose. The winners keep playing; the losers go to the end of the line.

Fouls? Fouls were called by mutual agreement, common consent, and sometimes by the force of personality. I don't want to say that bodies were dropping all over the place but I can say with complete confidence that a borderline foul was nonexistent.

The "give" part of New York "give-and-go" basketball comes out of these games, since you have to learn very quickly to keep the ball moving, to anticipate plays, to hit the open man as soon as you are double-teamed. If your reactions are slow, you will have three guys draped all over you.

The favorite foul was to cut off a guy as he was driving to the basket and sort of nudge him into the iron pole that held up the basket. There was universal agreement that anybody who found himself wrapped around the pole was entitled to consider himself fouled. (And, just incidentally, it is far from impossible that my traumatic arthritis started when I banged my elbow into one of those iron poles.)

Three-man basketball was much more than a neighborhood game; it was part of growing up in Brooklyn. There had developed, on a completely informal basis, a perpetual round robin of selective competition. In each neighborhood there was one park—and one basket—which was considered the challenge spot where the best players in the neighborhood would gather for what was always called the Big Game. The Big Game was completely open. If a team from another neighborhood wanted to come in and try you, they were welcome. Just as you were welcome to go into any other neighborhood and take on their Big Game.

When you'd go to East Flatbush, you'd find the guys who played for Tilden High, the same kids you'd be meeting in the high-school competition. When you'd go to Brownsville, you'd know you were going to find the best players from Jefferson.

The round robin not only went on day by day, it went on day and night. Some of the little neighborhood courts had lights; if they didn't, the Big Game would be played at the Y or some community center. In some neighborhoods the schools stayed open. Boy, there was pneumonia basketball for you. You'd play for a couple of hours and get yourself good and sweated up, and then the lights would go off and you'd be thrown out into the freezing winter weather.

From time to time, the Big Game in a given neighborhood would move to a different court, but somehow you always knew. I don't for the life of me know how you knew, but the word was on the grapevine and you somehow picked it up.

There was one Big Game that never moved, though, and that was the biggest of them all. THE Big Game was at Brighton Beach on the weekends, on the farthest court on the right as you entered. Brighton Beach is the farthest extension of Coney Island, and the best players in the whole New York area would descend on the big cement court adjacent to the beach. I'm not talking about only the high-school players now; I'm talking about the best college players, plus former college stars who had become successful professional men but who still came down on weekends to keep their hand in the game.

If you were going up against that kind of opposition, it was kind of foolish to come unprepared. There would always be twenty or thirty teams waiting to challenge, which meant that if you lost right away you'd have to wait a couple of hours before it swung around to you again. You could challenge on one of the other courts if you wanted to, but there was a sort of general understanding that if you thought you belonged in THE Big Game it was very poor form to take advantage of the lesser players. It was like a major-league team challenging minor-leaguers. If you won, what did you win?

Once you decided to go to Brighton Beach, then, the first job was to put your team together. Sometimes you'd call around before you left. Most of the time you had a pretty good idea who would be there and you'd pick your teammates from the pool of players who would be milling around the Brighton Beach subway station. If none of your people were there when you arrived, you'd wait for a few more trains. It was too risky to see who might already be on the court, because once you left the station it cost you another dime to get back in.

The great thing about Brighton Beach was that you were going up against guys who had received the best possible coaching. Not only were they great players, but they played the game the way it was supposed to be played, a far from minor distinction. A young boy eager to learn could absorb the finer points of the game through his skin.

I was always eager to learn. After a few weeks at the J the first year I had ever played the game, I was playing with the best basketball players in Bensonhurst, the kids who had been on the Lafayette team the previous year and would have been representing the school if the coaches had not been on strike: Mal Avchen, Jerry Masiffero, Asher Jagoda, Sid Yallowitz, Jerry Doren, Elliot and Arthur Greenfield. Instead of playing for the high school, they were representing the JCH against YMCAs and other community houses.

At the end of the year the National Jewish Welfare Board held the first of what were to become annual national championships, and we won by beating a team from Worcester, Massachusetts, in the finals.

When the strike was settled the following year, Lafayette got a new coach, Frank Rabinowitz, a red-headed man who had, as I remember, just come out of the Army. On the first day of practice, Coach Rabinowitz asked the former lettermen to step forward. Practically the whole JCH team moved out except me. My chances of not making the team under those circumstances were very slight, I knew, since I could assume that my teammates would be recommending me quite highly.

In those days the New York school system was conducted on a semester basis rather than a yearly basis. As a result, there were two separate graduation classes, one in January (at the normal midterm) and one in June. Since the midterm also split the basketball season right in half, the basketball teams could be ravaged. And ours was. All we lost were Mal Avchen, our center and leading scorer, and Asher Jagoda. That did two things. It ruined our chances of winning the championship, and it gave me a chance to play. The school paper welcomed me to the lineup by consistently spelling my name "Coufax."

In my senior year at Lafayette we started off as if we might win the championship, but once again the heart of our team graduated at midterm. Since I was the last of the old crew from the J, Coach Rabinowitz appointed me captain. Our record at midterm had been 3–1. With me as captain, we lost the next three games by a grand total of 7 points. The key game was against New Utrecht High, our crosstown Bensonhurst rivals. We lost when six-foot-seven Mike Parenti, who was to become a star at St. John's, came off the bench to beat us.

My own big game, when we still had a mathematical chance for the championship, came when I scored 24 points against Lincoln. At the end of the season I had 165 points in 10 games, the second highest in our division.

The great day of my basketball career, the kind of thing any kid dreams about, came when the Police Athletic League of

Bath Beach arranged for the New York Knicks to play a benefit game against us at our gym. The Knicks came in with six players, and among them were Harry Gallatin, Carl Braun, and Al McGuire.

I was a great Knick fan. I didn't go to many of their games, but I watched them whenever I could on television. My particular heroes were, naturally enough, Harry Gallatin, who was one of the great rebounders in the league, and Sweetwater Clifton, who had such big hands that he could do the kind of tricks with the ball that I would have liked to be able to do.

Before the game started, the various members of the Knicks held a sort of clinic to demonstrate the different shots to the audience. Gallatin, being the big man, was supposed to demonstrate how to dunk the ball. Well, Harry couldn't have been feeling very well, because he missed on two or three tries. We kids were standing back around half-court, watching, and all of a sudden Al McGuire was walking toward us and taking me by the elbow. "I've got a kid right here," he was saying to Gallatin, "who can show you how to do it." (I can only imagine that Coach Rabinowitz must have pointed me out to him.)

I dribbled in from the foul line, went up, and dunked it easily. Well, you can imagine how gleefully my classmates cheered. "I'll bet he can't do it again," Gallatin said, playing straight man for me. And so I did it again.

That sent me into the game pretty high. I'm not trying to say I belonged on the same floor with any of the Knicks. Obviously they weren't extending themselves against a bunch of high-school kids. But I got my share of rebounds. And I scored a few points too.

When the game ended, Gallatin came over, wrote my name on a piece of paper, and told me, "I'm going to be looking for you in future years."

Wow.

As far as my parents were concerned, there had never been any doubt that I was going to go to college. As far as I was concerned, there wasn't either. As with most kids, my idea of college included travel and independence. Maybe even more so in my case, since so many of my original teammates had gone all the way to California. In filling out the questionnaire for the high-school yearbook at the beginning of my senior year, I had written rather whimsically that I intended to go to UCLA, which I thought had a nice impressive ring to it.

I was very well aware, however, that if I couldn't get a basketball scholarship I'd be attending one of the New York colleges. While there was money enough to pay my tuition, there certainly wasn't enough to allow me to live away from home.

In the back of my mind, I suppose, I had always felt that when the time came an athletic scholarship of one kind or another was somehow going to materialize.

My father even had a favorite story about it. When I was perhaps ten or eleven years old, my mother and sister were attending some function or other at the high school. Finding ourselves alone, my father and I had begun to talk quite seriously and philosophically about life. "You know, Sandy," he said—we were crossing the schoolyard to pick up my mother and sister, I remember—"you know," he said, "it's getting to the time when your marks are becoming very important. If your scholastic achievement is high enough, you'll be able to have your choice of colleges. If it's not, you'll have to take whatever's left. In fact," he said, "if you finish high enough in your class, you might even get a scholarship."

And I had looked at him, in complete wonderment that anybody could conceive of my getting an academic scholarship, and said, "Gee, Dad, maybe an ath-a-*let*-ic scholarship. . . ."

My father got such a kick out of the pronunciation of the word that he has never forgotten it.

With the time at hand, nobody, unfortunately, was breaking down any doors to offer me any ath-a-let-ic scholarship.

Facing the matter realistically, I was fully aware that what talents I had were a big man's talents. While a small man could get away with playing a big man's game in high school, there was no guarantee that he could do it in college, where he would be whacked from both sides by guys standing around six foot seven. (Maury Wills has a theory that if you are a real competitor you will somehow manage to do whatever has to be done. I did grow a couple of inches in my freshman year. If I had stayed in college and followed Wills' Law to its logical conclusion, I might well have graduated at six foot seven.)

I had a few casual feelers from the city colleges, and a brief contact from Frank McGuire, the onetime St. John's coach who had gone down to the University of South Carolina and was bringing a healthy quota of New York players down with him. But nothing tangible. Nothing definite. Nothing even hopeful.

How I got interested in the University of Cincinnati is a puzzlement to me. It seems ridiculous, I know, that the details could be that hazy, but they are. Somebody who was recruiting for the university—officially or unofficially—talked to me, of course, but for the life of me I can't remember who it was or where I was talked to.

I know that I liked the idea at once. I also know that I asked both Coach Rabinowitz at Lafayette and Milt Gold at the JCH to write letters of recommendation for me, a sure indication that I was more interested in Cincinnati than it was in me. In the end, I was invited to come down to the campus a couple of weeks before school opened to work out with the squad in what amounted, for all practical purposes, to a tryout. But by then I had made up my mind that I was going, regardless. I had already sent in my application and been accepted. I paid my own train fare down. If I wasn't given a scholarship off the tryout, I intended to pay my own tuition, go out for the freshman team, and hope for the best.

I did show enough to get a scholarship. As I have said, I had already enrolled as a liberal-arts major, with some idea of transferring to the school of architecture. Because of its nature as a cooperative, the school of architecture was a five-year school. I was so delighted with getting anything that I didn't ask whether the scholarship would cover the full five years if I wanted to transfer. I figured that sometime before the end of the fourth year someone would let me know. No sense getting pushy.

The big player on the Cincinnati team was Jack Twyman, who had already made a national reputation for himself in his sophomore year. Twyman played the pivot in college, but he knew very well that at his height—six-six—he'd have to develop an outside shot if he wanted to play in the NBA.

The freshmen and the varsity practiced together. We freshmen, in fact, were always the opposition, adapting ourselves as best we could to each new opponent's style of play. After the rest of us had dragged ourselves back to the showers, Jack would still be in the gym, all by himself, practicing his outside shooting. When the time came for him to make the transition to the pros, he was able to show them one of the best outside shots in the business.

If I had played at Cincinnati as a sophomore, I'd have been on the same team with Twyman. If I had remained to the end, I would have been a senior when Oscar Robertson was a freshman.

The freshman year was the only one I played, though. Ed Jucker, also in his first year at the university, was the freshman coach. He was a winning coach from the very beginning, as our 12–2 record will attest. I was, again, the rebounder, and also the third highest scorer, with an average of 9.7. The best game I played was against Miami of Ohio, at Dayton, when I scored something like 23 points. One of the spectators, he later told me, was Walter Alston, who was just about to become the manager of the Brooklyn Dodgers.

If Walt never dreamed that he would have me on his hands as a pitcher in another year, neither did I. As a pitcher, I came to the party very late.

3

A Most Reluctant Conscript

When I first told my parents I had an offer to play baseball, my mother's reaction was: "Baseball? Whatever happened to basketball?"

Just about now, you may be thinking, "Basketball? Whatever happened to baseball?"

I did play a respectable amount of baseball. I did not do much pitching.

In my first year in Bensonhurst the kids in the neighborhood formed a team which we called the Tomahawks and entered in the Ice Cream League.

The Ice Cream League was a rather interesting phenomenon of those years in Brooklyn, since it anticipated in certain respects the Little League and the Babe Ruth League. It had been started and was run by one man, a brush salesman named Milton Secol, better known, for obvious reasons, as Pop Secol.

Pop got involved with baseball originally as a form of mental therapy. He had developed a weird phobia that he was losing weight, and he would fill his pockets with pennies and wander all over town, looking for scales so that he could weigh himself over and over. His doctor warned him that unless he found some kind of hobby to take his mind off himself he would be gone within six months.

That at least gave Pop something new to worry about. He had to worry about finding a hobby. His twelve-year-old son, Steve, suggested that he get the kids in the neighborhood together to play baseball. Although Pop hadn't been any great baseball fan, it obviously was a better idea than no idea at all. He told Steve that if he could round up a couple of teams, he'd umpire for them. To give the kids an added inducement to play, he promised that he would buy banana splits for the winners and ice-cream sodas for the losers.

Well, it isn't that easy to be a public benefactor these days. The kids came running, bats, gloves, and appetites at the ready, but when Pop went to the Parks Department for a permit to use one of the thirteen diamonds on the Parade Grounds—the huge baseball field in Prospect Park—he was told that the diamonds were allocated only to established, reputable, solvent organizations. Pop wasn't official. He wasn't authorized. He wasn't even sponsored. He was just a troubled little guy who wanted to get some kids together to play ball. Can't have any unauthorized, unorganized ball games going on around here.

Pop wandered back to the Parade Grounds and got to talking to the groundkeeper about his problem. The groundkeeper pointed to a little diamond over in the corner, which had no backstop and was not kept in any sort of repair. If Pop and his kids wanted to clean the diamond up, the groundkeeper told him, there was nothing to stop them from playing on it.

A purely unofficial little diamond for a purely unofficial little man.

Thus encouraged, Pop gave his boss notice that he was taking leave through the summer and went to work with his boys to clean up the diamond. The only trouble was that in the very first inning, a foul ball was hit straight back to where the backstop would normally be and broke a window across the street. The police came, the game ended, and Pop was out of pocket for ten banana splits, ten ice cream sodas, and one window.

That would have been the end of that noble experiment, except that Jimmy Murphy, who covered the sandlots for the Brooklyn *Eagle*, heard what had happened and immediately wrote a column calling upon the Parks Department to give Pop his diamond.

The power of the press. Pop, who had wanted only one diamond for one game, was immediately given complete control over three diamonds for the rest of the season.

Another column by Jimmy Murphy, suggesting that ice cream manufacturers sponsor individual teams, got the teams completely uniformed and equipped.

For Pop himself it turned out to be the best possible therapy. At the end of the season he threw a small dinner to reward the boys, and promptly disbanded the league so that he could go back to work. Except that they wouldn't let him. Applications from new teams kept coming in, and he found himself, like it or not, with a growing organization on his hands.

By 1951, when the Tomahawks joined, there were forty-six teams, divided into three leagues corresponding to the sophomore, junior, and senior classes of high school.

One of the teams came from across the bridge in Chinatown. The Chinese boys weren't that good, because they hadn't played that much, but they did have a rather unique, colorful, and ingenious way of giving the signs. The catcher just yelled them out in Chinese.

The Tomahawks had a very good pitcher, a kid named Mike Fields (who is now a surgeon). I became the catcher, partly because we didn't have anybody else, partly because I could make the throw to second, and mostly because nobody told us that lefties weren't supposed to catch. Personally, I was delighted. An outstanding pitcher in the sandlots completely dominates any game he is in. Since we had an outstanding pitcher, it meant that Mike and I were the only players really in the ball game.

There was that problem about a left-handed catcher's mitt, of course. We solved it rather cleverly, I think, by taking an old beat-up right-handed catcher's mitt and turning it inside out so that the thumb was on the right-hand side of the glove. We then ripped out the strap and sewed it back on what was now the outside of the glove. For padding, we filled it with excelsior.

Voilà! A perfectly good left-handed catcher's mitt. The only possible fault anyone could find with it was that every time I caught a fast ball a little bit of excelsior would squirt out through the lacing. By the end of the game, the area around home plate would look like the loading dock at a box factory, and the catcher's "mitt" would look considerably deflated.

While other teams, with standard-issue right-handed catchers, were practicing during the week, our team would be going around to fruit stores looking for a fresh supply of excelsior.

The next year we got a legitimate catcher with a legitimate right-handed catcher's mitt, and I became a flashy left-handed first baseman. We finished first in the junior division that year, winning all ten of our games—which meant that Mike Fields pitched ten straight victories. We still had to beat our runners up in the playoffs, though, and the playoffs were two games out of three. The way the playoffs were set up, a double-header was to be played on Saturday. If neither team won both games, the final would be played the next day.

We won the first game, as our fancy-fielding first baseman hit a triple with the bases loaded (I can remember a bases-loaded triple even when it was hit on the sandlots). If we had lost the first game, we'd have sent Mike Fields and his magic arm right back at them. With a game to play around with, we decided to let him rest for twenty-four hours. That meant we needed a pitcher. Well, I could throw the ball hard. All of a sudden everybody was looking at me.

I would like to be able to say that I pitched my team to the championship, foreshadowing the great things that lay ahead. What I *have* to say is that I walked five batters in the first inning, forcing across two runs. I walked three more in the second inning, but got out of that one—as we say in the sports pages—unscathed. My control improved a little as the game went on, but we lost it, 4–1. Mike Fields came back to pitch his usual game on Sunday, and we won the championship.

By this time Pop was throwing real banquets at the end of the season to hand out the awards to the champions and the individual stars. The dais was decorated by local politicians and judges and, to represent the Dodgers, Jackie Robinson and

Walter O'Malley. Mike Fields won the trophy as the Most Valuable Pitcher in the Junior Division, and one other member of the Tomahawks was there to receive an award too. Sandy Koufax. What did I win? Well, special trophies were awarded to the players in the league who had been outstanding in *other* sports in high school. I won the trophy as the Most Outstanding Basketball Player. Even in a baseball league, I was known primarily as a basketball player.

By the next year the Tomahawks had begun to drift apart. I had some friends in school on the baseball team, and they talked me into going out, mostly because they had nobody at all to play first base. The Lafayette coach, Charley Sheerin, is sometimes referred to snidely as the guy who decided I was a first baseman rather than a pitcher, which is not really fair. In the first place, I *wasn't* a pitcher. Pitchers and infielders didn't even sign up for the team on the same day. In the second place, Lafayette was loaded with pitchers that year. Our ace pitcher was Freddie Wilpon, a left-hander with a tremendous curve ball. We all thought Freddie was the guy who was going to make the big leagues. As a matter of fact, Freddie had been invited to Ebbets Field for a tryout a year earlier, and I had gone with him, sat in the stands, and watched him—tremendously impressed—while he pitched batting practice.

Behind him was a big redheaded right-hander, Jerry Boxer, who did make it to the big leagues briefly with the Kansas City Athletics. Behind them, was another good pitcher, named Stan Fishel, who ended up with a baseball scholarship to Long Island University.

Although I do everything else left-handed, I have always been a right-handed batter. No particular reason. I just happened to bat right-handed the first time I picked up a bat, and I never saw any reason to change. Which would seem to indicate, now that I think of it, a lamentable lack of imagination.

I fielded my position very well, but my hitting was just unbelievable. The school doesn't seem to have kept the old batting records, an oversight for which I will remain eternally grateful. I was once in the batter's box in a crucial spot in a game against Manual Training when Sheerin sent Walter Laurie, who was normally our first-string catcher, up to bat for me. It might not sound too humiliating to have a first-string catcher batting for you, except that the last time I had looked at Walter he had been sitting on the bench with a broken kneecap. They had sawed the cast off his leg and wrapped the knee in an Ace bandage so that he could hobble up to the plate to hit for me.

The thought of playing baseball professionally hardly enters the mind of a non-hitting first baseman. I stood in awe of the guys from the neighborhood who were professional ballplayers. Mike Napoli, who had come out of Lafayette a couple of years before I arrived, had signed with the Dodgers, and he was the big man in the neighborhood.

Another Lafayette kid, a big outfielder named Bobby Honor, had been signed by the Pirates and was supposed to be doing great things down at New Orleans, their top farm.

If I may be pardoned a little parochial pride, I doubt if any area in the country played better baseball than we did in Bensonhurst. Joe Pignatano, who was also a contemporary of mine, lived just around the corner from the high school. I believe he attended Lafayette for a short time and then transferred to a trade school. Bobby Giallombardo, who was with the Dodgers briefly, was the star pitcher the year after I graduated. There were Bob Aspromonte (whose brother Ken had been signed out of Lafayette too); Jerry Casales, who got a big bonus from the Red Sox; Larry Ciaffone, who pitched a little for the Cards; Larry Yellin, now with Houston; and Al Ferrara, who just could be the next big hitter for the Dodgers.

I wonder if there is a high school anywhere that can match that record.

There is a certain irony in having to graft the name of the worst-hitting first baseman in that glorious history onto the list, but that's the way it goes.

There was one man who did see me as a pitcher. Milt Laurie.

Milt was at most of our games because he had two sons on the team: Walter, the catcher, and Larry, an outfielder. Milt saw me whipping the ball around the infield and told me I should be a pitcher. More specifically, he wanted me to pitch for the team he managed, the Parkviews.

I didn't take him very seriously. "You've seen me hit, huh?" I told him.

He kept after me, though, and he had Walter keep after me too. "Not only am I not a pitcher," I'd tell them. "I'm not even a baseball player. I'm a basketball player."

"You've got a big-league arm," Milt would say. "I'd like to work with you."

Milt Laurie drove a newspaper delivery truck for the *Journal-American*, but his credentials were much stronger than that. He had pitched for the Bushwicks back in the late 1930s, when they were probably the strongest semi-pro team in the country. One of his teammates was Tommy Holmes.

Milt himself had been signed by the Boston Braves and was just about ready to report to spring training when his delivery truck skidded on a wet street, flipped over, and crushed his whole right side. His side, his arm, and his shoulder still showed the deep scars where they had operated.

Say what you want about baseball, it has always been able to exert its strong hold on the people who wanted so badly to make it and never could. Sometimes it seems as if the rejects— if we can call them that—love the game more than the people who are in it. Like so many others, Milt had transferred his dream of playing big-league ball to his sons. With both of them in high school and both of them very good ballplayers, he had formed his own team, the Parkviews, which had been strong enough to win the championship the year before in the tough Coney Island League.

When I saw that Milt was really serious about having me pitch, I explained that I wouldn't be around during the hot summer months anyway, since I always went up to Camp Chi-Wan-Da, near Kingston, New York, about ninety miles north of New York City.

I had started to go to the camp at the age of three, when my mother first went up to work on their books for them. As I grew older, I worked as a waiter to pick up a few dollars, although I had grown so close to the owners over all those years that I was always treated more as a member of the family than as either a camper or an employee.

That would have been the end of that—and quite possibly of any further talk of pitching—except that I wangled the job with my uncle's firm and remained in the city over the summer.

As long as I was in the city anyway, I pitched for the Parkviews.

I had already pitched two more games for the Tomahawks at the tag end of the school year, when they put in an emergency call for me. The first game was against a kid named Tony Balsamo, who was the star pitcher for Erasmus High. He went on to Fordham and was eventually signed by the Chicago Cubs. I got beat again, 6–2, giving me a career record of no victories and two defeats. Shortly afterward I pitched again and finally won, 4–2. What I remember more than anything else, though, was that I got myself three hits, an all-time record for me, and knocked in the winning runs.

As for my pitching, the pattern was always the same. I'd walk a lot of men and I'd strike out a lot of men.

When Milt Laurie got hold of me, I began to practice enough so that I had pretty good control of my fast ball, although I never got to the point where I had any idea where the curve was going.

I found that I liked pitching. The pitcher is always in the game. I also liked it because I found I could throw the fast ball past the hitters with pleasing regularity. In my first or second game for the Parkviews I pitched a no-hitter, got all the other players to autograph the ball for me, and brought it home proudly to present to my mother.

That alone must have been a shock to her, because I was always a kind of close-mouthed kid. (When I told her I was writing this book, she asked if I'd give her one of the first copies so she could find out something about me. "You never told *me* anything," she said.)

My folks had never seen me play any sport at all. They knew

I was a good enough basketball player so that I had a chance to get a scholarship. They also knew that I had played baseball in high school without any distinction at all.

"Who were you pitching against?" my father asked me, vastly unimpressed. "The Annandale School for the Blind?"

One of the first lessons I had learned about pitching was that it is very hard on the spikes. My old pair, which had seen their best days anyway, had begun to literally crumble on my feet. Since I also was the sole proprietor of the biggest feet on the team, there was very little chance of borrowing anybody else's.

With a game coming up on Saturday, I finally asked my father for the money to buy a pair. I must have caught him at the end of a bad week because when he found out that they cost $17 he was most unenthusiastic.

Later in the evening I deftly dropped the word where I would be pitching the next day and hoped he would come by to watch. I didn't see him there when the game started, but he apparently came by shortly afterward. When he saw me striking everybody out, he became so excited that he ran about three blocks to the nearest drugstore, phoned my mother, and, puffing for breath, shouted, "What's the idea of letting that kid play with old shoes? You want him to hurt himself? First thing Monday morning I want you to *make* him go out and buy a new pair."

Milt ran the Parkviews almost like a minor-league operation. Through the generosity of William Randolph Hearst, Jr., and his circulation department, we even had our own bus. To be accurate, let's put it this way: We didn't want to disturb such important men with our petty little transportation problems, but we were confident that if their consent had been asked it would have been given gladly.

Since newspaper delivery trucks have no need for seats in the back, we'd all sit on the floor, leaning back against the sides, yelling out to Milt to observe the speed regulations with infinite care since he was loaded down with such a valuable cargo of baseball ivory.

Milt may have started the team as nothing more than a way of developing his own two sons, but in the end we were all his boys. Walter and Larry both did sign with big-league clubs, Walter with Kansas City and Larry with the Dodgers. Each had one good year in the low minors, and then they both got married, quit baseball, and joined the police force.

It fell to me, Milt's most reluctant conscript, to become the chief beneficiary of his work and his dream. Life is odd.

We played tough ball. Most of the games, in the league and out, were money games, with each team putting up anywhere from $50 to $100. I pitched almost all the money games, which meant that I was pitching under pressure from the beginning. When I was broke and someone else put up the money for me, the pressure was even worse. It's bad enough to lose, but it's worse to lose other people's money. I pitched six league games and a few outside money games, and we won them all.

There were times I had a little help. We played one game against the Gravesend Youth Center, our toughest rivals in the league, in a fog that sometimes got so thick that I could barely see the batter. One kid didn't see the ball from the time I threw it to the time he heard it plunk into the catcher's mitt. When he heard the umpire call "Strike," he walked out of the box and absolutely refused to return.

I even had a couple of scouts show a little interest. The first scout who ever talked to me was from the Red Sox, although he did little more than introduce himself. The second was Joe Labate of the Phils. Labate, an oldtime spitballer, invited me to a general tryout he was conducting out on Long Island. Milt Laurie drove me out in my Parkview uniform. I pitched a couple of innings, striking out five out of six. Nobody said a word to us, though, so Milt and I just looked at each other, shrugged, got back into the truck, and drove on back home.

A couple of weeks later Labate offered me a contract for something like $1500 to play in a college league up in northern New York.

I didn't take it seriously. I had never followed baseball closely in the sense of watching the box scores or knowing the batting averages. I did follow it closely enough to know where the Dodgers were in the pennant race. You had to know that much in Brooklyn out of sheer self-protection.

I also knew enough about professional baseball to be aware that major-league clubs had to sign a lot of kids for the lower clubs in their farm systems just to flesh out the rosters so that the one or two players they were really interested in would have somebody to play with.

I had told Labate I wouldn't be interested in playing baseball unless I got a bonus large enough to pay my way through college in the event that I found, after a couple of years, that I was not good enough to make the majors.

The bonus rule at the time was that if you were paid more than $4000 they had to keep you on the big-league roster for two full years. I wasn't so naïve that I expected any major-league club would get rid of a proven pitcher to keep a raw kid like me. I think it would be accurate to say that I discussed it with Labate only because it seemed like the courteous thing to do after the interest he had shown and the trouble Milt Laurie had gone to.

The only importance of Labate's interest was that it put the idea of pitching professionally into my head. I was beginning to enjoy pitching. I knew I was pretty good. If you are at all competitive—and I had been competing all my life—you cannot help wondering how you would stack up against the best. I wasn't burning to be a big-league pitcher, but I had begun to wonder.

Still, when the scholarship at Cincinnati came through, I assumed I was going to be concentrating on basketball for the next four years. In my mind, I put baseball completely behind me except, perhaps, for an occasional weekend game for the Parkviews during the summer.

Instead, I found myself pitching for Cincinnati—for the varsity, yet—in my freshman year.

Maybe I was kidding myself. Maybe I was subconsciously committed—whatever that means—to reaching toward baseball all along. Perhaps I kept putting myself in a position where

I could find out how well I could pitch without having to admit to myself that I wanted to find out. But I don't think so. No fires were burning in me as far as baseball was concerned.

The same combination of circumstance, coincidence, and accident that had somehow got me pitching for the Parkviews got me pitching at the University of Cincinnati. Although this time, I must admit, the impetus did come from me.

This time it depended upon the coincidence that Ed Jucker, the coach of the freshman basketball team, was also the coach of the varsity baseball team. It depended upon the circumstance that, there being no freshman baseball team, freshmen were eligible to play for the varsity in non-Conference games.

And, in an odd, indirect way, it depended upon the sheer accident that Tony Trabert, who had left the University of Cincinnati to enter the Navy, had come back to school in glory during the second semester, having just helped the United States win its first Davis Cup in memory.

Next to Trabert, the greatest college tennis player in the country was Tulane's Ham Richardson, the NCAA Champion. A dual meet was hastily set up between Tulane and Cincinnati over the Easter vacation week, so that the two leading college players could meet, head to head.

All these factors converged upon my life unexpectedly while a few of us basketball players were hanging around Jucker's office after practice. Jucker didn't have time to kibitz with us. The baseball team, he told us, was going to accompany the tennis team down to New Orleans, and he was busily trying to put together a schedule, on short notice, so that both teams could stop off to play en route.

I heard those two magic words, New Orleans, and I could think of no other place in the world I would rather be.

"Coach," I said, "I'm a baseball player. I'm a pitcher."

He looked at me, as if to say, "Yeah, everybody's a pitcher these days. But what kind of a pitcher?—that's the thing."

I felt like telling him I'd had a *bona fide* offer from the Phils. Instead I said, "I'm not much of a hitter, but I can pitch pretty good."

The call for the pitchers and catchers went out almost immediately, well before the end of the basketball season. Since I was on a basketball scholarship, I would doubt whether I'd have been allowed to go out for baseball that early—if at all—if Jucker hadn't been wearing both hats.

We reported to Cincinnati's old, poorly lit gym. I whistled a couple of fast balls past the ear of the catcher, who was the fullback on the football team. He turned to Jucker, handed him the mitt, and said, "Get somebody else. I don't want any part of this guy."

By the time we headed south, my shoulder was so sore from showing everybody how fast I could throw that I almost didn't get to make the trip. To encourage Jucker to take me, I kept telling him that the warm weather was just exactly what the shoulder needed. And perhaps it was. It was feeling so good after a few days that I talked Jucker into letting me start against the Keesler Air Base, which was supposed to be stocked with minor-league players. I managed to struggle by until the fifth inning, when I walked two men and one of the old pros hit a home run. We tied it before we finally got beat, though, and if I emerged without glory, it was also without defeat.

The shoulder felt fine. Almost as soon as we returned to school I pitched a four-hitter against Wayne, striking out sixteen. On the next start I pitched a three-hitter against Louisville, striking out eighteen, a school record.

The scouts began to come around. I told them exactly what I had told the scouts in New York.

The first scout to approach me, really, was Bill Zinser, a bird dog for the Dodgers. Zinser asked me if I'd like to take a trip to Brooklyn at the end of the year to work out at Ebbets Field. "Gee," I told him, "I live in Brooklyn. They can get in touch with me any time during the summer without any trouble at all."

Zinser's report appears below. I should explain that in the Dodger system, A stands for big-league average. A+ is better than average, and A+++ is as good as it is possible to get. I should also explain, just so that nobody will think we deal in typographical errors here, that I hit better for Cincinnati than I have ever hit in my life.

The report is dated May 15, 1954.

Arm	A+	Running Speed	O+
Fielding	A—	Accuracy	A—
Hitting	A—	Power	A—

Very good prospect, also very good hitter
Has averaged 16 strikeouts per game this season
Aptitude—very good
Aggressiveness—Outstanding
Definite Prospect?—Yes

Physical description, Tall—muscular—quick reflexes, well coordinated
Other remarks: Going to U. of Cincinnati on Scholarship— not interested in pro ball until he graduates.
Also plays 1st because of hitting ability.

This was not the report that started me on my way to the Dodgers. Since I wasn't interested in pro ball, it seems to have been filed and forgotten.

Ed Jucker tried very hard to get the Reds interested in me. Buzz Boyle, their scout, apparently thought I was too wild, because, from what I heard, he recommended against making me a bonus boy.

Of course my last start, which was against Xavier of Cincinnati, our traditional rival, wasn't very impressive. I walked six and struck out seven in seven innings. I also lost.

Going into the sixth inning, the score was tied 2–2. I walked the lead-off man on a 3–2 pitch and, as so frequently happened in those days, I began to burn at myself. The next hitter was a big husky guy who looked as if he could hit the ball a ton. Our other pitcher, Don Nesbitt, had briefed me carefully on all the Xavier hitters, with particular emphasis on this guy. Nesbitt had played against him all his life, and he kept emphasizing that he was as helpless as a baby against curves and a regular King Kong against fast balls.

He had, as predicted, looked pitiful on curves the first two times up, but now I was mad and when I got mad I'd just rear back and bust the ball through.

Well, I had to admit that the information on him was great. This guy leaned into my fast ball and hit it farther than I had ever seen a baseball hit before. He hit a ball that went up over the top of the hill that surrounded the field. He hit that ball so hard and so far that I couldn't even get mad about it. Just ashamed.

I had a distinct feeling that any scouts who had come to look at me were now looking at him.

My record at the U. of Cincinnati was 3–1. My total figures, for any interested statistician, were 51 strikeouts and 30 walks in 31 innings.

My folks didn't know that I was playing baseball at Cincinnati, possibly because I didn't tell them. I could just hear my dad saying, "All right, you're playing basketball. That takes care of the winter. But winter and summer? That pretty much puts you into the sport business and out of the study business, doesn't it?"

My father got the good word when Gene Bonnibeau, the Eastern scout for the Giants, dropped into his office with a clipping about me from one of the Cincinnati papers. Bonnibeau wanted to set up a date for me to work out at the Polo Grounds. "When he comes home I'll pass on the message," my father told him. "If he wants to go down to the Polo Grounds to throw for you, it's all right with me."

Well, sure, I was willing to go down. It was something for me to do for the day. The whole business about scouts and tryouts was still an adventure for me. I was enjoying myself. I was having fun.

Enjoying myself, did I say? Fun, did I say? Yeah, enjoyment and fun, interspersed with an occasional fiasco. I have done my best to blot out the memory of my day at the Polo Grounds, and I am afraid I am about to open some old wounds.

Bonnibeau took me down to the clubhouse and introduced me to Frank Shellenback, the pitching coach. I had to open by telling Shellenback that I had forgotten to bring my glove, which was hardly a smash opening. It also wasn't true. I didn't own a fielder's glove. The only glove I owned was my first baseman's mitt. Shellenback looked at me oddly and asked whether I was right-handed or left-handed. When he found out I was a lefty, he brought me over to Johnny Antonelli, who had come in early with the pitchers. John was glad to let me use his glove. He gave me a wink and an encouraging slap on the back and said, "We lefties got to stick together, right?"

Antonelli always remembered me from that one incident. For years I couldn't meet Johnny in a ball park without him yelling, "Hey, Lefty, have you got your glove with you?"

They gave me some kind of uniform to go with the glove and took me out to the field. Let me tell you something. Walking out on a big-league field for the first time does something to you. What it does to you—what it did to me, anyway—is scare you to death.

The catcher was Bobby Hofman. "Just loosen up at first," Shellenback said, pleasantly. I wound up and heaved the ball over Hofman's head, loosening up about three rows of the grandstand.

And it didn't get much better. Boy, it was awful. It was terrible. While I hadn't planned on walking out of the park with a contract, I hadn't planned on making a fool of myself either. When they finally let me go, amidst sighs of relief from all sides, I ducked back to the clubhouse to take a quick shower. The only thing I remember clearly was that there was a Coke machine in the clubhouse and that suddenly I was thirstier than I had ever been in my life.

Having very little experience with clubhouse etiquette, I decided that the proper thing to do was to ask the manager, a kindly chap named Leo Durocher, whether it would be all right if I took a Coke. The kindly manager had a few other things on his mind, in the summer of 1954, like, for instance, winning the pennant. To borrow one of Leo's own pet expressions, he looked at me like I had nine heads. "I don't give a *blankety-blank what* you do," he snapped.

I slunk off into a corner to sip my Coke, then slunk out of

the clubhouse, averting my face as I went. Bonnibeau had left me a ticket to the game. It turned out to be way up in the second deck of the right center-field bleachers. I was still smarting too much from the memory of my brilliant workout to pay any attention to the game, which was just as well because I couldn't see anything from that seat anyway. It seemed to me that maybe they were trying to tell me something.

I was probably right too. When I began to work out with other teams, I found that the ones who were really interested in you put you in a box seat.

After about three innings I picked myself up and grabbed a subway home.

When my father got home that night he asked me how I had done at the Polo Grounds.

"It was a very memorable experience," I said, choosing my words with care.

"Oh?"

"Yes. There is a catcher by the name of Bobby Hofman who will remember me as long as he lives. I must be the only pitcher he's ever caught who hit the backstop more often than his glove."

I never heard from the Giants again.

4

How I Didn't Sign with the Pittsburgh Pirates

When the Dodgers announced they had signed me, I was identified as a University of Cincinnati pitcher. In point of fact, the Cincinnati interlude didn't have that much to do with it. Three clubs were willing to give me the kind of bonus I wanted: Brooklyn, Pittsburgh, and Milwaukee. All three offers came not out of the halls of learning but off the Brooklyn sandlots.

Back in Brooklyn over the summer, I pitched a few more games for Milt Laurie and the Parkviews. When the time came for me to go to camp I was eligible, in the glow of my new status as a certified college boy, to become a counselor. I'd come back over an occasional weekend to pitch. When it was a really important game, they'd make sure I was there by sending someone up to drive me back.

The first of the new clubs to show an interest in me was the Yankees. A pair of Yankee scouts even came to my house two or three times to talk to my folks, the first time any negotiations had ever gone that far. When it came to the point of trying to get our names on a contract, though, they sent an entirely different scout, a Jewish scout. It offended us. It was just a little too obvious.

Not that we'd have signed with them anyway. After all the talk about a bonus, the Yankees came up with nothing more than a $4000 contract for a Class D club.

The brief whirl with the Yankees did do one thing for me.

It forced me to sort out my thinking. After the first visit from the scouts, my folks wanted to know whether I was just playing around with the idea of becoming a ballplayer, just drifting along to find out what was going to happen, or whether I had really become so interested in baseball that I was willing to give up a college scholarship.

I had to admit to them that I didn't have any burning ambition to play baseball. "But," I told them, "I don't have any burning ambition to be anything else either. I've been in college for a year now, and I've got to be honest about it. After the basketball season is over I don't know why I'm there.

"All I'm really sure of," I said, "is that if a major-league club comes through with enough money so that I can go back to college if I don't make it as a pitcher—if I can get that kind of an offer and don't take it, I know I'll be kicking myself for the rest of my life for not giving myself a chance. I don't know how I know it, I just know it."

"That's good enough for us," my mother said. "Because whatever decision you make, you're the one who is going to have to live with it for the rest of your life."

Frankly, it didn't look as if I was going to have to make any decision at all. A few scouts approached me during the summer, but that dirty word "bonus" always scared them off. I pitched so intermittently, anyway, that it wasn't easy for a scout to get any kind of steady line on me.

Early in September, with less than a month left before I would return to school, everything began to happen. It started with a phone call from Ed McCarrick, the chief area scout for the Pittsburgh Pirates. McCarrick wanted to have lunch with me at Lundy's, a famous seafood restaurant in Brooklyn.

McCarrick turned out to be a relatively young man, in his early thirties, with a fighter's face but an easy, extremely articulate way about him. Scouts are salesmen, and they pitch their clubs' best features at you. The scouts for the winners, I had found, generally told you about their efficient organizations and their World Series checks; the losers, being unable to sell either efficiency or success, splattered their conversation with the word "opportunity." What they were offering, they made clear, was the chance to move right in on a club that was obviously in need of so much.

McCarrick surprised me by skipping the commercial. He just wanted to get acquainted with me, he said. He wanted to know what I was studying in college. He wanted to know what my plans were—long-range as well as short-term—as far as professional ball was concerned. I gave him what had begun to sound like *my* commercial; i.e., my willingness to leave college only if I could get a large enough bonus to protect myself.

My folks and I had reached a sort of tacit understanding by then that even if I did play ball I'd continue to go to college during the off-season. McCarrick, who was a graduate of St. John's University, warned me that it wasn't quite that easy. You start out with the idea that you can squeeze in a semester every winter, he said, and then you discover that the curriculum doesn't fall into place that neatly for you. The college has to be willing to readjust your schedule so that you can leave early for spring training. There are essential courses that never quite fit in. As you grow older, you can begin to feel uncomfortable attending classes with young kids. As your baseball career develops, you can just plain lose interest.

"I've signed a lot of boys who were going to finish their education in their spare time," he told me. "I don't know one of them who did. If your primary concern is to get an education, you'd better think twice before you sign a baseball contract."

I was aware that this was part of his sales pitch. Obviously, if my education had been my primary concern I wouldn't have been there talking to him. Nor was I so naïve by this stage of the game that I did not know that one of the most effective techniques for a scout or recruiter was to demonstrate, as they say, "an interest in the boy's welfare."

And yet, above and beyond all that, I felt that he was sincere. I felt that he was leveling with me.

And there was even more to it than that. This was, after all, no bird dog trying to set me up for a scout, this was one of the top men in the Pittsburgh farm system. From the beginning we both understood that he was accepting me at the valuation I had put on myself. We both understood that he was not going to come back, after a lot of chatter, with another of those minor-league offers.

If, under those conditions, he was still so anxious for me to think well of him, I had to conclude that he thought I was something special. For the first time I began to feel, in my own mind, that I might be worth what I was asking.

Ed McCarrick, as I have said, was no mere bird dog. As an outfielder for Durham, the Dodgers' Class B farm club, he had become a close friend of Branch Rickey, Jr., the Dodgers' farm director. (Remember that, because it is going to come up, as the final irony, in my rather bewildering experience with the Pirates.) Upon returning from the Army at the age of twenty-six, Ed decided he didn't have the talent to make it all the way to the big leagues, and so he accepted Branch Jr.'s standing offer to come up to the front office as assistant to the scouting director.

When Branch Rickey, Sr., moved over to Pittsburgh in December 1950, Ed was one of the handful of men he asked to come with him. What Mr. Rickey offered him was the choice between becoming general manager of the top farm club at New Orleans or the supervisor of scouting for New York and New England. Since Ed had just bought a home in the New York area for his growing family, he decided to take the lesser job. Joe Brown then accepted the New Orleans job and moved up to take over the Pirates when Mr. Rickey retired.

The story of my negotiations with the Pirates, when you come right down to it, is the story of how McCarrick lost me. Obviously I could not have been aware of the internal problems and stresses within the Pirate organization. But since those problems did play such an important role, I am going to try to tell it, in chronological order, by inserting the significant background material as we go along. Just remember that the italicized sections that will follow from time to time cover scenes, facts, and developments that I had no way of knowing about at the time.

All scouts have to develop a network of friends and bird dogs. When McCarrick moved from Brooklyn to Pittsburgh, a good part of his network stayed with him. One of the friends was a film projectionist at the Fox Theatre in Flatbush, named Ted Gale. Mr. Gale, a man with a crippled leg, had managed teams around the sandlots. He still worked the night shift so that he could spend his days around baseball.

Gale called McCarrick on a Saturday night to tell him to come to the Abraham Lincoln High School field the next day. McCarrick already had a commitment to scout someone else. "Cancel it," Gale told him. "I saw a kid pitch last week and I just found out that he's going to pitch again tomorrow. His name is Koo-fax. They call him Sandy. This kid has a great arm, and the beauty part of it is that no one knows about him because he wasn't a pitcher in high school."

Ed came down and saw me strike out fifteen men in seven innings.

The following Sunday he came down to see me pitch again. (Since we were into our league playoffs by then, I was coming down from camp every weekend.)

Before he got in touch with me, Ed made it his business to meet Milt Laurie and find out as much about me as possible.

After our conversation at Lundy's he phoned Rickey at his home in Pittsburgh to tell him he had come across a boy in Brooklyn with as fine an arm as he'd ever seen.

"His fast ball," he said, falling into the jargon of his profession, "has great velocity, and to make it even more attractive, he has a power curve. The only thing is that we are going to have to offer him a major-league contract at more than the four thousand dollars."

"Is this boy going to pitch again?" Rickey asked him.

"Yes, he's going to pitch one more time. Next Sunday."

"You're sure it's a bonus situation?"

"Absolutely. He'll be giving up a college scholarship. His parents are educated people and they feel very strongly about it."

Rickey told him that he'd not only send Branch Jr. down but that he'd also detach Clyde Sukeforth, the Pirates' bullpen *coach, from the club, so that he could take a look at me too.*

Branch Jr. and Sukeforth took a sleeper out of Pittsburgh that got them into New York early Sunday morning. McCarrick had arranged to pick them up at the subway exit on Montague Street, right in front of the old Dodger office where they had all worked so long. From there they drove over to Milt Laurie's house to pick me up for a private early-morning workout.

I had been picked up at camp a day earlier, so that I could sleep over at Milt Laurie's house and be rested for our final game, which was against the Falcons, the champions of the Shore Parkway League and our bitterest enemies.

I needed the rest. I had gouged out a hunk of flesh alongside my ankle in a swimming-pool accident a couple of day earlier, and the ankle was all bandaged up.

It wasn't until I arrived at Milt's that I found out about the imminent invasion of the Pittsburgh brass.

We drove out to Dyker Park, nearby, at about 8:30 a.m., early enough so that the field was completely empty. It was a cold, heavy morning. When I went out to the mound to throw to Sukeforth, there were still wisps of fog hanging in the air. McCarrick and Branch Rickey, Jr., stood alongside me on the mound. Milt Laurie remained more or less on the sidelines, just outside the first-base line.

From the beginning I didn't feel right. Either the ankle bothered me just enough to throw me off my natural rhythm, or the coolness kept me from loosening up. Probably it was a combination of both. At any rate, my shoulder stiffened up a little, and I was throwing with a cramped, strained motion. I didn't throw bad. I didn't throw good. But I had the distinct feeling that, when you're asking for a bonus, not throwing good is bad.

The workout over, we all got back into the car and drove to Erasmus Field, under the El.

The place was crawling with scouts. Milt had been promoting me all over town for two solid years, and all of a sudden everybody had become interested. About the only

54

team not represented was the Brooklyn Dodgers, which was curious because Al Campanis was known to be very high on Bobby Giallombardo, who was pitching against me.

Our games against the Falcons were always grudge games. Although we were in different leagues, we always played a couple of knockdown, drag-out money games against them during the season, and we always beat them.

There was a neighborhood rivalry involved; Milt Laurie's style of bunting, percentage baseball drove them mad; and, to top it all off, they had come to look upon me as a ringer. To really gall them, I had won my own game—and $50—the last time we had met by tripling off Giallombardo, the only time anybody on either team had ever seen me get a base hit.

While I was warming up, a blister came up on my middle finger. In the second inning the blister broke, and I was throwing up fast balls spotted with blood. If they came up to the plate bloody, they went back out battered, bloody, and bowed. With all the scouts in the world looking on, I got clobbered. Four runs in three innings, and I was out of there.

Poor Ed McCarrick, I thought. He had gone to all the trouble of bringing in the brass from Pittsburgh, and I had let him down. McCarrick didn't seem quite as discouraged as I was. In fact, he drove me back up to camp that night, so I had to assume that he was still interested. Branch Jr. came along with us. Sukeforth had disappeared, though, possibly in disgust. I had thought of Branch Jr.—if I had thought of him at all—as a quiet, diffident man completely in his father's shadow. He turned out to be a good-natured, energetic, exuberant man. I couldn't enjoy his conversation too much, though, because I was tired and dispirited. I'd spent a hard day and I'd done a lot of traveling, just to lose the most important game we'd played all year.

If I was discouraged, McCarrick wasn't. A couple of days later he put in another call to Rickey. "I know what kind of reports you got," he said. "Lackluster. They said the kid was all right but nothing to justify the raves I had given him. And

*from what they saw, they were right. But there were compli-
cations, Mr. Rickey. Before you make up your mind, I want
you to see him when he's right."*

*"All right," Mr. Rickey said. "Can you bring him to Forbes
Field?"*

The following Tuesday, McCarrick, Milt, and I took the
midnight sleeper to Pittsburgh. With us was Grover "Deacon"
Jones, an infielder from White Plains whom McCarrick was
also eager to sign.

By this time I had a busy schedule of tryouts set up. Shortly
after Ed had called me at camp to set up the trip to Pittsburgh,
I had received a call from Al Campanis and agreed to work out
for him at Ebbets Field on Sunday. Milt had been promoting
me to Honey Russell, the Milwaukee scout, and Russell had
arranged for me to fly to Milwaukee for a tryout. Since I would
be going back in Cincinnati the next week, we agreed that I
would fly to Milwaukee from Cincinnati on the following
Sunday, which also happened to be the last day of the season.

We were in Pittsburgh for two days. The first day I worked
out for George Sisler and Fred Haney and in the afternoon
watched a game against Milwaukee. Spahn pitched for Milwaukee, and everybody pitched for the Pirates. That's the kind
of team they had.

The next day was an off day, so we had the park pretty much
to ourselves. Mr. Rickey himself was there, sitting in a front
box just behind third base, chin in hand, watching me as I
threw. I knew I looked good. I knew I was fast.

*Rickey, McCarrick, Sisler, and Haney had a meeting later
in Rickey's office. Everybody was very high on me. Sisler was
every bit as enthusiastic as McCarrick. Haney wasn't far behind. Rickey turned to McCarrick. "Ed, we want this boy."*

*"You know what I said, Mr. Rickey. It has to be a major-
league bonus contract."*

"How much will it take?"

"I don't know," Ed said. "Not that much, I don't think. But

his folks may be very tough. They're not going to be happy about him leaving college."

Rickey had a problem. His four-year stewardship at Pittsburgh had been a complete bust, up to then. The Pirates were the worst team in history, anticipating the Mets. (If you don't believe it, ask Joe Garagiola.) That would seem like an excellent reason to spend money on new players. The catch was that Rickey had *been spending money on new players. He had spent so much money on bonuses that the budget had run dry. He personally was under fire from all sides. The team wasn't drawing flies at the box office. Badly as they all wanted me, Mr. Rickey had to tell McCarrick, he just didn't know how he was going to dig up the money.*

That's the kind of talk that can cast a pall over a meeting.

"I'll try to figure something out," Mr. Rickey finally told Ed. "Meanwhile, you go into his home and try to find out the thinking of the family. Take a sounding. If it takes no more than ten thousand, I'll find some way to get it."

Back we came on the sleeper Thursday night. Each of us had his own little roomette, which could be transformed from a sleeper to a sitting room. In the morning Milt dropped in to tell me that he was supposed to be sounding me out, without saying anything definite, as to whether a $10,000 bonus would do it.

I told him that, having sounded me out, he had discovered that I personally would be satisfied, but that I'd want the advice of my parents.

Ed came back to the house with me to talk to my folks. Now that I think of it, he had already gone to the trouble of checking with the Registrar at Columbia, the only New York college that offered a course in architectural designing. He was able to tell us that Columbia not only would accept my credits from Cincinnati but would be willing to adjust my courses to an off-season schedule.

To give him his due, he also told my folks, as he had told me, that he had never known a ballplayer to go the full route to a diploma. He went out of his way to tell them that a ball-player's life wasn't an easy one. There were constant frustrations and disappointments, he said. Somebody was always at your elbow, trying to take your job. The constant traveling and the public spotlight placed a strain on married life.

By painting the bleakest possible picture he once again made the best possible impression. There was only one thing that left us unimpressed. There was still no specific figure being mentioned and therefore no specific offer.

We, of course, had not the slightest idea that the Pirates were that broke. As for McCarrick, Rickey hadn't authorized him to make a flat offer of $10,000. He had only said he'd try to get it. Until he was sure that Rickey *could* get it, Ed didn't feel that he could offer it.

At last it fell to us to tell him that we felt the time had come for somebody to make a definite offer.

Besides, I'd be returning to Cincinnati in another week and I had to know where I stood. I didn't want to play basketball if I was going to be leaving in the middle of the season. And if I wasn't going to play, the only decent thing to do was to turn back the scholarship so that it could be given to somebody else.

"I'll tell you what," Ed said. "If the three of you are willing to go back to Pittsburgh and talk to Mr. Rickey, I'm sure we can get the whole thing settled."

We were willing. Back we went on the midnight sleeper, the same day on which I had returned.

This time McCarrick didn't go with us. After he saw us off, he phoned George Sisler from a phone booth to tell him we were coming. "It looks very good," he told him. "I think they're amenable to the ten thousand."

As far as we were concerned, we were going to Pittsburgh to sign a contract or, at the very least, to be told what Mr. Rickey was willing to offer. The trip between New York and Pittsburgh—as I had very good reason to know—takes exactly eight hours. For the trip up, we had a trip back. The most memorable part of our visit came when I spotted two very familiar faces in the hotel elevator.

"You know who those two men were?" I whispered after we'd stepped out into the lobby. "Stan Musial and Red Schoendienst."

My folks had never heard of either of them.

We had lunch with Mr. Rickey at the ball park, and we watched the ball game with him from his private box alongside the press box. It was the first ball game my mother had ever seen. Being quick of mind, she got the idea very quickly that you cheered when a run scored. Unhappily, St. Louis was scoring all the runs, which put Rickey in the position of having an enemy rooter sitting alongside him.

After the game, we all went into Rickey's office, arranged ourselves around his desk, and waited for his offer. He talked and he talked. His office was surprisingly small and, since the only window was of a translucent glass, rather dark and somber. So was the whole meeting. He talked for maybe an hour about the opportunities that could be found in baseball and about the virtues of Pittsburgh as a growing organization. I had come, frankly, to be bought, and he wasn't making the slightest attempt to buy me. Instead of telling me what the Pittsburgh organization could do for me, he seemed to be trying to sell the organization to me. At only one point did he touch even peripherally on the matter of a contract. The Pittsburgh organization, he said, would be willing to match any other offer I had. Since I had no other offer, that didn't bring me leaping out of my chair with joy.

It was all very confusing. When we were ushered out of Mr. Rickey's office and down into the street, the three of us just stood there, staring blankly at one another.

"Dad," I said. "I thought we came here to talk about a contract. What happened up there?"

"I was under the same impression," he said. "But we came here at Mr. Rickey's invitation, as his guests. It was his place to open contract negotiations, not ours. I didn't see why we should let him reverse our positions and maneuver us into naming a price as if we were the seller."

That was exactly the way I felt. It seemed to me he was willing to outbid anybody, as long as he was sure that he wasn't outbidding them by more than $500.

There is a steep curve on the railroad tracks between New York and Pittsburgh that is always taken on a high screech. It woke me up four times out of four in that one week, and it continued to wake me up when we were making the run with the Brooklyn Dodgers.

Back in Brooklyn, on Sunday night, Ed McCarrick called to ask how the visit with Mr. Rickey had gone. From the cheery tone of his voice, it was apparent that he was under the impression we had signed.

"Ed," I said, "he never made us any kind of an offer at all. We're still trying to figure out what we were there for."

"Oh my God, no," Ed said. And then there was a stunned, heavy silence.

I labored under a misconception for twelve years because McCarrick did not feel free to fill in the details while either of the Rickeys was alive. Mr. Rickey hadn't, as I had supposed, been waiting to outbid the opposition by $500.

From everything you now know, you may have come to the conclusion that he just couldn't raise the $10,000. That would make you just as wrong as I was

Mr. Rickey didn't try to raise the money. He was talked out of it ahead of time.

Remember Branch Rickey, Jr., and his own Sunday morning trip to Brooklyn?

Branch Jr. had not been able to get that game out of his mind. When he heard we were on our way up to be signed, he kept telling his father, "Don't do it. He's not ready. I've seen a sandlot team clobber him. All he'll do is take up space for two years and give the papers more ammunition to throw at you. And then when you need extra money again for some kid who will really be able to help us, you won't be able to get it."

Somewhere between the time we left Brooklyn and the time

we talked to Mr. Rickey, Branch Jr. talked his father out of signing me.

It didn't matter that much to me. The great irony, as far as Ed McCarrick was concerned, was that he lost me because he was undercut (for honest, logical, and understandable reasons) by his closest friends, the man who had brought him into the organization in the first place.

I wasn't left completely out in the cold by the end of the affair with Pittsburgh. Ed's call hadn't even been the first one I had got on the day we returned. Shortly after we walked into the house, All Campanis of the Dodgers was on the phone to find out how come I had missed my appointment to work out at Ebbets Field that morning.

The answer was easy. With all the running back and forth to Pittsburgh, I had completely forgot.

If you will bear with me, I'm going to flash back to show how the Dodgers finally stumbled across me. Jimmy Murphy of the Brooklyn *Eagle*, the same Jimmy Murphy who had god-fathered the Ice Cream League, had apparently seen me pitch the losing game against the Falcons too. Murphy had been far more impressed than the Pittsburgh brass had been.

Although I had never met Jimmy Murphy in my life, he had seen me pitch a few times, and Milt Laurie had kept him informed about my pitching at Cincinnati. Murphy already knew what I could do at my best, and he had been impressed by my willingness to keep throwing—however ineffectively— with a bloody finger.

A day or two later he happened to go to Ebbets Field— something he rarely did. He bumped into Al Campanis at the top of the grandstand behind home plate and began to tell him about me.

Jimmy Murphy, to Campanis, was just another old codger telling him about another phenom, another can't-miss kid— conversation which Campanis didn't hear more than six times a day. As much to get rid of him as anything else, he told Murphy he'd check me out.

Campanis, listening fast, had heard my name as "Kovacs."

He made no association whatsoever between a University of Cincinnati student named Koufax and a Brooklyn sandlotter named Kovacs. Murphy had told him that I went up to Camp Chi-Wan-Da during the week, so before he did anything else he sent a bird dog up to make sure I was at least built like an athlete. The report came back to him (1) that I was big and muscular and (2) that my name was Koufax.

At that point Campanis called me at the camp to set up the appointment. Just as he was calling me now to find out why I hadn't kept it.

Being nothing if not honest, I told him I'd just come back from Pittsburgh, where I had been working out for Mr. Rickey. I wasn't trying to show him I had other clubs after me. I wasn't that clever. I suppose, in fact, that I was just a little embarrassed at having to admit that I had broken an appointment with him because I had been out dancing with the competition.

Nevertheless, it was probably the best thing I could have said. The Pittsburgh scouting staff and the Brooklyn scouting staff had a friendly rivalry going, because most of them had worked together in Brooklyn under Rickey. Campanis and McCarrick had been particularly good friends, and were therefore particularly anxious not to lose any real prospects to each other.

Campanis asked me very quickly whether I had signed anything with Pittsburgh. I told him with a wryness that was undoubtedly lost on him that I most assuredly had not.

Thus reassured, he invited me to meet him for lunch the next day at Joe's, a well-known restaurant on Montague Street, just below the Dodger offices. One thing I had to admit, I might not be getting any bonus money shoved at me, but I sure was eating good.

While I was eating my veal Parmigiana and spaghetti, we set up a new tryout for the following day. It almost had to be the next day. Brooklyn was leaving town in three days, and I was returning to college in a week.

It turned out to be one of those days where you keep wishing that it would rain already, just to get it over with. Instead, there was just that intermittent light drizzle. Instead of taking batting practice, the players sat around the locked room, playing cards or reading their mail.

Since I had followed the Dodgers through the years, most of the players' faces were familiar, almost like one-column pictures come to life. And yet it was hard for me to be as over-awed as I had been at the Polo Grounds. Ebbets Field had a very small, very cluttered, very informal locker room. There was a kind of friendly, hospitable atmosphere about it. Or maybe it was just that I had become a veteran at this kind of thing.

When it became clear that there would be no batting practice at all, Campanis asked me, with a deference that surprised me, whether I'd be willing to go through with the tryout anyway, with the understanding that the adverse conditions would be taken fully into account.

Heck, I'd have gone out in a snowstorm. What did I care? Rube Walker came out to catch me. Campanis, Alston, and Fresco Thompson, the farm director, watched from O'Malley's box alongside the dugout.

I've got to say one thing. Everybody in the ball park watched my tryout. There being no batting practice, they had nothing else to watch. I was throwing very well, and I suppose the drizzle and the overcast skies made me look even faster. One of the customers not ooohing or aaahing was Ed McCarrick. I had let Ed know I was coming down, and he had decided to make himself a paying customer. I think I can say that it was the one time he wasn't rooting for me to look good.

All tryouts are pretty much the same. A tryout is a tryout is a tryout. Which means that a fast ball is a fast ball is a fast ball. Because that's all they're really looking for. Everything else can be taught. The fast ball is what you have to bring to the park with you.

They asked me to throw the fast ball for about five minutes and the curve for about five minutes. Then they alternated them for a while, fast ball, curve, fast ball, curve. Then two fast balls, two curves; three fast balls, three curves. Somewhere along the line they ask you to throw your change-up, and sometimes they even look at it. I always had the feeling they only ask for the change-up because they have to grade it on their report.

Control doesn't really concern them that much either, as long as you're somewhere around the plate. My definition of control was very simple. If you threw the baseball and the umpire called it a strike, that was control. In a workout like this, if I got it close enough to the plate so that Walker didn't have to jump around too much, I was happy. Try to throw to spots? Try to hit the catcher's glove? You've got to be kidding. If Walker had moved his glove from pitch to pitch, I wouldn't even have noticed.

There's one way you can tell if you're doing well. If they like what they're seeing, they'll keep you throwing for at least a half-hour. Because there's one final thing they have to know. They have to know how much of your speed you lose as you go along.

They must have kept me there for close to an hour. I had good stuff, good enough control, and my stuff held well enough to the end.

After I became a member of the Dodgers, Rube Walker told me that when they asked him for his assessment of me he had told them, "Whatever he wants, give it to him. I wouldn't let him get out of the clubhouse."

When I did go into the clubhouse, they asked the trainer, Doc Wendler, to give me a quick alcohol rubdown to get the dampness out of my bones. I had the distinct impression that they really wanted him to let them know whether I had the kind of body that might run to fat. I had put on a lot of weight up at camp during the summer. I must have been up around 220 pounds, the heaviest I have ever weighed.

Campanis's scouting report, dated September 17, 1954 (three days after the tryout), follows. Remember, again, that A stands for big-league average. The grades are based upon a scale of 80.

Fast ball	A+	Good velocity and life	77
Curve	A+	Breaks sharply	72
Change (F.B.)	A—	A bit too fast	60
Control	A—		60
Definite Prospect?	Yes		

Remarks: Athletic build, good musculature
Good poise and actions—smoother delivery—many clubs interested. Two are willing to make him a bonus player. Lad appears to possess confidence in himself. He has the tools. Whether or not to make him a bonus player is the question.

Al's comment that two other clubs were willing to make me a bonus player is interesting, because I had only said that they were interested in me. I suspect that Al, anticipating some resistance to making me a bonus boy, was giving himself a position of strength from which to argue. If so, it worked. Buzzie Bavasi, the Dodgers' general manager, immediately gave him permission to go after me.

Even before I left for college, Al had set out to woo my folks. He invited them to the Latin Quarter to meet his wife, and he began to visit our home almost nightly. He was pretty shrewd, too. He kept reminding my mother that if I played for Brooklyn I'd be able to live at home and save on living expenses. I would not want to say that Al was also implanting the idea that she would have her boy at home that much longer, except that he was.

When it got down to the money, my father told him it would take $20,000 to sign me.

"I'll be perfectly honest with you," Campanis said. "This is not an unreasonable amount of money to ask for. But this is my first big bonus case, and I was thinking more in terms of ten thousand. I'm going to have to go back to Buzzie and find out whether I can get it for you."

When he came back, Campanis asked if we would be willing to include my first year's salary in the $20,000. Since the minimum salary was $6,000, that would give me a bonus of $14,000.

Just before our trip to Pittsburgh, we had sat down to figure out just what a college education would cost and—allowing for the income-tax bite—the figure had come out to something very close to that.

There was one complication. A big-league team can carry only forty men on its roster over the winter, and the Dodgers still had to clear a space for me. Bavasi told my dad that he intended to trade Preacher Roe before the next season and asked for enough time to make the best possible deal. In the meantime, he wanted to sign a private agreement with us, whereby I would commit myself to sign, on the stipulated terms, whenever they got around to offering me the contract.

In passing the Dodgers' offer on to me, my father told me that he had a very strong objection to that kind of binder. We would be binding ourselves to sign when they wanted us, he said, but they weren't binding themselves to a thing. Not only did that kind of one-sided agreement offend him to the depths of his legal instincts; it was, he told me, illegal. There was a law on the books in New York at that time which rendered any contract that benefited only one of the parties null and void.

What he proposed to do, he said, was to make a handshake deal with Walter O'Malley, Dodger president, as fellow lawyers and gentlemen, whereby they would both commit themselves to live up to the terms of the agreement.

That sounded fine to me.

"Now wait a minute," he said. "I want to be sure you know what you're doing. Knowing human nature, you've got to understand that if word gets out about this—and we have to assume that it might—it is quite conceivable that other clubs are going to evaluate you on O'Malley's judgment and, knowing that you are not legally bound, make you a better offer. Even a fantastic offer.

"If I make a handshake deal with O'Malley, I am morally bound as a gentleman, but you're not bound, either legally or morally. If somebody comes along with a fantastic offer, you just might find yourself tempted. I want to ask you one thing.

Are you sure that you're satisfied with the terms the Dodgers have offered?"

I told him that I was.

"All right," he said. "Now I am going to ask you whether if you did receive a better offer would you hold up my right arm or would you let me drag my nose in the dust?"

I said, "Dad, I'm not that concerned about more money or less money. All I want is to find out whether I can pitch in the major leagues. But *any* deal that you make for me, even if I never pitch another game in my life, I will stick by."

No deal had been made, though. I was still committed to go to Milwaukee, and the season was running out.

The trip to Milwaukee remains one of the weirder events in my life as a free-lance, free-loading bonus boy. I recall it as through a sleepwalker's mirror, because that's exactly how I went through it, sleepwalking.

Since I didn't have either the scholarship or the contract when I returned to Cincinnati, I had gone to work as a stockboy at Rollman's, a department store that has since gone out of business. After working my first late shift Saturday night, I went to the airport and caught a plane that set me down in Milwaukee at six a.m. A scout was there to pick me up. He drove me to the Schroeder hotel, told me to report to the park at ten o'clock, and drove off.

Now, that was a mistake.

I flopped down on the bed, fully clothed, and the next thing I knew I was being shaken rather vigorously. Swimming into view came my scout and, behind him, two other men. I had slept through the ten-o'clock appointment. I had slept through their subsequent phone calls, I had slept through the pounding on the door. They had finally had to get the bell captain to let them in.

"My god, kid," one of them said, while I was yawning sleepily. "We almost broke the door down. Didn't you hear *anything?*"

Hear anything? I just barely managed to stay awake through the ride to the ball park. One of the scouts kept muttering, with something akin to awe, that he had never seen such a nonchalant kid before. That wasn't nonchalance. That was lack of sleep.

The only thing I can remember about the workout—for no reason at all—is that my catcher was Johnny Cooney, the bullpen coach. No, I also remember that Charlie Grimm, the manager, came over to say hello. That's all managers ever seem to do in these tryouts. I suppose they are taking a good look, but they keep themselves very much in the background. The lines of authority are so precisely drawn in baseball that it would be considered very bad form for anybody—even a manager—to inject himself into an area which is looked upon as the special province of the scout, the farm director, and the pitching coach.

Dazed as I was, weary as I was, I must have showed them something, because Milwaukee made me the best offer I ever received. There must be some moral in there somewhere, but I'll be darned if I know what it is. Maybe the moral is that it pays to be nonchalant.

The figure that John Quinn, the Braves' general manager, quoted to me was, if I remember correctly, $30,000. That's the kind of talk that will clear the cobwebs out of your head in a hurry. I'm not sure whether the first year's salary was included or not, or even whether that aspect of it was discussed.

There was a catch to their offer, though. The Braves already had two bonus boys, Joey Jay and Mel Roach, whose two years wouldn't be up until the middle of the next season. The club was hardly prepared to write either of those investments off without giving them both a better look, and they were certainly not prepared to carry three bonus players.

Their proposition was for me to stay in school, pitch another year of college ball, and join the club in June, after graduation. As far as I was concerned, joining a team in mid-season, especially a team that figured to be in contention, would be a complete waste of time. As a practical matter, I recognized that I would probably be spending my first year on the bench in the best of circumstances. Still, I did permit myself to do a little dreaming. The one place I'd get a chance to pitch, I knew, would be in spring training. Maybe, just maybe, I could pitch well enough to convince the manager that he could use me every now and then without making a travesty of the game.

I was also aware by this time that a promise to sign me in June was not completely binding. Not that I doubted Quinn's motives. It just seemed to me that if I came up with a sore arm or a broken leg I could hardly expect—or want—them to hand me $30,000 and wish me good luck in my new career.

I told Mr. Quinn that I wanted to sign before the end of the year. It was left at that. I didn't turn them down completely. They didn't turn me down completely.

I went right back to the airport and caught a plane back to Cincinnati so that I could catch a few hours' sleep before my first class in the morning.

I called home the next night to tell my father about the Milwaukee offer. He hadn't signed anything with Brooklyn yet, he said, but he had just made the handshake deal we had talked about.

"Fine," I told him.

My father had relayed his objections about the binder to O'Malley before they got together, and O'Malley had recognized the problem.

When they met in O'Malley's office to discuss the matter further, my father suggested that O'Malley might want to know a little more about him.

"I know quite a bit about you," he said. He ran down O'Malley's complete background, telling him that he had graduated from the University of Pennsylvania in 1926 and received his law degree from the Fordham Law School in 1930. He told him that he had practiced law in Brooklyn for five years, and had become attorney for the Dodgers in 1942, as the representative of the County Trust Company, the bank which was handling the Dodgers' affairs.

"You are no longer a practicing lawyer," he said, "but the point I want to make is that you *are* a lawyer."

He then went into his own background. As a young lawyer

in Dutchess County, he had practiced law with Judge Mack, the man who had nominated Franklin D. Roosevelt for President, and he had worked as assistant corporation counsel for the city of New York in the LaGuardia administration before going into private practice.

"The point I want to make about myself," he said, "is that in Dutchess County lawyers do not do business with each other as they do here. In Dutchess county, lawyers do business without written stipulations, and without written agreements. Their word is their bond."

With the biographical exchange out of the way, he told O'Malley that we were willing to accept the bonus that had already been agreed upon, with the proviso that O'Malley agree to proffer the contract by December 20 so that the income tax be paid for the current year.

"If you are in agreement with this deal," he told O'Malley, "just step up two paces and take my hand."

O'Malley took a long look at Bavasi. "You know, Buzzie," he said, "up in Dutchess County, where Mr. Koufax practiced law, a lawyer who wouldn't keep his word with another lawyer was ostracized from the legal community."

He stepped around the desk, took my father's hand, and said, "I'll take that deal."

The handshake deal, then, was made in late September. Cliff Alexander, the Dodgers' area scout, dropped by the dormitory to introduce himself and welcome me to the fold. My plans were to finish out the semester and check out at the Christmas vacation, just after the contract was signed.

Before I left, there came, out of nowhere, one last, rather painful echo from the Pittsburgh Pirates. In the first week of December, Ed McCarrick came to town and invited me to dinner at a fancy Chinese restaurant not far from the campus. I liked Ed, and I was glad to see him. The only difficulty was that when the talk turned to my future in baseball I didn't know what to say. I wasn't sure whether I was free to talk about the deal with the Dodgers, or whether the handshake had included an agreement of silence.

I went as far as I thought I could by telling him that I was still in close touch with the Dodgers, that Cliff Alexander had been down to see me, and that as soon as they were able to clear their roster they were going to make me a concrete offer.

"Well," he said, "you know how I feel. I'd give you anything you asked. We're just so tight for money right now that we can't come up with it."

When I got back to the dormitory, I couldn't sleep. The more I went over the conversation, the more I realized that McCarrick may not have picked up my broad hints. The thought that I was still on the market and Rickey wouldn't come up with the money was obviously driving him nuts.

First thing in the morning I wrote a letter to Ed, telling how much I appreciated everything he had done for me and how much I would always value his friendship. But, I emphasized, there was no doubt at all that I would soon be signing with the Dodgers.

A few days later my father received a call from Ed McCarrick. "Have you signed anything with the Dodgers yet?" Ed asked.

My father told him, quite truthfully, that we hadn't.

"Then don't do anything until I can talk to you," he said. "Whatever their offer is, we'll give you five thousand more."

"Well," my father told him, "when I said we hadn't signed anything, that was true. But I think I had better tell you now, in all candor, that I have an understanding with Mr. O'Malley on a lawyer's handshake, which is just as binding upon me as a written contract. Unless they fail to come up with the contract by December twentieth, in which case we will be happy to entertain all other offers."

A day or two later a call came from New Orleans, this time from Mr. Rickey himself. "Mr. Koufax," he said, "have you signed a contract with the Dodgers? There's a rumor around to that effect."

My father gave him the same answer he had given McCarrick, and Rickey repeated that the Pirates were prepared to go $5000 above the Dodgers or anybody else.

"Mr. Rickey," my dad said, "some months ago, you invited us to Pittsburgh at considerable expense to yourself and some discomfort and inconvenience to us. I was told you were inviting us for the purpose of discussing a contract. We were there almost two days, and you didn't mention one word about a contract. How is it you're so interested now?"

Rickey told him that money had been tight at the time, but that the club had just sold its New Orleans farm club. "And we are now anxious to spend money on bright young prospects like Sandy."

We could only imagine that Rickey had been told about the handshake deal and was giving my father another opportunity to change his mind about honoring it.

My dad couldn't quite resist the temptation to call Al Campanis and tell him about it. Al just waited, without saying a word, for whatever was coming next. "Don't worry, Al," my dad said, laughing, "I'm going to keep my word."

What had happened was that Ed McCarrick, unable to get me off his mind, had asked Rickey for permission to fly down to Cincinnati to keep up his contact with me. When he received my letter a short time afterward, he interpreted it not, as I had intended, as a final statement that I was committed to the Dodgers but as a warning that he had only a very few days to act himself. He immediately called the Pittsburgh office to make one final plea. Mr. Rickey was in Sea Island, Georgia, on a hunting and fishing expedition with some friends. There was absolutely no way, Ed was told, of getting in touch with him.

"We've got to do something," Ed told Sisler. "I just got a letter from Sandy, and he's going to sign with Brooklyn."

Either Sisler managed to get word to Sea Island, or Mr. Rickey came out of the woods. Two days after Ed had put in his frantic call, Rickey called him at his home in Westbury, New York. "Mr. Rickey," Ed said, "this is the kind of prospect a scout comes across once in his life. I don't want to lose this boy, Mr. Rickey."

And so Rickey, at that late date, had finally given him the go-ahead to make the offer.

If I have been under a misconception for twelve years about why Mr. Rickey hadn't offered us a contract while we were in Pittsburgh, Ed McCarrick has been under a misconception too. Since he thought he still had a chance to sign me when he received my letter, he assumed that the handshake deal my father told him about must have been made between the time he received my letter and the time he was finally able to get in contact with Mr. Rickey. In other words, he has been living for twelve years with the belief that he lost me because Mr. Rickey had been out of communication with the world for two full days.

To make it even more galling, from Ed's point of view, I would have preferred to sign with Pittsburgh because I knew I'd have a much better chance to pitch for them. Brooklyn was fighting for a pennant, and Pittsburgh was fighting to stay alive. The Pirates could afford to let me learn and let me lose. The Dodgers couldn't.

The Dodgers sold Preacher Roe and Billy Cox to Baltimore on December 14 and immediately proffered the contract to my father. After he had signed, it was mailed down to Cliff Alexander. Cliff picked me up at the dorm and took me to dinner at a small Italian restaurant. I signed while we were waiting for the meal to be served. The negotiations with the Dodgers ended as they had begun, over a plate of veal Parmigiana and spaghetti.

In signing the bonus contract, I was also signing a contract for both 1955 and 1956, at $6000 a year. That was fair enough. Since a bonus contract freezes you for two years, it was reasonable enough to wrap the whole deal up in one package.

It gives me great pleasure to be able to point out, in the pursuit of better management-labor relations, that Mr. O'Malley is more flexible than his detractors will admit. His rule against multi-year contracts does not extend to contracts that call for the minimum salary.

The announcement was made to a vastly uninterested world as a footnote to the story that Roe and Cox had been sold. The photographers were waiting in the Dodger offices when I arrived, looking not too excited with their chore for the after-noon. I put on the customary Dodger baseball cap and the customary Dodger shirt and posed with Al Campanis and Fresco Thompson in front of a blackboard that listed all the Dodgers' farm hands.

There is nothing like photographers to stamp an event as official. Historic. Irrevocable. It had happened. What had started so casually, almost as a lark, had become a career.

For the first time I felt a little fear. For the first time I felt the weight of my inexperience. I was on a big-league roster, frozen there for two years. Behind me were the names of minor leaguers, all of them vastly more experienced than I was.

How could they have given me all that money? I thought to myself. How could they have dared to clear the roster for me? Why, I hadn't pitched twenty games in my whole life!

The photographers, focusing away, asked me to smile. I gave them my very best forced smile at first, the way you do when you're not used to posing. But all at once the smile began to spread, almost of itself, and it was a smile that had nothing to do with the photographers. The feeling that had come over me at that moment—to my own astonishment—was the sense of sheer pleasure that comes when you have set off on some im-possible course and have unexpectedly brought it off. *I got away with it*, I thought.

In the brief moment it took for the flash to go off and the blindness to clear from my eyes, I thought: I've fooled them. All these experts who are supposed to know so much, and I've fooled them all.

That wasn't how I had expected to feel at all.

5

La Dolce Vita *of Vero Beach*

Normally spring training begins on March 1, but the pitchers report a week or two early so that they will be prepared to throw batting practice to the incoming hitters and so that, when the season opens, everybody can nod wisely and say that the pitchers are still ahead of the hitters.

In 1955, for reasons that must have seemed good to the collective wisdom of the rulesmakers, there was a rule that nobody, pitchers included, could report before March 1. Since rules are made to be evaded, I went down to Miami a week early and worked out at the Miami Stadium with Roy Campanella, Don Newcombe, and Joe Black.

I was delighted. It was all an adventure to me. Besides, I wanted to get in as much work as I could down South. I was eager to be in the best possible shape, even though I had not the slightest idea what being in shape meant.

The trip to Miami really started as our own idea. My father hadn't been feeling well, and we all thought a vacation would do him good. Since we had relatives around the Miami area, we had decided that we would drive down together.

To make the great adventure perfect, my father had just bought a new Chrysler. I grabbed the wheel after the first lunch stop, and I don't think he got it back for the rest of the trip.

After spending a few days with our relatives, we checked into the Lord Carlton Hotel in Miami Beach. A day later I met

Campy, Newk, and Joe at a luncheon at the Algiers Hotel. I imagine that the reason they were beating the March 1 opening was that Campy was coming off a bad season and a couple of operations on the nerves of his left hand. It was important to him and to the Dodgers to put the hand to the test as soon as possible. Campy still didn't have the complete lateral movement of three of his fingers at Miami, and I don't know if it ever did come back completely. All he was able to do was to grip the bat and the glove well enough to win his third Most Valuable Player Award in 1955.

I didn't do much more than throw a ball around with them for three or four days, but as an adventure in the big-league life it was great. Irving Rudd from the Brooklyn front office was down there early to get the Miami Stadium into shape, and he appointed himself as our guide. The first thing he did was to introduce me to Jimmy Durante—*in* person. The manager of the hotel had the TV cameras there to shoot some film of me showing Durante how to pitch and—to show how much they knew—to hit.

I also got myself my first award as a big-league ballplayer, a key to the city of Miami. Campy, Newk, and Joe were being feted by the Algiers Hotel, and when I turned up as a rather anonymous fourth member of the Dodgers they dug up a key for me, too.

Upon leaving the affair, my dad and I found yet another award from the city, a parking ticket. As we left quaint, colorful Miami, gateway to Vero Beach, we had two souvenirs of our visit, one of them deserved.

The camp at Vero Beach is really an old reconditioned World War II Navy base. What you see upon driving in is a dingy gray cluster of long, flat two-story buildings, set off behind rather nicely landscaped shrubbery. The main building —the club offices, dining room, and general recreation room— is in the middle. The old officers' quarters, which are now players' dormitories, are on either side.

There are two kinds of rooms. One—apparently for the junior officers—was no more than that, just a little old YMCA-type room, with a common shower down the hall. As a very junior ballplayer, I was, needless to say, assigned one of the little rooms. I was also assigned a roommate, Chuck Templeton, another left-handed pitcher.

If a rookie hangs on, a life of luxury and ease awaits him. In a couple of years, through time and natural attrition, a suite opens up in the larger building. *We* call them suites, anyway. The Waldorf-Astoria might call them something else. Our suites consist of a small bedroom, a small sitting room, and, at last, a small built-in private shower.

The Dodgers had a legitimate phenom in camp, Karl Spooner, who had broken in with the team at the end of the previous season with a couple of tremendous strikeout games. Since we were both fastballing lefties, Karl and I found ourselves working side by side quite frequently, and, as almost always happens in baseball, the guy you're thrown into contact with becomes your closest friend.

Baseball aside, there were three of us from the same neighborhood, Joe Pignatano, Mike Napoli, and myself. Karl would join us after practice almost every day to do what you would expect three boys from the streets of Brooklyn to do—go fishing. That in itself should give you an idea of *la dolce vita* of Vero Beach.

During spring practice the players wear their last year's uniforms, which means that the new players take whatever is around that fits. The first day I walked into the dressing room, I was assigned number 32, a number that had been knocking around among utility players for years. Cal Abrams had worn it, Rocky Nelson had worn it. Joe Antonello had worn it in 1953, and it had lain fallow in 1954. Antonello (another Brooklyn boy, incidentally) had been built along the same lines as I, and so I got his old uniform, complete with number. Old or new, there is something almost ceremonial about pulling on the uniform for the first time, like being initiated into the fraternity. Maybe it's because the uniform has the name of the team written so prominently across it, the same familiar emblem that you have seen gracing the chests of great ballplayers for as long as you can remember. I had worn a Dodger uniform in my tryout, of course, but this was altogether different. This time I was a member of the team, one of twenty-five men. This time I knew that I was supposed to make some contribution to the over-all effort.

And I was so green. I was so green that I didn't even speak the language. When I heard that someone "had good wheels"— which in baseball parlance means he can run—I thought he was being praised for having a good head on his shoulders, as in "his wheels are always spinning."

Here's how green I was. Our first exhibition game was in the Miami Stadium. After batting practice we all came back to the dressing room to change into fresh sweatshirts, and I suddenly realized that I had not the slightest idea what I was supposed to do. "Just follow me," Joe Black told me, "and whatever I do, you do too."

Joe stationed himself halfway between the infield and outfield and relayed balls back in to whoever was hitting fungoes. I staked myself out an inconspicuous spot of my own and alternated between throwing balls back in and staying out of the way.

I was easily the most inexperienced kid ever to come to a major-league camp. But I was not—repeat not—as green, as wild, or as awkward as some of the taller tales make me out to have been.

One of the stories that seems to follow me around is that I was so wild and awkward in my first two or three springs that Joe Becker, the pitching coach, used to take me behind the barracks so that I could warm up without being embarrassed. Walter Alston was supposed to have said that he had never seen such an uncoordinated pitcher. One of the hardiest perennials is that I blushed crimson and pawed at the dirt with my toeplate upon overhearing a tourist say that I threw like a girl.

Nothing like that happened at all, of course. Common sense tells you that no major-league team would have wasted time, let alone a place on the roster, on a pitcher who looked that bad. Without a basic sense of coordination you'd have as much chance pitching in the big leagues as you'd have dancing for the Rockettes. Coordination isn't anything that can be taught; you either have it or you don't.

What happened in the first couple of springs, and happens still, is that when you first start to throw, your arm gets sore. I had assumed, from my vast inexperience, that you eased your valuable arm into shape slowly by throwing a day and resting a day. I discovered very quickly that you just kept throwing. Every day. Your arm was sore? So what? You were expected to throw through the soreness. Your shoulder was stiff? What a shame! You were expected to work it out by exercise. I don't know about anybody else, but my shoulder stiffens up pretty good when I first begin to throw in the spring. It takes me ten or fifteen minutes just to get loose. While you are trying to loosen up a sore shoulder, you are going to look stiff and awkward.

Becker did take me behind the barracks. It wasn't to hide me, though. All the pitchers were taken behind the barracks for the excellent reason that the pitching area—commonly called "the string area"—is back there. (From a couple of the practice mounds, you throw to a visible strike zone blocked out by two horizontal and two vertical strings.)

I'm not trying to say I wasn't wild. For one thing, Dixie Howell wouldn't let me. Dixie was standing innocently along the batting cage one quiet morning, well out of the line of fire, he thought, since I was throwing on the sidelines. I threw a fast ball so wild that it caught him on the shin and sent him hobbling to the trainer's room for first aid. For years, I couldn't bump into Dixie without his saying, "You dirty so-and-so, every time it rains I get a remembrance from you."

I didn't start to earn my pay by throwing, anyway. I started to earn it, it seemed, by running. In my limited experience, I had never run at all. It never occurred to me that running kept you in condition to pitch, and I never dreamed that you were supposed to run every day.

Joe Becker taught me different. Becker, a rough-hewn old catcher, had just become the pitching coach for the Dodgers. My first day in camp was his first day too.

Joe walked around introducing himself to his pitchers and then made himself something less than a prime candidate for Man of the Year by telling us he wanted us to go twenty-five laps around the ball park.

"Twenty-five," one of the veterans moaned. "Let's start with fifteen and work our way up."

"No," Joe said. "Let's start with twenty-five and work down. If you're going to get sore, you might as well get as sore as it's possible to get the first day."

This, I discovered, is the war that never ends. Pitchers complain about running the way soldiers complain about the food, partly because it's expected of them and partly because nobody likes to run just for the sake of running—not even runners. The coach can only tell you that you have to run because it's good for you, which is like telling a kid to eat his spinach.

Any pitcher worth his salt tries to cut his running down by making the outfield turns as small as possible. The coach's job is to make you go as wide as possible. Joe would stand there with his bag of balls and he'd hit fungoes to you, and he had this fiendish, maddening, and uncanny ability to place the ball so that, if you ran as hard as you could, you could just barely catch it. If you didn't catch it, the ball would roll a good distance behind the "track" you were running, so it was always better to exert yourself to make the catch than to have to chase the ball down and then hustle to get back in the group again.

By the end of spring training I might not have been ready to pitch big-league baseball but I was in excellent shape to run a marathon.

The year after we moved to Los Angeles, Art Fowler, a very funny fellow, joined the club. Every day Art would have a new argument to put forth in his debate with Joe. "I got a mule at home can run all day long," Art would tell him, "and he can't get *nobody* out."

Or: "If running was that good for you, Jesse Owens would win forty games."

I'm overstating the resistance, of course. Nobody, for instance, ever worked harder than Don Newcombe. Newk, I discovered, was a fanatic on running, which was surprising, in that most people looked upon him as a big, slow, lazy kind of guy. Newk was a big man, and he felt he had to do a lot of running. He warned me from the beginning that I had better get into the habit early. "It's important now," he said, "and it will be more important later. It just never stops."

That wasn't why most pitchers ran, though. You ran, it seemed to me, because Joe wanted you to run, and because you knew it was part of his job to make you run. Maybe you didn't feel like it, maybe you didn't think it was good for you, maybe you thought it was a lot of nonsense, but you ran anyway.

When the rest of the team was gone, the pitchers left behind would get in some hitting and some throwing, and then, even without Becker there to crack the whip, we'd run our laps. We were "Becker's Bastards"—that's what he called us—and we felt we were members of a select corps.

Joe commanded that kind of loyalty because he treated everybody exactly the same whether he had won twenty-five games or none. You were one of his boys, you belonged to him. He was like the shepherd of the flock. If you were going badly, he worried with you, and if you were going well, he rejoiced with you. The great thing Joe did for me in those frustrating early years was to make me feel that somebody looked upon me as a legitimate member of the team, that somebody was interested in whether I ever became a pitcher or not.

Joe helped me where he could. For one thing, he told me I was leaning back too far in my wind-up. The farther I leaned back, he said, the more room I was giving myself to make a mistake and the tougher it was to keep the ball low. To put it the other way, the less you do before you throw the ball, the less trouble you can get yourself into.

I did tighten up my wind-up a little. It was not until 1961, though, that I really scrapped my somewhat exaggerated wind-up and made it as compact as I could make it while still building up the body motion I needed for my momentum.

I believe I've made it plain that I like Joe Becker, and that I appreciate everything he did, or tried to do, for me. I was his special project from the day he first drew on the Dodger uniform, and for years I suspect he looked upon me as his greatest disappointment.

But nobody can make you into a pitcher except yourself. The physical part of it just isn't that difficult. Throwing a baseball is not the incredibly complicated, esoteric, and scientific undertaking that some people try to make it.

You have to be careful. In telling one writer how inexperienced I was when I reported, I said that I didn't even know how to stand on the mound, which is the same kind of exaggerated humor as saying that you don't know which end of the bat to hold. He took me at my word, though, and one of the stories that keeps popping up, in the name of research, is that Becker had to show me how to stand on the pitcher's mound.

The way to stand there is to stand there. I'm not sure how it could possibly be done wrong.

The same thing is true about the correct way to hold a ball, another highly technical point in which I presumably needed instruction. I'll tell you all you have to know about holding a ball: if you hold it too tight, your muscles will tense up and you'll be throwing with a stiff wrist; if you hold it too loose, you'll drop it. So if you don't drop the ball and don't squeeze the juice out of it, you're in excellent shape. If you hand your ten-year-old son a baseball, he'll hold it quite nicely.

Now that we've established that you stand on the mound by standing there and hold the ball by holding it, there remains only the problem of throwing the ball correctly. There *is* no such thing as the right way to throw a baseball. No two pitchers throw exactly the same. You throw it the way it's most comfortable for you to throw it. You can do anything you want to do as long as you do it every time. The act of pitching is a mechanical exercise. Purely mechanical. The same movements over and over and over. If the mechanism is in good working order—motor, swivels, hinges, levers—every picture taken at the same point of your delivery should be exactly the same in every detail down to the wrinkles on your uniform. As long as the mechanism follows the prescribed pattern every time, the ball is going to follow the same path.

Once the mechanism is operating smoothly, it becomes a matter of making the necessary adjustments to change the flight of the ball. By stepping an inch or two to the left on your stride, you will move the ball four or five inches to the left at the plate.

Control, the ability to put the ball *where* you want it, is purely physical. The mental part of pitching comes in knowing *why* you want to put it there.

There has been a lot of highly technical jargon written about "bending your back" and having your hands in the proper position after delivery. All that means, in simple English, is that you should follow through, just as you should follow through on a golf swing or a basketball shot.

You don't throw a ball with your follow-through, any more than you hit a ball with your follow-through. They are only the indications that the whole mechanism is in good working order.

When I reported to camp I threw straight overhand—over the top—just as I throw now. I had a fast ball and a curve, just as I have now. As a matter of fact, my fast ball was faster, because I was younger and stronger. My curve ball was sharper too. That's normal enough. During the All-Star break in Washington in 1962, Warren Spahn came over and asked me to show him how I threw my curve. Come on, Warren, I thought, you're putting me on. But he wasn't. Spahn told me that he had never had a good curve.

My curve is more effective now, because I know where it's going. But it isn't bigger. Quite the contrary. I threw a bigger curve on the Parade Grounds than I've ever thrown at Chavez Ravine.

I had to learn *how* to pitch. And that, I'm afraid, is something you have to learn yourself. You watch and you listen and, as we say in our line of work, you "have an idea." I had darn little idea what it was all about that first spring.

In those days the Dodgers spent only a couple of weeks at Vero Beach and then went to Miami to play their exhibition games. Before we left Vero, the big team played an exhibition game against the Dodgertown All-Stars, the best of the minor-leaguers who had been invited to camp. I started against the All-Stars—Jim Gentile is about the only All-Star I can remember offhand. I went three innings, striking out five and walking one, and Pignatano threw out the guy I had walked. In all honesty, I felt I had done well. In all honesty, I also had to admit that the lights at Vero were pretty bad.

Still, I had wanted to use the spring training period to show what I could do. I felt I had shown something. I also felt, just looking around me, that I was not going to see too much work during the season.

6

Bonus Boy

When the historians of our civilization list the more foolish and self-defeating measures imposed by any profit or non-profit organization upon itself, let them not forget baseball's ingenious bonus rule, a notable improvement upon the ancient Phoenician custom of throttling their young.

The purpose of the rule was to discourage big-league clubs from paying too much money to too many promising young ballplayers at the one point where the player still had the opportunity to bargain. The method, as we know, was to force the club to keep the bonus boy on the roster, as a sort of neutral observer, for two full years. The inevitable result was to cut the most promising players off from active duty at precisely the point where they most needed the work and the competition and were most open, physically and mentally, to instruction and improvement.

If we assume that the bonuses went to the best players, a not unjustified assumption, we can only conclude that baseball was deliberately hobbling its future stars, the players upon whom it would one day have to depend to draw customers to the box office. It was a brilliantly conceived program from beginning to end.

They finally repealed it—from what I understand—not because they had grown weary of cutting their own jugular but because too many clubs were cheating on their own rule by paying the bonuses under the table.

The bonus rule penalized (a) the team, (b) the boy, and (c) baseball itself. It also penalized (d) the fringe player, the most penalized figure of all. When the bonus boy took over the no. 25 slot on a roster, somebody, after all, got pushed over the edge.

The fringe player is the guy who is always hanging on by his fingernails. He is the guy who is trying to get in his fifth year so that he qualifies for the pension. He is the guy who needs the big-league salary to live on, and prays for a World Series check (or first-division cut) to pay off his accumulated debts and maybe even put away a few dollars for his kids' education. It really made him feel good to see some untried kid, without a responsibility in the world, push him back to the minors.

Happily for me, I was too green to have any self-consciousness about being a bonus boy. Other teams, after all, had wanted me and had been willing to pay an even larger bonus. Besides, the Dodgers, as anyone who was around the league those days can tell you, were as great a group of men as has ever been put together. They didn't throw a party to welcome me to the clubhouse, but they didn't make me feel like a stranger either.

And then there was this: we won our first ten games, a major-league record, lost two out of three to the Giants, and then came right back with eleven more straight victories. With everybody else breaking even, we had the pennant won almost before anybody else got untracked. If I was taking up a place on the roster, it was a place that could obviously be spared. By the time our pitching began to fall apart, we were so far ahead that it still didn't matter. Not to downgrade myself too much, I must say this: at the low point of the season for the Dodgers, they called upon their bonus boy (there being nobody else), and their bonus boy won them a ball game.

In the first couple of weeks I wasn't even in the bullpen. I was on the bench. The trouble with putting me out in the bullpen was that you can't see what's going on from out there. In order to keep the two years from being a total loss, the Dodgers wanted me sitting alongside Erskine or Newcombe so that I could ask questions and absorb the wisdom of their accumulated years. There were at least two basic misconceptions there. The first misconception—and I mean this quite seriously—was that I knew enough about pitching to ask an intelligent question. The second was that pitching is an academic subject that can be taught in a lecture course, like medieval history. It was simply the least bad of the two possible alternatives, the other alternative being to put me in a ball game.

That first week was something. The Dodgers started six different pitchers, Erskine, Newcombe, Loes, Meyer, Podres, and Labine, and only Newk got hit. Watching them, I felt my chances of ever getting into a game fading away. This was a team that simply never made a mistake. I could see very little reason why they should want to put me in to prove that they were human.

It was an extraordinary team in every way. The infield was Hodges, Gilliam, Reese, and Robinson. The outfield was Snider, Furillo, and Amoros. The catcher, of course, was Campanella. Not only could they all hit the ball out of the park, they could all field their positions with anyone.

With it all, it was a particularly confident team. Not cocky, not complacent, just absolutely sure of itself. It was a team that had been winning pennants (or just barely losing) for so many years that there was a settled air about the locker room, a lack of tension—meaning job insecurity—that, I later learned, was very rare in a big-league club. There was not quite so much exultation after a winning game (unless it had been a particularly dramatic win) and not quite so much gloom after a losing game (unless it had been a particularly galling loss). When the Dodgers won, they expected it; when they lost, they expected to win the next day.

The nucleus of the club had been together for an inordinate length of time, even for a winning team. Reese was in his sixteenth year, Furillo in his tenth. Snider, a graying eagle, and Robinson, even grayer, were in the ninth year. So was Hodges. Campanella was in his eighth year; it was Newcombe's and Erskine's seventh. They were all, for the most part, good friends; in some instances—Reese, Snider, and Erskine—extremely close friends. Besides just liking one another, each felt good about the others because they had all helped one another become winners.

And then there was that friendly ball park itself. As I have said, the dressing room in Ebbets Field had a cozy, sandlot atmosphere about it. Here's how small it was: there were two huge pillars right in the middle of the room, and we were so tight for space that there was a locker on each side of each pillar. The *visitors'* dressing room in Yankee Stadium is luxurious by comparison.

Unlike the lockers in any other dressing room I have ever been in, those at Ebbets Field were not set up numerically. The old settlers had laid claim to their own spots through the years, and there was no kind of order or sense. Duke Snider and Carl Erskine, close friends, had their lockers on opposite sides of the first pillar—which put them completely out of sight of each other. Campy had his locker set up in front of the second pillar, which put him directly across from Erskine. Pee Wee Reese had his locker in a sort of corner alcove along the far wall, but looking out toward the back of the room. Next to Reese came Hodges, and next to Hodges came Jackie Robinson.

Except for Reese, everybody has a simple, ordinary stool in front of his locker. Reese has a big black solid armchair. It is the captain's chair. Pee Wee sits there comfortably, one arm draped over the side, sipping a beer after the game. He is entitled.

Reese and Hodges will always be needling each other in a dry, deadpan sort of way. From Hodges will come innocent throwaway remarks about aging ballplayers, since Reese has been losing half a step for half a dozen years. Reese will offer asides about Hodges' saintly nature and superhuman strength, the picture of him (and a true one) that is always presented by the press. If Pee Wee is being interviewed about the futility of arguing with umpires, he will point out that the competitive fires must be fed and, without cracking a smile, he will lift his voice so that it can be heard throughout the room and say, "Why, even Hodges, as meek and mild as he is, was once seen arguing with an umpire."

Reese's and Hodges' lockers form a triangle with Snider's. Add Erskine and Robinson right alongside, and you have the core of the room. Tucked in between the two pillars and Robinson's locker is the big steamer trunk, filling up all the extra space. It is the all-purpose card table. There will usually be a game of bridge or hearts going on, with Jackie—always the competitor—noisily involved.

The other two members of the Old Breed are Newcombe and Furillo. Furillo has the end locker on the Reese-Hodges-Robinson side of the room. Carl is kind of a loner, in that he tends to go his own way. In my second year I will begin to room with Carl on the road and get to know him for the solid guy that he is.

Big Newk has the end locker on the other side of the room. He is big and good-natured and helpful and hard-working. He is all the things that somehow never came across to the public. A shame.

My own locker is on the near side, almost across from Campy's. I am an observer. I am with the team but not of it. I am wearing the uniform, but I am contributing nothing. I am denied even the therapy of being allowed to be unhappy. The problem of every manager—as every manager knows—is to keep the players who are sitting on the bench happy. Or, at least, not too unhappy. If you have a guy who isn't playing and doesn't care, you don't want him. If, on the other hand, he is always grousing, he is a troublemaker, sharpshooter, and clubhouse lawyer. When a team is spreadeagling the field you can't second-guess the manager for anything, not even for failing to see how much better off he'd be using you. All you can do is sit.

The players give the locker room its tone and a great deal of its spirit. The real spirit of the room, however, comes from Charlie DiGiovanna, better known as the Brow. A great boy, Charlie. Charlie must have been, oh, twenty-three or twenty-four years old when I came to the club. He was sometimes called "the world's oldest batboy." He was also the world's best-paid one, because he was always voted half a share of the World Series money.

Charlie almost went into the Little Red Book as the only batboy ever to get thrown out of a ball game. He got on an umpire real good one day, a practice considered somewhat beyond the legitimate aspirations of your normal everyday batboy. When the umpire turned around to find out where all that noise was coming from, Charlie, brought suddenly back to reality, went racing into the clubhouse while we all roared.

By the time I joined the team Charlie wasn't only a batboy, he was practically the assistant clubhouse man. Ask a ballplayer what he does when he comes into the locker room, and he'll probably run through everything except the one routine, faintly irritating task that he has become so accustomed to that he does it without thinking: signing baseballs. I'm not sure what they do with all those balls, but someone must be stockpiling them in underground caves in Arizona, because no matter how many of them you sign one day, there are always a couple of boxes of fresh new ones waiting to be signed the next.

One of Charlie's jobs was to get the balls signed. As you walked into the locker room, Charlie would be chanting, "Everybody loves to sign baseballs. Jablonski signs balls, Repulski signs balls, Baczewski signs balls and Kluszewski signs balls. If Repulski, Baczewski, Jablonski, and Kluszewski can sign balls, *you*, Sandy Koufax, can sign baseballs too."

Or he'd catch the star of the previous game coming in and give him the real spotlight treatment. "Yes, you've heard of him, you've seen him, you've read about him in your favorite daily journal. And now you can see him in person—the Dook, the one, the only, the original Dook. Yes, you too can see Duke Snider, star of the National League, scourge of the right-handed curve-baller, sit down and sign baseballs."

Since it was impossible for us to sign all the baseballs and still find time to play the ball game, Charlie took up the slack by signing a reasonable percentage of them himself. Through perseverance and dedication to the job, Charlie had become a highly skilled forger, an ambidextrous forger. The man was amazing. He'd be standing there, talking to someone, and he'd be rolling the ball in his hands, shifting the pen from right hand to left, as he signed for the entire Brooklyn roster. He apparently followed a definite pattern, placing each signature in precisely the same spot on every ball. Once the season was under way, and the roster was set, he scarcely had to look down at his work.

The nickname "the Brow" originally came, it was evident enough, from his rather heavy eyebrows. The name stuck, however, because it had that extra connotation of intelligence and shrewdness. It had a Runyonesque dash about it, as of a professor who had joined the carnival.

We all knew that Charlie had had some kind of rheumatic heart condition from his youth, but nobody paid much attention to it, least of all Charlie himself. Once each year he'd take a road trip with the club and simply take over every town we were in. He was so lively, so full of life, that you couldn't believe he could go overnight. But he did. He came to Los Angeles with the team and died suddenly, after our first season.

It is impossible to think of the Ebbets Field locker room without thinking first of all of Charlie the Brow. You also think of John Griffin, who came to Los Angeles with us also and died almost in front of my eyes.

Griffin was known as the Senator, probably because he looked like one to somebody with a highly jaundiced view of Senators. John had a round paunch and a round cigar. By the time I came on the scene he'd been with the Dodgers for something like forty years. Hard as it was for me to believe at nineteen, he went all the way back to the days when Casey Stengel played for the club. It's more difficult to describe John's impact on the clubhouse because his personality was exactly the opposite of Charlie's. The Senator was a generally quiet, generally gruff man. The first time I ever spoke to him I had just come out of the shower and wanted to know if there was an extra towel around somewhere. "No," he barked, scaring me half to death. A few minutes later I looked around, and there, hanging on my locker, was a fresh towel. That was the Senator. He liked to bark but he never bit.

The Senator's great contribution was to the flavor of the club. The quiet, gruff man was a clown at heart. The Senator always had a special outfit to wear or, at the very least, a special hat. It might be a stovepipe or a coonskin or a derby or a football helmet or a baby's hat, or he might tap some outrageous model from that inexhaustible supply, women's headwear.

Usually John would wear the whole costume: not just the baby's hat, but a diaper—yes, I said diaper—bib, and rattle; not just a cowboy hat, but the whole darn outfit, complete with chaps. You haven't lived unless you've seen John walk through the lobby of a swank hotel wearing a beanie hat with a propeller on top, and smoking a big cigar. Only a magnificent human being could pull something like that off. The Senator's secret was that, no matter how outrageous the costume or startled the stares, he never acted as if he was wearing anything out of the ordinary.

The theory behind it all was that the Senator continued to wear the same outfit for as long as we kept winning. We had an early-season winning streak one year that extended right through a visit to Chicago, and Chicago in the springtime is *cold.* The Senator was wearing that baby costume at the time, and he gamely wore the diaper right through the whole series.

John was all things in the clubhouse, by which I mean he was given the right, through longevity, of doing whatever he felt like doing. Every once in a while, when he felt the team needed to be picked up, he'd call a clubhouse meeting and announce that he was going to go over the signs. He'd run through all kinds of signs, all of them graphic, all of them humorous, all of them indescribable, and none of them usable in a ball park.

Pitchers were his favorites, I suppose because John was the man in the clubhouse when the pitcher came storming in after he had been knocked out of the box. The first time I came out that I can remember, I heaved my glove angrily against the wall. "If you threw that hard out there," the Senator said calmly, "you'd probably still be there."

John was in his fifties when the team moved to Los Angeles, and there was some question as to whether he'd be brought along. He came, though. After forty-five years, he'd have been lost without the club.

He and I were talking casually in the Pittsburgh clubhouse in 1963, and he was flexing his left arm from time to time and complaining that it was bothering him.

In Pittsburgh, the home and visiting clubhouses are side by side. When you leave the clubhouse, you go through the under-pinnings of the park to the runway leading to the first-base dugout. There is usually a seat outside the clubhouse door, probably for the special guard to sit on when you want to keep everybody out.

John got up and walked outside. Shortly afterward I started out, and just as I got to the doorway he toppled right off the chair. I let out a yell to the trainers. A call went out for a doctor, but by then it was too late. He was gone.

But that was much later. In Brooklyn, we had the Brow and the Senator and the nicest group of guys in captivity. The only trouble was that I wasn't getting in any ball games. To be perfectly honest, I had made it very easy to ignore me. On the fifth day of the season, I was shagging flies dutifully in Pittsburgh when I either stepped into a hole or hit the sprinkler head embedded in the ground. Very embarrassing.

Less than two weeks later, back in Brooklyn, I was running in the outfield again, getting in my work, when I strode grace-fully into another sprinkler head and twisted my left ankle good. I went limping over to Joe Becker to explain why I couldn't run any more, then went inside to let Doc Wendler have a look at it. Doc probed around a little and sent me to the Long Island College Hospital in Brooklyn to have it X-rayed. I had spent two weeks in uniform, my contribution had been zero, and I had developed a fascinating talent for stepping into holes. Idiot!

I didn't look upon it as a serious injury, though, nothing more than a slight sprain. The ankle loosened up after a couple of days, and I was back into my routine again when Doc Wendler called me in to tell me that I had a hairline fracture on the ankle and was being placed on the disabled list for thirty days.

A very slow-drying X-ray.

I'm sure it was purely coincidental that, with the May 15 cutdown date coming up in a week, my unfortunate injury gave the club a chance to hold on to another pitcher for three extra weeks. Actually, the Dodgers were protecting themselves even further by carrying ten pitchers and only four outfielders, which means I was really replacing an outfielder. When my thirty-day vacation was over on June 8, Tom Lasorda was sent down to make room for me. Lasorda eventually became a scout for the Dodger organization, and he still likes to point me out in a crowd and say, "You wouldn't believe it, but this is the guy who drove me out of the big leagues."

The Dodgers still had the ten pitchers. The day after I came back, Joe Black was traded to the Reds for an outfielder, Bob Borkowski.

I celebrated my return to active duty by promptly spending another two weeks doing nothing. Well, not exactly nothing. I pitched batting practice every other day. I also ran. Someone passed me as I was making the big turn on one of the laps around the outfield, and he welcomed me back to the fold by advising me, "Be careful now. Don't trip over the foul line." It's great to know they're that concerned about your welfare.

What do you do when you're the ninth man on a nine-man squad? Well, you very quickly realize that the only way you are going to get into a ball game is for your team to be so badly beaten that there's nothing to lose by putting you in. With the Dodgers this wasn't easy. The Dodgers were such a strong hitting team, especially at home, that we were never really out of a game.

You don't root against your own team. Under no circumstances can I imagine any ballplayer rooting for something to go wrong. But you know that in the course of the season there are going to be some games where you're going to get clobbered. You can only keep working and hope that you have a good day when your chance to mop up comes.

It didn't work quite that way with me. What happened was that the entire Dodger staff, except for Newcombe and Labine, began to have arm trouble, separately and in concert. My chance came when Erskine began to have trouble with his elbow. Early in a night game at Milwaukee, Carl felt the elbow tightening on him again, and Alston sent me down to the bullpen. That wasn't unusual. It was customary for me to start every game on the bench and be sent to the bullpen when they wanted me to throw. Not infrequently I was there as a decoy. Walt wanted the other manager to see a left-hander out there to discourage him from sending up a left-handed pinch-hitter.

I had great stuff warming up. Just great. Still, I didn't expect to be called. I had been up and down so many times by then that I had given up any idea of pitching in a game. My role on the club had become quite clear to me. Some guys pitched, and some guys threw in the bullpen. My job was to throw in the bullpen.

I was throwing to Rube Walker. Somebody else—it may have been Labine—was throwing to Dixie Howell. When the bullpen phone rang, Becker got it. If he said anything at all, I didn't hear it. All I know is that when he hung up and turned back he said, "It's Koufax. Go get 'em, Sandy."

The date was June 24. We were playing the sixty-sixth game of the season. It was the last half of the fifth inning, and we were trailing, 7–1. It was a Friday-night game, the Braves were in second place (a scant fourteen games behind us), and there were 43,068 people in Milwaukee Stadium, only a handful below capacity.

As I started the long walk in from the bullpen, I wasn't the least bit scared. I felt great. I knew I'd been throwing well. I was overjoyed—if somewhat astonished—that I was finally getting into a game.

By the time I reached the mound, all that had changed. Remember, now, I had never walked onto a big-league field to pitch before. Let me see if I can describe it: the bullpen in

Milwaukee was in right center field, and there were no bleachers behind us at all. The only bleachers were way over in left field. That meant you were not surrounded by people, you were walking into the people, *into* the sound. More specifically, you were walking toward a double-decked grandstand filled with people. A weird thing happened. As you got closer and closer to the infield, the grandstand seemed to rise up in front of you, to become higher and steeper. The crowd noise, which you had been completely unaware of, became louder and louder, and you yourself became increasingly—and, don't kid yourself, frighteningly—aware of the sheer solid mass of humanity staring down at you.

The closer I got to the mound, the less cocky I became. By the time I was ready to pitch, all the cockiness had leaked out of me.

The announcer waited until I was almost on the mound before he announced my name (undoubtedly he had to scurry through the program to find it), then pronounced it, of course, Koo-fax. As I walked onto the mound I could hear the stands answer back, "Who?"

I may have lost my cockiness, but I still had pretty good stuff. The first batter I ever faced was Johnny Logan. The first pitch was in there for a called strike. The next two weren't. And then Logan hit a little blooper off the end of his bat that fell behind first base for a base hit.

Eddie Mathews took a called strike and then bunted right back to me. Easy double play. With all the time in the world, I wheeled to whip the ball to Pee Wee. The only trouble was that I threw it to Duke out in center field.

A rookie pitcher in his first game, you think, and he panics. Maybe that's what they thought in the stands, too. I don't know what they were thinking on the bench. You don't panic on plays like that, though. You don't think at all. All your training is directed against thought. You react. Fielding is reflex action. Being wild, I had thrown wildly to second base, that's all.

There were now men on first and second. The batter was

Henry Aaron. I walked him on four straight balls, which may have been the smartest thing I did all year. There have been many times since when I wished I had been wild enough to walk Henry Aaron. I am usually backing up third as I am wishing it.

The bases were loaded; there was nobody out. Just like the good old days on the sandlots and in college. The batter was Bobby Thomson. I had tried a couple of curves on Aaron, without getting them within whispering distance of the strike zone. Now that I was in real trouble, I just reared back and threw fast balls. Harder and harder. The first two pitches to Thomson were balls, and I just kept throwing harder. I got a strike in there, another ball, another strike. Thomson swung and missed on the 3–2 pitch, and I had my first big-league out. And my first big-league strikeout.

That brought back some of the confidence. Until you get that first out, you press. Even today I don't feel that I've settled down to pitch a game until that first out goes up on the scoreboard.

A strikeout, under those conditions, gives you confidence anyway. You throw that fast ball through there, and you're showing them you're a pitcher, right? I had thrown it past them in the sandlots, and I had thrown it past them in college. Well, I could throw it past the big-leaguers too.

It was probably the worst thing that could have happened to me, getting my first out by striking out a big hitter. Because that became my pattern for five years, trying to get out of trouble by throwing harder and harder and harder.

Still, the first out is something special, something unforgettable. Every pitcher can remember it clearly. And yet I have a confession to make. I can remember that inning, pitch by pitch, but I had to check back through the records to be sure it was Bobby Thomson who struck out, a strong indication that my mind had been locked to everything except the necessity of hammering the ball through.

Joe Adcock was the next batter. Him I remember very well.

Joe fouled off a pitch, took a couple of balls, and hit a nice ground ball down to Pee Wee. In professional baseball, they make the double play.

And now I'm so cocky again I'm thinking: This is great. This is a breeze. You can get two outs on one ground ball up here.

The next inning was easier. I was facing the bottom of the lineup, Danny O'Connell, Del Crandall, and Lew Burdette. Each of them took the first pitch, and each of the pitches was a strike. O'Connell grounded out to Pee Wee, Crandall flied to center, and Burdette took a called third strike on a 3–2 pitch.

Five days later, back in New York, I was sent in to pitch the final inning against the Giants. It had been another Willie Mays day. The Giants were leading, 6–0, and all Mays had done was knock in all six runs with a grand-slam home run, a solo home run, and a single.

The third batter this time was Mays, and I found him in the same situation I had found Aaron, with men on first and second and nobody out. This time it was Alvin Dark who had singled and Whitey Lockman who had beat out a bunt. I was shrewdly wild again, although I did manage to get one strike over to Willie—on the 3–0 count—before walking him. Again, the bases were loaded and nobody out. Again, I got out of it rather easily. On only five pitches. Don Mueller hit a short fly to left field. Henry Thompson fouled to Jackie Robinson and Gail Harris hit a ground ball to Pee Wee.

The pattern had been the same. You load the bases, and you fight your way out of it.

It got me my first start, against Pittsburgh, a week later, on the excellent grounds that there was nothing to lose. We were thirteen games ahead, and the Pirates were in last place, a few light years away. Where there had once been a strong pitching staff, there was now a collection of sore arms. Despite the lead, the extra pitcher, unusable, had become more of a luxury than anyone would have thought.

I didn't load the bases before I got a man out this time. All I did was walk three of the first four batters. Actually, I had a one-hit shutout for four innings, which looks very good if you don't count the six bases on balls. In the fifth I walked two more men behind a couple of singles to force in the first run against me. When my first pitch to the next batter, Gene Freese, was a ball, Alston rushed in Ed Roebuck, who got Freese, but we eventually lost the game in the eighth.

I had already had a pretty full day, 105 pitches. Just under half of them—52—had been balls. Of the 26 batters I had faced, I had gone to the 3–2 count on nine of them, 3–1 on two others and 3–0 on one—the pitcher yet.

It was another good crowd, oddly enough, more than 20,000, one of the biggest crowds in Pittsburgh all year. Not all of them were rooting for the Pirates to destroy me, either. After I pitched the no-hitter in 1964, a woman wrote Al Abrams of the Pittsburgh *Post-Gazette* to ask if I could possibly be the same Koufax (or even a reasonable facsimile thereof) whom she had seen years ago on her first trip to the ball park. She had felt so sorry for me, she wrote, that she had almost cried. If it was that sad from up there, think of how it must have felt down on the field.

Just as a curiosity, only once did I ever walk more men than I walked in half a game on my first start. That was in 1960, when I walked nine men in a thirteen-inning game.

A week later the Dodgers brought up Roger Craig and Don Bessent, who filled the breach more than adequately. Both of them, in fact, pitched brilliantly. Borkowski was sent down, and I was filling in for an outfielder again—if you can call it filling in. I didn't start another ball game for fifty days.

It was seventeen days, in fact, before I got into a game at all by pitching the final two innings of a lost game against Milwaukee. The next day I pitched the final inning in another lost cause, and then I sat for over a month. For all the action I saw, I might as well have been on the disabled list again.

In mid-August the Dodgers went into their only tailspin of the year, losing eight games out of eleven. I got a call finally, in the last inning of a Thursday twilight game against Cincinnati. We were behind, 8–3, we had a night game coming on, and there was no sense wasting a pitcher.

The first two batters struck out on six pitches, and Alston said, "If he gets the next man I'm going to start him Saturday." I got the next man on a pop fly to Hodges.

Back in the clubhouse, Don Zimmer told me what Alston had said. Rube Walker, who had also overheard him, told me about it while we were driving home. I didn't really believe it, though, until Alston gave me the word himself after we had dropped another game on Friday.

Since we were still ten games ahead, there wouldn't seem to be any reason for a Dodger fan to lose any sleep. And if it had been any other team there wouldn't have been. But the Dodgers were the team that had blown a thirteen-and-a-half-game lead in 1951, and sore arms were breaking out all over the pitching staff again. All things considered, I was pitching a game of some importance.

Since I was starting, I got to the park even earlier than usual. While I was getting dressed, Jake Pitler, our first-base coach, went into Alston's office. I could hear him say, "Well, Skip, who's going to pitch today?"

"I've got a pitcher," Walt told him and immediately changed the subject.

As Pitler was leaving he asked him again.

"Koufax," Alston said.

And I could hear Pitler moan. "Oh, no."

The Reds had a strong hitting ball club. Next to the Dodgers they were the best offensive team in the league. Their four power hitters were Kluszewski, Gus Bell, Wally Post, and Smoky Burgess, three lefties out of four. Which meant that Cinci saw all the left-handers in the league.

I had good control from the beginning. The lead-off man, Johnny Temple, took a ball, took a strike, and flied out to center field. That big first out. Burgess, one of those rare catchers who batted second, took a called third strike. Big Klu hit the first pitch through the hole for a single, but Post flied out to right field. An easy inning. Eleven pitches.

Control, to me, meant throwing strikes. When you're not getting into the strike zone—when you walk too many and get behind too many batters—you will lose. This is the "promising" pitcher, the pitcher with the perpetual .500 record. He always seems like a better pitcher than he is, because his good games are so spectacular. But that's the best he'll ever do; he'll win a game and lose a game. He has to have his best stuff to win, and you are simply not at your best that often. I didn't know that then. All I knew was that I was striking out an awful lot of Cincinnati Redlegs.

In the second inning Bell took a called third strike and Rocky Bridges went out swinging. In the third inning I got both Roy McMillan and Art Fowler on called third strikes.

Kluszewski walked in the fourth on a 3–2 pitch—he was still the only man to get on base—but the inning ended with Bell going down swinging on a 1–2 curve ball.

The Reds had been waiting me out in the fourth inning. Both Klu and Wally Post had gone to the 3–2 count. In the fifth I was throwing nothing but strikes. Mele went down on the 1–2 count, Bridges flied to center on a two-strike pitch, and McMillan went down swinging on the 1–2 pitch. Eight strikeouts in five innings.

We were already ahead 5–0.

Milt Smith, a pinch-hitter, led off the sixth and was called out on another 1–2 pitch. But from there the control went. Temple walked on four straight balls. I went to 3–2 on Burgess, and lost him too. Two men on, and Big Klu up there, looking tough. I got ahead of him, though, just firing the ball, and he flied out to short right.

I couldn't get out of the game without one moment of embarrassment. While I was delivering the first pitch to Post I lost my footing and slipped off the mound. Both runners advanced on the balk, and I was in the first real trouble of the game. Post hit the next pitch good to right field, too, but Furillo went back and got it.

It turned out to be the only inning where I didn't strike anybody out. Gus Bell, who had already struck out twice, fouled off the first two pitches in the seventh. I tried to waste the next pitch, and my control was so bad that I got it just in far enough to nip the corner of the plate for the third strike—the best pitch I made all day. With two out, I got wild again, walking both Bridges and McMillan. Chuck Harmon came in to pinch-hit and struck out.

A pitcher has no right to go a strong nine innings in his first start in fifty days. I was riding on sheer excitement and adrenalin, and I actually got stronger as I went along. Temple flied out on the first pitch in the eighth, which gave me a boost, and I got Burgess and Klu on strikeouts.

As I came out for the ninth I had thirteen strikeouts and a one-hitter. I was in shock. I wasn't thinking of the strikeouts or the shut-out or anything like that. All I was thinking of was that I needed three more outs.

Post grounded out to third base. Two more to go. I hadn't done a thing wrong on Gus Bell all day. Even my curve ball had been breaking better on him than on anybody else. He had gone down on strikes three times, and he went down swinging again. One more out to go. The batter was Sam Mele. I got a called strike over, then a ball, way too high. On the next pitch he lined a double down the left-field line. One out still to go. The batter was Bridges, who had been running the count down on me all day. This time he swung at the first pitch, a pop fly to Reese. It was over.

There was a post-game television show on which the—ahem —stars of the day were interviewed, meaning me. When I finally came back to the locker room, all the players were still there, even those who normally dressed quickly and ducked out. Ballplayers don't praise each other unduly. When praise is called for, it usually comes in the form of insult. Pitch a no-hitter, and you can be sure that your teammates will drop by to let you know what a lousy hitter you are. It doesn't matter what they say, really. The real message is perfectly transmitted and perfectly understood.

This time the Old Breed of the Brooklyn Dodgers had waited around to shake my hand and offer some words of congratulation. What they were doing, of course, was welcoming me to the team. The message, again, was perfectly transmitted and perfectly understood.

Gil Hodges was one of them. Gil had been the guy I had always rooted for, probably because he was a first baseman like me, and also, I suppose, because everybody in Brooklyn knew he was a nice guy. Although I had rarely gone to ball games, I had been in the ball park the day he had hit four home runs. Obviously, then, we had a great deal in common. Only Gil didn't know it. Gil, who was never any part of an extrovert, hadn't spoken very much to me from the time I joined the team, and so it was a particular thrill to have him pat me on the shoulder and tell me that I had done just fine.

The photographers were waiting there too, to take my picture holding a baseball in front of a blackboard which announced the fourteen strikeouts.

It was great. It is the kind of memory I wish to every kid who ever signs with a major-league team. Since I had known I was going to be pitching, my folks had been there to watch me. When we got home there were kids waiting in front of the house for my autograph. The phone rang all evening with congratulations from friends and relatives.

Four days later I pitched an inning of relief against Milwaukee and got bombed. This game can't wait to humble you.

After every exceptionally good or especially important performance you are asked, as sure as there is a writer with a notebook, whether it was your greatest thrill. (I understand that after Don Larsen pitched his perfect game he was asked whether it was the best game he had ever pitched.) You can't compare thrills, of course. Each performance is relative to its own time, place, and situation. (I don't want to sound as if I'm ridiculing the writers. I'm very well aware that nine times out of ten the writer is really asking whether there was anything of special interest I'd care to volunteer about the game—anything different, anything unique, *anything*.)

I always answer, if I'm pressed on the Great Thrill Sweepstakes, that it's hard to beat the first win, especially when it was

103

a two-hit, fourteen-strikeout shutout, and you are nineteen years old.

And I suppose it goes even deeper than that. As time goes on and this whole business about pitching becomes so exciting and rewarding, I feel obliged to direct a small, fond nod toward that bonus boy who scuffled around for so many years and came so close to giving it all up.

It's funny. After the fifth Series game in Los Angeles last year I bumped into Sam Mele, by then manager of the Minnesota Twins, as I was walking out toward the parking lot. I had been asked about the biggest thrill so often in the preceding few days that the Cincinnati game was fresh in my mind. I just naturally started to talk to Sam about it, assuming that a routine ball game played ten years earlier had remained green in his memory too. It became evident at once that he didn't have the slightest idea what I was talking about. What? Could it be possible that Sam didn't remember lining that double down the left-field line with two out in the ninth inning, the only hit since Klu's single in the first? It was possible all right. Sam didn't remember the hit. He didn't even remember the game. To get right down to it, Sam couldn't remember that he had ever faced me in his life. It was like writing an article about "The Most Unforgettable Character I Ever Met," and finding that the most unforgettable character had forgotten all about me.

After the Cincinnati win Walt had promised me another start against Pittsburgh the following week. Despite the bombing by the Braves, I got it. Karl Spooner, whose arm was coming around, had shut Pittsburgh out the day before. I shut them out with five hits, striking out only six but walking only two.

Two shutouts in a row. This game wasn't so hard, after all. I had to wait slightly longer for my next shutout. Four years.

Five days after I beat the Pirates, we clinched the pennant, the earliest it had even been clinched in the history of the National League.

From there on in, it was just a matter of getting the pitching ready for the World Series. We were playing the Yankees, which meant no days off for traveling. From the beginning, word got to me—unofficially but reliably—that there was a strong possibility either Spooner or I would pitch the sixth game.

I started two games in the final weeks of the season, struggling six and two-thirds innings against Cinci and taking my first loss, but pitching a pretty good four innings against St. Louis before being removed for a pinch-hitter. Facing the Cards gave me my first look at Stan Musial. It also got me my first home run hit against me. Those two statements are not unrelated. Musial looked at my fast ball, found it to his liking, and hit it over the screen at Sportsmen's Park. Rip Repulski was the next batter, and he hit the second home run ever hit against me. After that I stopped counting.

The night before the season ended, I was down for the middle three innings against the Pirates.

Disaster.

I started by walking Gene Freese, then walked Jerry Lynch on four pitches. Dale Long topped a ball back to me on the 0–2 count, and both runners advanced as I threw him out.

Then came the play. Roberto Clemente, who was in his rookie year, came up as a pinch-hitter and hit a ground ball into the hole. Hodges made a good play, bobbled the ball slightly, but recovered in plenty of time and looked over to throw to me at first.

Who, me? I was standing on the pitcher's mound, admiring his mobility. Freese scored, Lynch went to third, and Hodges picked up the error that rightfully belonged to me.

I promptly showed how quickly I could shrug these things off by throwing a wild pitch to Frank Thomas to score Lynch.

It was not covering first base that did it. Anybody can be hit, and anybody can throw a wild pitch. But any pitcher who doesn't have the basic reflexes to break for first base on a ground ball hit toward the right side of the diamond can hardly be looked upon as a World Series pitcher. As of that moment, I knew I was scratched.

The Dodgers had been trying to win a World Series—and beat the Yankees—from the time they changed their name from the Superbas. All they ever needed, it became apparent, was me sitting on the bench, watching.

Everybody remembers how Johnny Podres came off his arm troubles to win two games, including the avenging shutout in the seventh game. My clearest memory of the Series is the key play. I was sitting on the steps at the far end of the dugout, and I had a perfect view of Sandy Amoros following Berra's curving fly ball down the left-field line, holding out his glove hand and having the ball drop into the glove as if it were dropping into a basket.

And I can see very clearly the quick throw to Pee Wee and the perfect relay to first base to double up the runner.

The only other play I remember in the whole game is Elston Howard hitting a Podres change-up to Pee Wee to end the game and make the Dodgers—us—the World Champions for the first time in their—our—history.

I had already enrolled in Columbia University, not because the season had convinced me that my future in baseball wasn't particularly bright, but only because it had been understood all along that I would. Classes had begun the day before the end of the Series, which made everything very nice, since it enabled me to go to school directly from Yankee Stadium, which was only a couple of miles away.

After the seventh game I stopped off at Columbia to ask one of my professors if I could be excused so that I could go to the Dodgers' victory party.

"Is it really that important to you?" he asked me. "Are you really that much of a rooter that you'd miss class just to go to a party?"

"Well, it isn't that I'm such a rooter," I told him. "It's just that I'm on the team."

"You're a member of the Brooklyn Dodgers?"

"Well, yes. I'm one of the pitchers, although I don't pitch too much yet."

"Well, I'll be darned," he said. "I thought I knew all the players. Koufax, huh? I'll have to watch for you next year."

I was still so well known the next year that once, when I was pitching the second game of a double-header, I came to the park late, as is the custom, and almost didn't get in. The policeman at the gate didn't believe I was a player, and it was only after a great deal of arguing that I was able to get him to call the chief of the park police force so that he could identify me.

My education ended with that one semester at Columbia. The next winter the Dodgers were touring through Japan. I could have passed that up all right, but Al Campanis advised me to get some experience by pitching in Puerto Rico. Under the rules then in force, you were not allowed to play winter ball if you had been in the major leagues for more than two years, which meant it was the only chance I would ever have.

I had to sit down and ask myself, "What is your profession?" If it was baseball, and if I was serious about doing well, I knew I had to go to Puerto Rico and, I hoped, find out what it was like to pitch in a regular four-day rotation. The following winter I went into the Army. Ed McCarrick had been right. It just wasn't that easy to get a college degree in your spare time.

Everything considered, my first year hadn't been bad. If I can't say anything else about it, I can always say that it was a heck of a lot better than my second year.

7

The Last Pitcher
for the Brooklyn Dodgers

Early in my first year I had come to the conclusion that I would serve out my two-year sentence in the majors sitting on the bench, then go down to the minors and give myself another three years to establish myself as a big-league pitcher. My original instinct about signing with a second-division team like the Pirates had been right, but there was nothing to be gained by second-guessing myself. Having made my own bench, I would sit on it.

As it turned out, I didn't go down at all, which was unfortunate. My three years with the Brooklyn Dodgers—before the team moved to Los Angeles—may not have been a total loss but . . .

A Dick Young column of June 14, 1956, in the New York *Daily News,* sums up my second season very nicely:

> For some reason that escapes me, Alston manifests very little confidence in Koufax. A pitching pinch has to develop before Walt uses the kid. Then, it seems, Sandy must pitch a shutout or the bullpen is working full force and the kid will be yanked at the first long foul ball.
>
> Koufax didn't start until the club got to Cinci on the second western trip. Then, only because Drysdale had a sore arm, Koufax drew the assignment originally planned for Don.
>
> The score was 3–3, as Brooklyn batted in the seventh. Koufax has thrown a home run ball to Frank Robinson in the first, and a 2-run triple in the fifth which Gilliam should have caught. All

told, the Redlegs had seven hits. Koufax had walked one. The first two Dodgers up in the seventh went out. Koufax was due to bat next. He didn't. Amoros was sent in to pinchhit. Clem Labine pitched the seventh and eighth, was tagged for 3 runs and Brooklyn lost.

Koufax next started in St. Louis the other night. He was leading, 3–1, in the fourth when he walked the leadoff man and threw two balls to the next hitter. Carl Erskine, who had been warming up since the first inning relieved. Erskine gave up seven hits in 4 innings, Koufax had given three hits in three innings. After the game, Alston said Koufax didn't have good stuff, but Erskine did.

Dick makes only one mistake in here. My first start, after Drysdale had come up with the only sore arm of his life, had been in Chicago, five days before the Cincinnati game. I won it, 4–3, but I didn't go all the way. I was taken out in the ninth inning after walking the lead-off man.

I didn't pitch a complete game all season. In Cincinnati I went into the ninth tied 3–3, but was removed when Brooks Lawrence opened the inning with a bloop double to left field. Lawrence eventually scored, and I took the loss.

Five days later I had a 4–1 lead with two out in the ninth. Two men were on base, however, both on walks, and Walker Cooper lined a double off the left-field fence to score them. Don Bessent was brought in to get the final out.

Over the last half of the season we were chasing the Milwaukee Braves, and we caught them when the Cardinals beat them in the last series of the year. In the last two months, I pitched only once, starting against the Giants when the situation must have really been catastrophic. Going into the fifth we were behind 2–0 on home runs by Mays and Castleman. With one out, Schoendienst singled, Mays doubled, and Koufax was removed, never to be heard from again through the rest of the season.

I'm not here to take pot shots at Walter Alston at this late date. Walt can stand on his record. I could even see his problem. Walt was hired in 1954, as everybody knew, to win not only a pennant but a World Series, the prize that had eluded

Brooklyn from the beginning of time. In his first year he hadn't even won the pennant. The Giants had sneaked through and Alston's Dodgers finished third. In his second and perhaps crucial year, with the pressure on him to produce, they had saddled him with a bonus player. In his pre-season planning, he had to discount me. When his pitching, which had started so strong, began to crumble, he would have been less than human not to resent having me hung around his neck. He couldn't use me, Walt felt, and he couldn't get rid of me.

My own view was, of course, entirely different. I don't feel I would have disgraced myself at the beginning, and I am sure I would have become a winning pitcher years earlier. If I didn't feel that way I'd be in the wrong business.

I have already pointed out that when you come to the park day after day without getting into a ball game there is a danger that you will come to think of yourself as a non-player. Something far more dangerous can happen in the manager's mind.

Alston began by discounting me. I would suppose that, in going over his rotation plans, as his staff thinned out, he fell into the habit of letting his eyes skip right over my name. I was the Great Unwanted. I was the guy he couldn't afford to take a chance with. That impression, carried over a year . . . two years . . . three years . . . four years, can get to be very difficult to shake. Years later—*years* later—I couldn't put a couple of men on base in the late innings without being pulled right out of there. And if the game was close in the late innings, I could count on going out for a pinch-hitter. To be fair, I made that very easy. In my first year I came to bat 12 times and struck out 12 times. My hitting over most of my career has moved the most respected critics in the game to flights of nostalgia; it has moved them to compare me with the worst hitters of all time.

I needed experience; I needed work. Walt needed to win. I had always prided myself that I would come through in the clutch; Walt left me with the clear impression that he didn't think I had it in the clutch.

My record over my first five years was nothing to convince any manager that I wasn't being used too much, instead of too little. The record of any pitcher who isn't being used with any regularity, in any specific job, isn't going to be very impressive.

A big-league pitching staff usually consists of nine men, four starters and five bullpen pitchers. Three of the pitchers in the bullpen are important out there, the two long men and the last (or short) man.

The long man is up and ready to take over in case the starting pitcher is knocked out early. He is loose at the beginning of the game, and he is up at the first sign of trouble. The last man is the real gunfighter. He's the guy who has to come riding into town to take care of any trouble in the last three innings. He'll start throwing automatically at the beginning of the seventh inning in close games. He will get his share of work by the nature of the game, and if he has gone without work for any length of time the manager will look to get him in for an inning or two just to keep him sharp.

The problem for the other two guys, the number 8 and number 9 men, is simply to stay alive. In the natural course of events you won't get into the ball game. That means, as I have said, that you must sit there and wait for a catastrophe to overtake the team, for the other bullpen men to get knocked out or for the club to fall so far behind that there seems little sense in wasting them.

You are still supposed to do what a pitcher does, of course. You are supposed to hold the other side until the manager can pinch-hit for you.

It isn't that easy. You haven't been pitching in the game, which is the only way a pitcher can find his groove. You have hardly been throwing at all. You can't pitch batting practice, because there's always a chance that you might be used that day. You can't indulge yourself in a hard workout in the late innings of a close game in which you are obviously not going to be used, because they might have to use you the following day. You are being squeezed at both ends. Although you are the pitcher getting the least amount of actual game time, you are also getting the least amount of practice.

What can you do about it? Nothing. It's part of being the

low man on the totem pole. It always has been and it always will be.

Even if you are penciled in to pitch the second game of an upcoming double-header, when the pitching gets a little tight, you cannot prepare for it by the customary hard workout followed by the customary day of rest. There is always the possibility that the manager might have to call on you either of those two days. The start? As a starter, you're eminently replaceable. Your name, having been "penciled in," can easily be penciled out. A minor inconvenience, at the worst. What the heck, the manager isn't counting on you to win that game you were scheduled to pitch. If he could count on you, you wouldn't be a number 8 or number 9 man.

If one of the regular starters is injured and misses a couple of weeks, he is not really expected to pitch at the top of his form. Everybody gives him a huge discount on his first couple of outings because everybody knows what he can do.

A number 9 man who hasn't worked for two or three weeks doesn't get any discount at all. On the contrary. If he gets shelled, everybody just thinks, "What do they keep that stiff around for?" When *he* says, "Well, what do you expect, I haven't had any work," they put it down as an alibi. Everybody *knows* he can't pitch.

It's nobody's fault. It's the system. There are only seven regular jobs on a pitching staff. The strong get stronger because they are working steady, following a regular regimen of exercise and rest, improving themselves in combat (the only way you can improve). The weak get weaker because they become starved for work.

Occasionally the low man on one team's totem pole is involved in a trade, gets a quick start, and looks good. The new team, having no preconceptions about him and wanting the trade to look as good as possible, keeps pitching him. He looks better and better. And now everybody nods wisely and says, "The change of scenery worked wonders for him." No, not the change of scenery. Regular work. The chance to pitch. Witness Pete Richert's work when he went to Washington in the Osteen trade. Claude Osteen himself was the number 9 man for Cincinnati in 1960 before he moved on.

The young strong-arm pitcher isn't depending on fine control, of course, but without regular work he is sometimes going to find it difficult to throw the ball into the strike zone. Since control is what he's probably having trouble with anyway, it gets to be a vicious circle. They can't pitch you, they say, until your control improves. The less you pitch, the worse your control becomes.

And worst of all is the fear that overcomes you. When I did get a chance to pitch, I felt I had to look good in every game, in every inning, on every pitch, or I'd be taken right out of the game.

I was pressing. When you press you're afraid to let anyone hit the ball, because if they hit the ball it can go out of the park, or at least in between a couple of fielders. The one way you can be safe is to strike everybody out. There's one built-in limitation the rulesmakers placed upon the strikeout, a limitation which very frequently eludes strong-arm young pitchers. You cannot strike anybody out until you have two strikes on him.

You don't care about that, though. You're going to throw the third strike past him three times.

Everything suffers when you press. Your control suffers, your stuff suffers, your fast ball doesn't move, your cordination and timing are bad.

So you walk a couple of men, and now you get angry. You're finally getting a chance, you think, and you're not doing the job. The back of your neck begins to glow, and now you're pitching out of both fear and anger.

In my three years in Brooklyn I was never a pitcher, I was an arm. A pitcher—a real pitcher—uses his arm the way a horseman uses his horse. He isn't going anywhere without it, but he has to know where he wants the horse to go and why he wants it to go there. It gets down to the basic question of who's in charge here, the horseman or the horse?

A ballplayer has a limited number of years. It may be possible to make up in salary for what you haven't been paid in the early years, but there is no power on earth that can give you back the years you have lost, especially those years when you were young and strong. I cannot help feeling that some of my prime years were wasted.

I could be wrong. It could be argued, I know, that I was brought along slowly, nurtured carefully, and worked into the rotation when I was ready to put what I had learned to use. The only thing is that you can never convince me of it.

The one good thing that happened to me during the 1956 season was the arrival of Sal Maglie, the old enemy from the Giants. Maglie had been shuffled off to the Cleveland Indians in the middle of 1955, and the Indians were letting him go at cutdown time. Sal's listed age was thirty-nine. His back was chronically stiff. Obviously he was all washed up. Obviously we were witnessing another example of good instinct for publicity. "Maglie in the Enemy Camp," a great two-week story. After which the Dodgers could quietly hand Mr. Maglie his release and let him fade into oblivion.

All Mr. Maglie did was win thirteen games for us. All he won for us was the pennant.

To me, a Dodger rooter, Sal had been the darkest of villains. He was Sal the Barber, wasn't he, the man who had set off the annual Dodger-Giant rhubarb?

I had begun to room with Carl Furillo that year, and nobody had tangled with Sal more than Carl. When the news came through that Maglie was now in our camp, Carl just nodded grimly and said, "Well, he's going to have to show me."

Sal reported a day late because there had been a death in his family. Furillo, who had been in a slump, had come to the park early to get in some extra hitting. When Sal walked in, unannounced and unexpected, only Carl and a couple of pitchers were there. John Griffin told Sal where he was supposed to dress. Nobody else said a word to him. And so Carl, who happens to be a good guy, went over and said, "Hello, Sal. Welcome to our side."

After the game that night, the photographers took some posed shots of Carl welcoming Sal to the fold. Carl even lathered up so they could take the inevitable gag shot of Sal the Barber pretending to shave him.

But they were only pictures. Sheer accident may have turned Carl into a one-man welcoming committee, but he did not accept Sal immediately. As he had said, he had to be shown.

You know who became Sal's best friend on the club, don't you? Of course. Carl Furillo.

You look at Maglie on the mound, and he looks like he has to be, at best, the second meanest man in the world. Off the mound he is a very soft-spoken, very amiable man, extremely thoughtful and extremely intelligent.

Or maybe it was just the old story about the healing powers of a winning ball club. Sal, from whom nothing could reasonably be expected, was keeping us in the pennant race. You could see it begin to happen. Slowly but inevitably, Carl and Sal began to talk, to find common interests, to become good friends. Since Sal had come to the club late, he had no roommate. By the second road trip the three of us were going out together to eat.

From my point of view—starting from scratch and taking him as I found him—I found that he knew as much about the art of pitching as anyone I could possibly hope to dine with. This man didn't guess about pitching. He *knew*.

He was also a born teacher. Sal ran a little seminar for Don Drysdale and me, and he had himself two eager students. We would sit alongside him on the bench and listen to him analyze what was happening. Drysdale, of course, benefited more directly because he and Maglie were both right-handers and both threw with a three-quarter motion. Don's best pitch is his fast ball, while Sal's was his breaking ball but, even there, their breaking ball was very similar. (As far as sheer technique was concerned, it was far more helpful for me to watch Erskine and Podres. Especially Podres. John was a left-hander, and we threw pretty much the same kind of stuff.)

Where I was able to benefit was in theory. Watching Maglie play with a batter, once you knew what he was doing, was worth a semester at Heidelberg to an aspiring young duelist.

Sal would get two strikes and no balls on a batter, and you could watch him go all the way to 2-2 or even 3-2 to set him up for the one pitch he wanted him to hit.

He would do more than that. Sal was the first man I ever noticed work from *behind* a batter. In other words, Sal would be behind the hitter two balls and no strikes, and yet he'd pitch to him as if he were ahead. He would pitch exactly as if he had the batter in a spot where the batter had to go for Sal's pitch.

The ideal place to do this is when you are in a situation where you don't care whether you walk the man or not. If he goes after your pitch, fine. If he doesn't and you miss the corner, no harm done.

You can also do it if you know or suspect or feel or hope that the batter, confident that he has you where you have to come in with the ball, is mentally primed to swing. You can do it, once, on a big hitter in a clutch situation where he doesn't dream you'd have the guts to do it.

If I were pitching from behind the batter, I'd assume he was looking for a fast ball on the 2-0 count—as well he should—and so I'd throw a curve. If I got that over, I might throw another curve. Now, if I've got them both over and he hasn't hit the ball, I can throw anything, depending on the situation and the batter, without feeling that he's looking for a particular pitch.

If you get away with it, you've not only got him out, you've given him a great deal to think about. There is nothing pitchers like more than thinking hitters.

For all his reputation as Sal the Barber, he was hardly that with the Dodgers. Really. Sal was an in-and-out pitcher with us. He depended on catching the inside corner and the outside corner, and just as little of it as possible. Basically, he pitched down. The curve was the pitch he wanted you to hit, the low curve at the knees. He would show you the fast ball often enough, but he'd throw it to you three or four inches off the plate, either inside or outside. If you wanted to chase it, good luck to you, but it wasn't the pitch he wanted you to hit. If a batter was close to the plate, sure, Sal's fast ball would move him back. When you work the way Sal worked, that's to be expected. And his next pitch would probably dip down and catch the outside corner. That was to be expected too.

We caught Milwaukee right at the end of the season, with Sal pitching a no-hitter against the Phillies to put us in a tie with four games to go. Four days later he and Labine won both ends of a double-header on the final day of the season to give us the pennant. The no-hitter was something special. I can remember Sal sitting by his locker afterward, toward the end of his career, talking about how he had always wanted a no-hitter and had given up all hope.

Young as I was, deeply disappointed as I was over my own lost year, I recognized that I was witnessing the triumph not only of skill but of the human spirit. I had the glimmer of another idea, too. I had the merest glimmer of an idea that you could will yourself to win. The best way I can put it is to say that character counts. Not character in the conventional sense, but character in the sense of finding the grain of your craft and never wavering from it.

Everybody remembers that Sal ran into Don Larsen's perfect game in the World Series. They forget that Sal won the opening game for us. They also tend to forget that Sal pitched a tremendous game himself against Larsen, setting down the first eleven batters before he lost 2–0.

What they don't know is that Sal was originally down to pitch the day before, but had been held back to give him the advantage of pitching with a National League umpire behind the plate. The National League umpire, as I suppose everyone knows, is supposed to give you a lower strike zone. I've never noticed any difference myself. If there is, how much could it be?

At the end of that second year I did get a chance to put some of what I had learned to the test by playing those few months of winter ball in Puerto Rico, the closest I have ever come to minor-league experience.

One of the things I feel I have missed as a ballplayer is the background of coming up through the minors. You sit around a locker room and you hear the stories about the buses that broke down and the meals that were never eaten, and you are suddenly an outsider. You are suddenly aware that you have not participated in what is a shared experience of almost everybody else in your profession.

"Boy," they'll tell you, "you don't know how lucky you are. You never had to ride those minor-league buses and play under those minor-league lights."

And you wonder whether they're complaining or bragging.

You hear the players who were at St. Paul talking about how they always played double-headers against Minneapolis on holidays, one game in each park. They're grousing about how they had to scramble from one park to the other, and you know that it was not only funny but fun.

I'm not volunteering to go back for my basic training, understand. Not at my age. But when you're young you don't worry about comfort. As a matter of fact, we slept on the bus during that trip to New Orleans when I was at the University of Cincinnati, and we had a great time.

At any rate, the Dodgers made some kind of agreement for me to play for Caguas, which had a working agreement with Milwaukee.

We had a good club. Ben Geraghty was our manager. Vic Power, who had started with Caguas as a teen-ager, was an infielder. We also had Felix Mantilla, Wes Covington, Luke Easter, Charlie Neal, Leon Wagner, Jim Landis. Timmy Thompson, from our own system, was the catcher. The other pitchers were Corkie Valentine, Karl Drews, and Taylor Phillips.

Tommy Lasorda was there too. His role is probably best described as pitching coach and pitcher-in-waiting. The one thing you discovered very early was that you had signed for the season—as long as you did a good job. There were always four or five guys sitting around looking hungry, and if you didn't show up well immediately, it was *buenos noches* time.

It's not that different up here, now that I think about it, except that up here they usually assign your contract to someone else.

I had been warned that the Puerto Rican fans were a bit

excitable. I never saw any wild fights, though, nor did we ever have to go roaring out of any town while the populace was pelting our bus with stones and bottles. Sure they got excited. They'd be sitting there betting on every pitch, a practice which can give a man more than a casual rooting interest in the outcome.

Traveling through the island was the real experience. On the first trip we made, the club rented private automobiles. We were riding five players to a car, plus the driver. When you drive to the western part of the island, you are traveling on a narrow road which winds through the mountains. Looking back down, you can see a five-mile ribbon trailing behind you. Beautiful but frightening. You wonder what happens if a car is coming the other way, because there seems to be just enough room for two cars to slip past each other. Well, we had a driver who let us know. He went zipping up through the mountain at a safe and sane 60 miles per hour, pulling out to pass cars on curves, blowing his horn wildly, and never, but never, hitting the brake.

When we finally straightened out on a fairly long stretch of road, Luke Easter, who was in back, tapped the driver on the shoulder and uttered exactly one word: "Stop!"

The driver pulled the car to a stop and looked back to see what could possibly be on Luke's mind. Luke jerked his thumb toward the door and uttered one more word: "Out!"

The driver got out of the front. Luke got out of the back. Luke slipped in behind the wheel. The driver, getting the message, took Luke's place in back. Not a word was said. We proceeded on to Mayaguez at a reasonable speed, passing nobody.

For the next trip we had a caravan of station wagons, which permitted us to stretch out in back and grab a little sleep as we went. It was only on rare occasions that the driver would have to come to a screeching halt so that he could go out and talk a cow into removing herself from the middle of the road.

When I went to Puerto Rico I knew that the Dodgers had to keep me for thirty days into the 1957 season to make up for those thirty days I had spent on the disabled list. If it were not for that, I would undoubtedly have been assigned to a minor-league club, as I had anticipated.

There is no question in my mind that it would have been the best thing that could have happened to me. At the time, though —to be perfectly honest about it—I was happy that they were being forced to hold onto me. Logic has nothing to do with it. Once you're in the big leagues, you want to stay there. Sure, I wanted to pitch. I wanted to pitch for the Dodgers. Sure, I wanted to learn. All right, I'd learn in the big leagues. I was never lacking in the confidence that I could do the job.

On May 16, my last day on the bonus list, I started a game in Chicago. I can only surmise that it was a test to help the Dodgers make up their minds about me.

I had started one game, earlier in the season. We were leading that one, 3–2, when I was taken out for a pinch-hitter in the last of the fourth, one inning less than I needed to get credit for the win.

I had pitched a little in relief, though. I had even picked up a win by pitching the fourteenth inning of a 4–4 game against Milwaukee after we had run out of pitchers. I retired the side in order, and Gino Cimoli immediately ended it with a lead-off homer.

In Chicago I had the best stuff I'd had since that first win against Cincinnati. By the end of seven innings, I had twelve strikeouts. There had been only two hits, a bloop double in the second inning and a line single to center in the sixth. The Cubs had scored a run in the fifth inning when I forced in a run with three walks around an error, but we were leading, 3–1.

In the eighth, Chicago scored another run when Amoros dropped Lee Walls's fly, and Walls went around on a single and a sacrifice fly.

In the ninth inning I chalked up my fourteenth strikeout and followed it with my seventh walk. Bobby Morgan then hit a dribbler I couldn't get to, and there were men on first and second. Normally I could have expected to be taken out with the game on the bases like that. I'd pitched a ball game and a half by then, anyway. This time Alston was staying with me all the way. Moryn fouled out behind third, Banks popped up to short-stop, and it was over. I had made the team again. I had also pitched my first complete game in two years.

I have often wondered what would have happened if I had been shelled that day.

Briefly, and for the first time, I was in the starting rotation. In the next two weeks I won a game and lost two, departing fairly early in all of them.

I was out of the rotation again.

But not quite. Sal Maglie was supposed to pitch against the Cubs back in Brooklyn, on Better Brooklyn Night. Sal had jammed his thumb while catching a fly ball, though, and when he came to the park he found that the thumb was still bothering him. I got a quick call. Oddly enough, Campanella had to leave the game after being hit by a pitched ball, and Joe Pignatano came in to catch his first big-league ball game. It really turned out to be Better Brooklyn Night. Or Better Late than Never Night. It wasn't Better as You Go Along Night.

I started well, striking out two men in the first and three in the second. At the end of five innings I had a no-hitter and a 7–0 lead.

Bob Speake's two-run homer in the sixth, and Ernie Banks's three-run homer in the eighth made it a 7–5 game and brought Ed Roebuck in to pitch.

In seven and two-thirds innings I had struck out twelve men. Although I had only pitched fifty and two-thirds innings, I was actually leading the National League in strikeouts, with fifty-nine. And even with the five runs that had been scored against me, I had an ERA of 2.94. I didn't consider that bad pitching. I even thought I might have earned another chance.

I didn't start again until July 19, forty-nine days later.

In those forty-nine days I had two widely spaced relief jobs. On June 27 I faced the final two batters in a game in Milwaukee and struck them both out. On July 4 I pitched the final two innings against Philadelphia, striking out two, walking one, and allowing one hit.

And that was all.

The start finally came because my good friends from Chicago had come to town again. In seven innings I allowed only two hits, but both were home runs. I also struck out eleven batters. We were trailing 2–1 in the last of the seventh, though, and, with a runner on second and two out, Furillo pinch-hit for me.

Even Chicago couldn't keep me healthy indefinitely. I did beat them once more, striking out eleven men, but in my final starting assignment of the season I lasted only an inning.

And that was the way it went in the final year in Brooklyn.

By the end of the year we knew we were going to Los Angeles, even though Mr. O'Malley didn't make his announcement for another week. I doubt if it meant much to any of the players. It didn't to me. A baseball player is always aware that he can go to sleep belonging to one team and wake up belonging to another. As you say when it happens, "That's baseball." All it meant, to be practical about it, was that they had traded the whole franchise instead of a few individual players.

I had never been to California. Duke Snider and Don Drysdale, the natives, kept telling me how great everything was out there, and I have to confess that, Brooklyn boy or no, I was rather looking forward to another adventure. It's only when you look back that you become a bit nostalgic about what was left behind when baseball left Brooklyn.

Ballplayers liked to play in Brooklyn because Brooklyn fans knew baseball better than any other fans in the league. Hard as they rooted for the Dodgers, they appreciated a great play or a great player no matter where he came from. There were certain players on the other teams they adopted—Stan Musial in particular. Musial murdered us. He wore out that right-field screen. He beat us, in all probability, more than any player in the league. And yet Brooklyn fans loved him. When Musial came to the plate, you would have thought it was Pee Wee or Duke.

Walking to the dugout for the start of the game was an experience in itself. To get from the clubhouse to the bench, you had to walk down a long dirt runway, which was separated from the main concourse by a high picket fence. Every day, as you left the clubhouse, there would be a mass of fans lined up from one end of that fence to the other. The march to the bench was a triumphant procession. They'd be reaching through the picket fence to shake you by the hand or pat you on the back. They'd be yelling, "Newk, you're the greatest pitcher in the whole wide world. . . . Get 'em today, Pee Wee baby. . . . Today's the day, Gil."

When you went back, they'd be there to shower you with affection. If you had won.

You'd lose the game, though, and, as Leo Durocher puts it, "You gotta go back the same way you came." They'd be waiting there, the same loyal rooters, and they'd be screaming, "You bums! You bums couldn't beat nobody, you couldn't beat my grandmother! What's the matter with you?" They'd throw sand through the fence, and sometimes a dislodged rock or two. If you were in the wrong position in the line of march, you really needed a shower by the time you got to the clubhouse.

Nobody paid any attention to me, of course. I almost longed to be important enough for somebody to yell, "Sandy, you bum . . ."

That was the Dodger fan of blessed memory. They came to root, and they rooted for their own. Brooklyn against the world. It was an exciting park to play in, and they were exciting fans to play for. Even as an observer I could recognize that. Something went out of baseball when the Dodgers left Brooklyn, and not all the king's horses or all the king's men can ever put it back again.

If the move had come overnight, my reaction might have been different. But it was really no part of a surprise. In my very first season we had played seven games in Jersey City. In the two years that followed, there had been a string of indications. Mr. O'Malley had even sold Ebbets Field and purchased the Los Angeles franchise in the Pacific Coast League. I didn't believe all the talk myself, at first, probably because I couldn't believe it. Early in the 1957 season, though, the National

League granted permission for the Dodgers and Giants to draft the Los Angeles and San Francisco territories in the Pacific Coast League. How could you doubt it after that?

Because Mr. O'Malley came out as the villain of the piece (East-Coast division) there seems to be a misconception around that he announced he was going to Los Angeles first and then Horace Stoneham slipped quietly into the resulting uproar to whisper that he was going along for the ride. That wasn't the way it happened at all. Mr. Stoneham made his announcement well before Mr. O'Malley. Mr. Stoneham made his announcement in mid-August, with the season still on. At that point nobody except the most dedicated optimist could doubt that the Dodgers would be going west too.

We closed out the Brooklyn Dodgers in Philadelphia. And glad we were to bring that long, dreary, disappointing season to an end. The Dodgers had dropped to third place, well out of it. For the first time there was no World Series to look forward to. Just the Army. Don Drysdale and I were all set to report for our first six-month tour of duty under the reserve program.

Roger Craig started the final game for us against Seth Morehead. I was in the bullpen. We were behind, 2–1, in our half of the eighth, and Campanella pinch-hit for Craig. The call came for me to go out and pitch the Phils' half of the inning. I walked two men before striking out the final batter, Willie Jones, on three pitches. I left the game exactly the way I had found it, still 2–1. We didn't score in the ninth, and that was that.

The game was over, the season was over, the Brooklyn Dodgers were over. History can record that the last pitcher to throw a baseball for the Brooklyn Dodgers, formerly the Superbas (1890–1957), was one S. Koufax, a local boy about whom it could be said that he had once shown some promise.

In my three years for the Brooklyn Dodgers, I had won nine games and lost eight. In twenty-eight starts I had gone the distance only four times. The best game I had ever pitched had been my first one at Ebbets Field.

8

California,
Here We — Oops — Come

The Dodgers did not get a glimpse of Los Angeles until after the season had begun. We had opened the season in San Francisco to help the Giants introduce themselves to their new fans in the old Seals ball park. If anybody ever asks you over a beer who pitched the first game for the Giants in San Francisco you can tell him that it was Ruben Gomez. You can also tell him that he shut out the Dodgers 8–0, summing up our season with 153 games still to play.

After flying to Los Angeles, we were driven to the Biltmore Hotel for a welcome dinner given by the LA branch of the Baseball Writers Association of America. What I remember most was the mayor telling us how lucky the city was to have us. There had been unsuccessful negotiations with the Browns and Senators in earlier years, he said, and now, for its faith and perseverance, Los Angeles had not just a broken-down second-division club but the storied Brooklyn Dodgers, a certified pennant-winner.

It was a memorable speech, a speech to stir the hearts and hopes of all Los Angeles fans. I thought of it often during the following winter, since it was far less painful than thinking about our seventh-place finish.

In the morning open convertibles were lined up outside the hotel to take us to City Hall for the long motorcade to the Coliseum, a trip of almost ten miles. If I remember right, Piggy and I shared a car at the tag end of the parade, where we would not distract anybody's attention from all those big-league ballplayers.

There was a tremendous turnout all along the route. It was the biggest parade, according to the police, since General Mac-Arthur returned from Japan. There were bands playing "California, Here I Come"—a tune we heard no more often than the President hears "Hail to the Chief." There were drum majorettes, and there were plastic baseballs being thrown along the route as souvenirs. It made us feel as if we were part of it all, especially when an occasional citizen, in hot pursuit of a ball, found himself draped over the hood of our car like a strapped deer.

I was not greatly impressed with Los Angeles at first. The trip from the airport had taken us through the downtown area, which is not the prettiest section of the city. After listening to Duke and Don for three years, I had been prepared for palm trees and breaking surf and movie stars in dark glasses, and all I saw were bars and department stores.

Of course the Los Angeles fans weren't very impressed with me, either. They scarcely knew I was a member of the team. Don and I had been in the Army at the start of spring training, stationed at Fort Dix. We had been able to spend our two-week leave at Vero Beach early in March, though, so we were not in bad shape at all.

Don actually was able to join the team four days before I was, for the excellent reason that he was discharged four days earlier. Don's home was in Los Angeles, which entitled him to four days' travel time. Since my home was across the river in Brooklyn, I got none. Army records aside, both of us were heading for the same place—wherever the Los Angeles ball club happened to be. I caught up with them in Fort Worth as they were traveling north—or should I say west?—for the start of the season.

My first glimpse of the Coliseum came when I stepped onto the field before the game. I had always looked upon the Coliseum as a place where 100,000 people came to see USC and

UCLA play a football game. For baseball, the capacity had been sliced to 93,000.

I don't know about anybody else, but my first impression was of seats, just rows and rows of seats rising miles and miles into the sky. The impression came back strongest when we played an exhibition game with the Yankees early in the season for the benefit of Roy Campanella. There were 93,103 people in those seats (and another tidy crowd rioting outside, trying to get in), the largest crowd ever to attend a baseball game. In the course of the ceremonies, all the lights were put out and everybody was asked to light a match for Campy. It was one of the most impressive and moving sights I have ever seen.

Don and I had heard about Campy's accident over the radio while we were at Fort Dix. It was impossible to believe. Not Campy, the good-humor man. Campy, the kind, friendly man who had helped me down in Miami. I thought of all the nights during spring training when Campy would hold court in his personal little spot in back of the kitchen and spin his yarns about the old Negro Leagues. He always said you had to have a lot of little boy in you to play baseball, and nobody fitted his description more perfectly than himself.

We all knew that the loss of Campy was going to hurt us. There was no way of knowing how rough the whole season would be on everybody.

The second thing you noticed about the Coliseum was the high screen that had been erected in left field, where it was only 250 feet down the foul line. There was no doubt from the beginning that when a right-handed hitter was at bat you'd have to forget the inside half of the plate. The predictions that all home-run records were going to fall went the way of most predictions. It wasn't the home run that killed you at the Coliseum. The home runs were usually pretty well hit. What killed you was the short fly that just nicked the screen on the way down—especially when you had two men on and two out. (I did lose a game during the year when Wally Post hit a high fly ball that came down on top of the screen and fell over on the other side for a home run. The ball didn't even go into the stands. It landed in the tiny space between the screen and the front row of seats.)

The opening-day crowd was 78,672, the largest of all time. We beat the Giants 6–5, when Davenport neglected to touch third on Willie Kirkland's triple. After that it was all downhill. We were starting life in Los Angeles with a nineteen-day home stand. By the time we left, the crowds had become the story rather than the team. Not that big numbers weren't involved in the scores of our games, too. San Francisco belted us 11–4 and 12–2 before they left town. I got into my first ball game—our seventh game at home—to pitch the last inning of a 15–2 rout. It turned out to be a landmark game in Dodger history because Don Zimmer replaced Pee Wee Reese halfway through the game, hit a home run and single, and took over as the regular shortstop. In his twentieth season, Reese finally moved to third.

The change would probably have come anyway, even if we had remained in Brooklyn. The Old Breed was growing older. But all changes seemed to be emphasized by the move to Los Angeles. There was the feeling that it was a new team, a new start, with most positions up for grabs. Robinson had retired. Campy was gone. Reese was moved over to third base. Newcombe and Erskine had chronic arm trouble. Hodges and Furillo were getting no younger.

And then there was the Coliseum. Whom age did not destroy, the park drove mad.

When Willie Mays stepped out onto the turf that first day, he is supposed to have said, "Poor Duke." What poor Duke said was probably unprintable.

The fences ran from 390 feet to 440 feet in right and 415 feet in center. Duke would hit the ball solidly and you would automatically think to yourself, "That's out of here." And it would be just another 400-foot fly. It was like hitting fungoes in an airport.

If a pitcher has to win when he has his good stuff, a hitter has to get his base hits when he hits the ball as well as he can. A great hitter like Duke will hit the ball solidly three times out of five. To hit his average, he has to look for the ball to fall in two of those three times. He also has to figure that when he gives it his best shot the ball will fly out of the park. Not that park.

The Coliseum took the home run away from Duke, and most of the extra-base hits. After the first shock, he tried to adjust by going the other way. To some extent he succeeded. But Duke had been schooled for years to look for the ball that he could pull. For a power hitter in Ebbets Field—and for power hitters in most parks—to pull was good; all of a sudden, to pull was bad.

In addition to the physical change that was necessary, there was the mental adjustment. Everything he had trained himself to do, and had done so successfully that he was recognized as one of the game's great hitters, was now wrong.

It wasn't natural for him, and it wasn't comfortable for him. It probably made things more difficult for him on the road too, since it upset that great swing of his. Add a sore arm and a bad knee, and the season became somewhat of a trial for Duke.

The park killed Rube Walker, too. With Campy gone, Rube was finally getting his big chance. In that first week Rube must have hit fifteen balls that would have gone out of any other ball park in the league. The Coliseum just sat there, growing grass and laughing at him.

There are variables that must be taken into account, of course. At Ebbets Field the opposing pitcher would have been trying to prevent Rube from pulling, while at the Coliseum he was happy to let him pull the ball all day. Still and all, the Coliseum probably made Rube a coach two years before his time.

It didn't help Carl Furillo, either. I can remember Carl hitting a fly ball to Ashburn in right center that was so deep that Pee Wee tagged up and scored from second base, the only time I've ever seen that happen.

What hurt us most, I think, was that, playing there day after day, we became too conscious of the screen. The pitchers could feel it looming over their shoulders, and the hitters would swing with one eye on the ball and the other on the fence. The secret of playing in that park was to forget the screen.

As for myself, I started my brave new career in Los Angeles by getting misplaced again. I mean it was just like those good old days in Brooklyn. My first start came in our twenty-first game. I had a one-hitter and was leading 3–0 until the sixth inning, when I served up a home-run ball to Chuck Essegian, walked a couple of men, and was relieved.

My next start was in Milwaukee, in our thirty-third game. We were in last place. Why not try Koufax?

It turned out to be one of the key games, I think, in my career. In the first inning Schoendienst walked and Johnny Logan hit a blooper that just cleared Reese's glove behind third base and dropped along the foul line for a single. Schoendienst went to third as the ball was juggled in left field. After Harry Hanebrink had flied out, we purposely walked Aaron to load the bases. I then threw a wild pitch past Roseboro to score Schoendienst, and when John's return throw went past me at the plate, Logan scored and Aaron wound up on third. Aaron scored on Joe Adcock's fly, and the Braves had three runs right off the bat.

That was just great. Next start, July. Next stop, St. Paul. I breezed through the second inning, though, and when I came up in the third there were two out and nobody on. Walt let me bat.

In the fifth inning I was due up with men on first and second and only one out. If the score had still been 3–0, I'd probably have been gone right there. Fortunately we had picked up two runs in the fourth inning on three walks and two sacrifice flies, bringing the score to 3–2 on a total of one hit by both sides. By then I had set down eleven batters in a row. Walt let me bat again.

The consecutive outs ran to fifteen before I walked Johnny Logan with one out in the sixth, wild-pitched him to second, and purposely passed Hank Aaron. There had still been no other hits, but we were still behind.

John Roseboro, the fifth batter in the lineup, was leading off the seventh inning, which meant that if two men got on base and neither of them had scored, I would undoubtedly be taken out for a pinch-hitter. Roseboro put an end to that kind of speculation by hitting a home run.

Johnny Logan got the second hit for the Braves, a double down the right-field line with two out in the eighth. He was also the last Brave to reach base. The game went into the eleventh inning, where Duke Snider broke it up with a pinch double.

I had allowed only two hits. Over the final ten and two-thirds innings, I had allowed only one hit and one walk (not counting the intentional one).

I began to pitch regularly after that, starting and in relief. There was one road trip where I appeared in seven of the eleven games we played. I was in five games in five days, including both games of a double-header in Cincinnati. In three days I had two wins and a save. All of a sudden I was "a strong-armed lefty" and "Handy Sandy."

At the end of the road trip I started two games and won them both, bringing my record to 7–3, an all-time personal high.

Back home, the strong-armed lefty started against the Chicago Cubs and in the first inning I struck out Tony Taylor and Ernie Banks. In the second Jim Bolger hit a ground ball to Norm Larker at first base. Handy Sandy, starting late, arrived at the base to take the throw a fraction of an inch before Bolger. Bolger came down on the side of my ankle, and I went head over heels. The ankle was cut and badly sprained, and I was out for two weeks.

Injuries are part of the game. There isn't much you can do except to accept them. It never occurred to me to think, "Just when I'm going good this has to happen!" I felt I'd come back and pitch at least as well as I had been. I didn't, though. I was a different pitcher after I came back. It was like two different seasons.

With two games left, we had risen to sixth place, a game ahead of the Chicago Cubs, who were in Los Angeles to finish out the season. It may not be of vital importance to the Free

World whether you finish sixth or seventh, but when it's the only thing you have left to play for, you would be surprised how important it becomes. Sixth place sounds so much better than seventh.

I was pitching the first of the two games. Al Dark singled off the screen in the ninth, breaking a 1–1 tie and bringing my record for the year down to 11–11. It was, nevertheless, the only complete game I pitched at the Coliseum all year.

On the final day we were leading 4–3, into the ninth. All we needed were three more outs to clinch sixth place. The Cubs batted around and scored four times.

It was that kind of season.

How can a team finish seventh one year and be World Champions the next? I'm not sure. There's a difference of attitude between a winning team and a losing one, no question about that. When everything begins to go wrong, a team can go out just waiting for something bad to happen. Once you're in that frame of mind, it generally does.

But even there, a team like the Dodgers with a winning tradition behind it always feels that things are going to straighten out tomorrow. Nothing that a few base hits won't cure, we'd say. One thing we know, it's got to get better because it can't get any worse. A ten-game winning streak in August, and we're right back in the middle of this thing. Athletes are like politicians; you have to feel in your bones that you're a winner or you wouldn't be in this business to start with. The spring optimism that runs through all the training camps isn't faked. Everybody can see how with a break here and there—if this veteran comes back and this rookie comes through, if they can fill this one spot or if they get maximum production out of every man on the squad—his team can move right into contention.

We were not really as bad as we had looked in the Lost Year in Los Angeles, no doubt about that either. It took us a year to accommodate ourselves to the Coliseum. But in the end it always comes down to talent. You can talk all you want about intangibles, I just don't know what that means. Talent makes winners, not intangibles. Can nice guys win? Sure, nice guys can win—if they're nice guys with a lot of talent. Nice guys with a little talent finish fourth, and nice guys with no talent finish last.

We had not only become accustomed to the screen by 1959, we had picked up a hitter who could play a symphony on it. Or have you forgotten Wally Moon and his famous Moon-shot?

The screen had not only been irresistible to the right-handed hitter, it was also very tempting to the left-hander who could hit to left. Moon became a master of inside-outing the ball so that it would arch, not necessarily majestically, over the screen.

What Moon did was to turn what is normally a liability into an asset. When a strong right-handed hitter popped one off the screen, you at least knew that he was trying to go that way. What really aggravated you was when you jammed a left-hander, fooled him, and saw the resulting fly ball bounce off the screen.

Moon did it deliberately. Moon looked for the inside pitch so that he could get his hands out in front of the bat and slice the ball up against the screen or over it.

The beautiful part of it was that when the other teams read that Wally was hitting home runs over the screen, they naturally assumed that he was popping the outside pitch over the fence. For the first time around, everybody came in and deliberately jammed him, setting him up with exactly the pitch he wanted.

I had the best seat in the house to observe the Moon-shot being launched on the night I struck out eighteen men. But that was very late in the season, on August 31, long after everybody had figured out what he was doing.

My own start in 1959 had to be seen to be believed. I had finally been given some starting assignments in April, and I had been knocked out early four times out of four. The club had bailed me out and, indeed, gone on to win all four games, but that didn't change the fact that my rhythm was shot and no amount of practice seemed to be helping.

Two days after the last of the fiascos I went out to the bullpen during the game so that I could get in some extra work. When we fell behind 9–4 in the sixth inning, Alston decided to give me a chance to pitch myself loose in competition. "Come on," Becker said, "here's your chance to show Walt you should be back in the starting rotation."

I showed him all right. When I came out of the game it was still the sixth inning and the score was 14–4. In two-thirds of an inning I had given up four hits and four walks. Over the year I had pitched eleven innings, allowed fifteen runs, nineteen hits, and seventeen walks. My ERA was a glittering 12.27.

The ball club, I suspect, was very close to getting rid of me.

Joe Becker was being quoted as saying, "He has no coordination and he has lost all his confidence. His arm is sound, but mechanically he is all fouled up. . . ."

Alston was being quoted as saying, "You can't give up on him," which has the odor of a man who has pretty much given up and wishes the front office would stop being so stubborn about it too.

I was only hoping that if they did ask waivers somebody would claim me and keep me in the big leagues.

In mid-June it all came back, and I pitched three consecutive complete games for the first time in my life.

My fourth complete game of the season, two months later, had been in Philadelphia on my last time out. That's what had got me the start against San Francisco, in the final game of a crucial three-game series.

The Giants had come to town two games ahead and held on to that lead by getting themselves a split in the first two games. If they won, they would be leaving town three games ahead with twenty-three games left in the season. If we won, we'd be going into the final month only a game behind, the closest we had been all year. Although it was a Monday night, there were 82,794 fans in the stands, the largest crowd of the year.

I didn't start out with anything more than average stuff. The first two men struck out, then there were doubles by Mays and Cepeda to give the Giants a quick run. Of the first ten outs, only three were strikeouts.

The fast ball came alive by the fourth inning, though, and in the late innings the curve was exploding too.

To get eighteen strikeouts, all I needed—if I had been thinking about it, which of course I wasn't—were fifteen strikeouts in the final seventeen outs. And that is, of course, what happened. One of the outs was a two-strike sacrifice bunt by Jack Sanford. The other was a fly to left field by catcher Bob Schmidt to end the eighth.

But that doesn't mean Schmidt was the only batter to hit the ball. I threw four straight curves to Willie McCovey in the fifth inning. Then I threw an inside fast ball and threw him another curve ball in tight. Willie hit it out of the park. Sanford had bunted after Danny O'Connell led off the seventh with a double. And, finally, Felipe Alou had dropped a single into center with two out in the eighth, the only hitter who didn't go to a two-strike count in five and two-thirds innings.

I wasn't thinking of a record, though. I had enough trouble staying in the ball game. We had scored a run in the first inning on a walk, a stolen base, a passed ball, and a force-out. When Roseboro led off our half of the seventh with a single to right, we were still trailing 2–1. Maury Wills, who was batting eighth, was given the bunt sign. I was sitting at the far end of the bench alongside Carl Furillo, and while Wills was waiting for the first pitch Alston called over for Carl to get ready to pinch-hit. As Carl got up to go to the bat rack, all I could say was, "Pick me up, roomie."

Wills didn't get John over. Maury's bunt was right in front of the plate, and Schmidt threw to second to force Roseboro. Carl was just beginning to leave the dugout, but Walt called him back and looked over at me. "You see if you can bunt him over now, Sandy," he said. "We might as well keep you in the ball game." I almost fell down running for the batting helmet.

I managed to get the bunt down, and Junior Gilliam brought Wills home with a single.

It was still a tie ball game when I came out to pitch the ninth. I was aware that I had a lot of strikeouts. With that large a crowd, the Coliseum was always filled with transistor radios—

some of the fans were seated so far away that they needed guidance and instruction—and broadcaster Vince Scully had been keeping count.

In the middle of that three-game winning streak in June, I had gone into the ninth inning against the Phillies with sixteen strikeouts (which turned out to be a record for a night game). I had known how many I had in that game. I had known that I needed one to tie Dizzy Dean's National League record, two to tie Bob Feller's major-league record, and three to set a new one.

I got none. All I got was a laugh. As I was ready to pitch to the first batter, a passing stranger came toward me from the third-base stands, letting off shrill blasts from a whistle and marching as if he were in a parade.

Los Angeles had a city ordinance against drinking beer in the Coliseum, which had done not a thing to cut down the beer consumption in the park. There had been a great deal of publicity about these "smugglers," and policemen had even been stationed at the entrances to check the more suspicious-looking packages. My first thought was, "Oh, oh, here's a smuggler for sure."

The guy kept trying to hand me his card, and I kept telling him, "I don't want it. I'm busy. I'm working."

There had also been a lot of publicity that week about a basketball scandal, and I was determined that I wasn't going to take a card from a stranger, a reaction which was, of course, insane, since no gambler was going to come marching out to try to bribe me in front of thousands of people. Johnny Roseboro, who thought a little faster than I did, took the card to get rid of the guy. Satisfied now, the guy went marching off toward first base, where he was greeted by some members of the park police, who suggested that he hold his parade somewhere else. In fact, they insisted on it.

The marcher didn't bother me, though. If anything, he relaxed me. I had two strikes on the first two batters, Joe Koppe and Richie Ashburn, but they both flied out to center field. The last out came, oddly enough, on a base hit. Dave Philley lined the ball to right field and, although his team was behind 6–2, he was out trying to stretch it into a double.

I had better luck two months later with the Giant hitters. I got them on ten pitches. The Giant batters in the ninth inning were Eddie Bressoud, Danny O'Connell, and Jack Sanford. Bressoud took the curve for a called strike, fouled off the fast ball, and missed another fast ball. O'Connell took the fast ball for a strike, swung and missed on the curve, and was called out on a fast ball. The crowd had been cheering after every strike. The roar that went up when O'Connell was called out made it clear that I must have tied some record or other.

The oddity of the record, I think, was that I got the chance to tie it, with two out in the ninth, against the opposing pitcher, something that can happen only when you're in a tie game. Sanford is a good hitter for a pitcher, but he's still a pitcher. I wasn't giving him anything except fast balls. He swung at the first one, took the second (which was outside), and swung at the other two.

Now all we had to do was win the ball game. I was the second batter in our half of the ninth, and darned if I didn't single to left field. Gilliam singled right behind me, which put me on second base with Wally Moon coming to bat.

Al Worthington was brought into the game to pitch. While Worthington was taking his warm-up pitches, Danny O'Connell came over to second base and said, "Are you hoping you won't score so you can strike out some more?"

That thought had never entered my mind.

Moon had tripled in the ninth inning the day before to knock in the tying run and, eventually, score the winning run. With a 1–1 count, Worthington threw him a slider. From where I was standing I could see the ball break in sharply on his fists. I could also see Wally give it his best inside-out swing. The ball went arching up toward the screen, and I was off and running. At worst, it was going to hit the screen and I was the winning run. I was halfway home when the roar of the crowd told me that it had gone over.

There was some talk the next day that the record couldn't really be compared to Feller's because the lights at the Coliseum weren't too good. Everybody's got a right to an opinion, of course, but I must admit that it was annoying to be put down when I had finally done something that seemed worthy of praise. Three seasons later, on April 24, 1962, I struck out eighteen men again. This time it was in Wrigley Field, where they play only by God's sunlight. I struck out three men in the ninth in that game too, but it was an entirely different story.

The whole pattern was turned around in that game. Against the Cubs, I had a big curve ball at the beginning of the game. I struck out the side on ten pitches in the opening inning, and had nine strikeouts out of the first ten men.

In the middle innings, however, I ran into control trouble and began to aim the ball. In the fifth inning I walked three men to force across Billy Williams, who had opened with a double.

And even though I struck out the side in the last inning, I could hardly say it was done with a flourish. Billy Williams opened the inning by hitting a hanging curve for a home run. After that, we forgot the curve and just threw fast balls.

After Bob Will, the right fielder, and Elder White, the shortstop, had struck out, Moe Thacker, the Cubs' catcher, hit a high fly between first and second, which was blown away from the second baseman and fell safely beyond first baseman Tim Harkness's last-second lunge. Which meant I got a second chance at the record-tying strikeout. Moe Morhardt came up as a pinch-hitter and took a called third strike on a 2–2 pitch.

It was an entirely different situation from the Giants game anyway, because we were ahead 7–0 after five innings and I was trying to get the first pitch over to make sure I got ahead of the hitters. The crowd was small (8938) and not particularly enthusiastic. I had no idea I had struck out that many until my teammates came rushing out of the dugout to congratulate me with an enthusiasm that hardly seemed called for in a 10–2 ball game.

One interesting sidelight was that Tony Balsamo, who had beaten me in the Ice Cream League playoff, pitched the sixth and seventh innings for the Cubs.

The greatest difference of all between the two games was that I had become a pitcher by 1962. In 1959, when I struck out eighteen Giants, I was still a thrower. The game against the Giants had been only my eighth win of the year. It was also my last.

The 1959 pennant race had been a peculiar one for us. We had been chasing San Francisco all season, and when we finally surged into a tie on the last two days of the season, the team we found ourselves facing in the playoff series was the Milwaukee Braves.

We defeated the Braves in two straight games, pulling out the second one after we had gone into the ninth trailing 5–2. I hardly covered myself with glory in that one. I went in to pitch in the eighth, got two outs, and then walked the bases full before I was yanked.

In the opening game of the World Series I did much better, pitching two perfect innings. The only trouble was that they didn't mean a thing. The White Sox were beating us 11–0. It's always better to do well than to do poorly, of course. Beyond that, I doubt whether that performance had very much influence in getting me a start. It was important from my point of view only because it did give me a good workout, just the kind of tightener I needed if I did get to start one of the games.

And I had felt from the beginning that if the Series went to five or six games and it was not a suicide game—that is, if we had a 3–1 or 3–2 lead—I could easily be tapped.

I got the call in the fifth game, after we had come back from the opening-day trouncing to win three straight.

By sheer coincidence I pitched before a lot of big crowds in my early years. The eighteen-strikeout game had been the biggest regular-season crowd of the year, although not one person had paid his way into the park to see *me*. All three World Series games in Los Angeles were played before capacity crowds, with the attendance figure going slightly higher on each game as the number of standing-room tickets was increased. Since I pitched the last of the games at the Coliseum, I was pitching before 92,706, the largest crowd of them all. Unless another ball club plays in a Coliseum someday, a most unlikely prospect, it may be the largest single crowd that will ever watch an official ball game to the end of time.

I'd have swapped at least 90,000 of it for a run, especially after the White Sox scored in the fourth. Jim Landis had singled to lead off the inning, and Nellie Fox punched a fast ball back through the middle, sending him to third. Lollar sent a ground ball to the second-base side of Maury Wills, and since it was still early in the game Maury went for the double play.

In the seventh inning, with the score still 1–0, Duke Snider was sent in to hit for me.

Duke and I went back to the dressing room and watched the rest of the game on television. I had an extra reason for rooting for the Dodgers to pull it out. I was reporting to Fort Dix the following Monday to put in my two weeks in the Reserves. If the Series went the full seven games, the last game would be played on Sunday, and I'd have to miss the victory party.

In the last of the eighth inning we loaded the bases with one out. Carl Furillo was sent in to pinch-hit for Roseboro. *Come on, Carl!*

Although Carl had been relegated to a pinch-hitter role most of the year, he had still managed to have his moments. In the final playoff game against the Braves, he had come through with a long fly to tie the score in the ninth inning. Remaining in the game, he had singled his next time at bat and finally hit the tricky ground single that brought in the winning run and put us in the World Series. In the third game of the Series he had pinch-hit in the eighth inning with the bases loaded, two out, and knocked in the winning runs. If my roomie was going out, he would go with style. But Carl popped up to the third baseman.

And that brought up Don Zimmer, who would be an even better story. Zip had lost his job to Maury Wills halfway through the season and had played very little over the second half of the year. He was coming up to bat now, for the first time in the Series, only because Wills had been taken out for a pinch-hitter. Here was Zimmer, who had almost been killed by pitched balls twice and who had hung in there, putting out his 100 per cent, despite the danger. And now it had come down to this. The bases were loaded. There were two men out. He could hit the ball out of the park and win the World Series— even a good single would do it.

He hit a high fly to short left field.

They just don't write stories the way they used to.

We flew to Chicago and wrapped it up quickly by winning the sixth game. The victory party was held on Saturday night.

It was a very, very nice party.

9

Suddenly, That Summer

Before the players depart at the end of the year to go their separate ways, there is a housecleaning ritual to be taken care of. Everybody cleans out his locker, throwing the worn equipment, the almost-empty bottle of after-shave lotion, and the old magazines onto the garbage pile in the middle of the clubhouse floor. If you are going to work out during the winter (or think you're going to work out) you take a glove and a pair of spikes and maybe even a pair of uniform pants home with you.

Each player has a wooden box into which he puts the rest of his equipment. The boxes are inserted, like shelves, into big steamer trunks, and they will be there waiting for you when you report to Vero Beach the following spring.

After the last game had been played in 1960, I put nothing at all into my drawer because I was disgusted with my performance during the season and uncertain about my future. I took a new pair of spikes and my best glove, in case I wanted to play softball in the park on Sunday afternoon. Might as well come out of this mess with something. Everything else I heaved onto the garbage pile.

"There it is," I said to Nobe Kawano, our clubhouse custodian. "Do whatever you want with it."

"What are you shipping down?" he asked me.

"Nothing," I said, indicating the empty drawer. "Including myself."

He looked at me as if he wasn't sure whether I was serious.

"If you want to quit, go ahead," he said. "But I wish you'd leave your arm."

That summed me up pretty well. Great arm; no head. All potential; no performance.

It wasn't that I had any regrets over the choice I had made. It was just that, having given myself six years, a full apprenticeship, I was convinced that the time had come to admit to myself that I wasn't going to make it.

It wasn't that I hadn't gotten my chance to pitch in 1960, either. I had been given more chance than ever. Nor did I feel that I hadn't learned anything about pitching. After six years you cannot help learning something about pitching. There are things you see just by watching the pitchers who do win. From my first couple of years in Brooklyn, the message had been clear. You watch Newcombe pitch, and it's almost exclusively the fast ball. You watch Maglie, and it's almost exclusively the curve ball. But both with great control. Then you watch Erskine, who has the fast ball and the curve and the good change-up, all with control. You understand very quickly that there are as many ways to pitch as there are pitchers, and that there is only one constant: CONTROL. And you also get the glimmer of an idea that more important than anything else, more important than how hard you can throw or how much your ball breaks, is the ability to put the ball where it is difficult to hit.

The Newcombes and the Maglies and the Erskines disappear. You watch Warren Spahn change from a fast-ball pitcher to a finesse pitcher, a pitcher who looks very easy to hit except when you are in the batter's box. You watch Stu Miller, who looks very easy to hit even when you are in the batter's box, and you realize that he is a master at changing speeds. I doubt if anybody else could get anyone out pitching the way Stu Miller does, and yet he not only gets them out, he makes them look ridiculous. And as time goes on that glimmer of an idea glows brighter and brighter, and you know that it is only a matter of putting it all into practice and executing it all correctly.

As long as you feel that you have only to grasp the idea, to learn the batters, to improve your control, you have something to look forward to. The most frustrating thing in the world, I had discovered, was to feel that you knew what you were doing and were doing it about as well as you could, and find that you were still losing. It was like focusing your camera on a beautiful scene, taking due account of color and composition, etc., running it through the developer, confident that you have a prize-winning picture, and having it come up blank.

I had come up blank.

In my first start I had given up five runs without getting a man out, a grand beginning but hardly untypical for me in April. A week later I relieved against San Francisco, walked three men, and was taken out.

I had never gone to the manager to ask to pitch. I had never gone to the front office to complain. It's not that I believe in sitting back and taking whatever fate serves up. I have always believed that if I did a good job I'd get a chance. I was not doing a good job for the Dodgers. I could not see why they should keep giving me chances. I had been on the club too long and had failed too often. There had been times when I felt I'd be traded. There were times when I was surprised the Dodgers were still holding on to me.

When I finally spoke my piece to Buzzie Bavasi, it was purely by accident. To get from the dressing room to the dugout in the Coliseum, we had to walk down a tunnel that let you out behind home plate. Just as I got to the end of the tunnel, I ran into Buzzie coming in. "Buzzie," I said, "why don't you trade me? I want to pitch, and I'm not going to get a chance here."

"How can we pitch you," Buzzie said, "when you can't get anyone out?"

"How can I get anyone out when I'm sitting around in the dugout?" I said. "If I can't do the job for you, why don't you send me somewhere where I can get a fresh start. Maybe you can even get a ballplayer you can use. I don't want to sit around and just watch."

We went around a couple of more times, and that was that. A week later I got a start against the Phillies, just where I'd have got it, I'm sure, if I had never opened my mouth. I had seven strikeouts in the first three innings, fifteen strikeouts in the first nine innings. But I had allowed a home run by Bobby DelGreco in the sixth inning, Don Cardwell was pitching a two-hitter himself, and we were tied 1–1.

In the tenth inning, with one out, B. G. Smith hit a ground ball down to third base, and just as Aspromonte got set to field it on the bounce behind third, the ball hit on top of the base and scooted through. A walk, a safe bunt, an error, a sacrifice fly, and Dark's home run, and I was a loser, 6–1.

Okay. Five days later against the Pirates I was leading 3–1, with two out in the eighth, having allowed two singles. Stuart singled, Baker walked, Hal Smith singled them both in and went to second on the throw to the plate. Out I went, with the score tied, but I was still responsible for the man on second. Gino Cimoli singled off the relief pitcher, and I had another loss.

Eight days later I got another chance against the Cincinnati Reds. I hadn't pitched a complete game against the Reds since that winning game in 1955. This time I came within one strike. With two out in the ninth, we were leading 4–3. Elio Chacon laid down a bunt, which was not what he should have been doing at all. With two out, he should have been swinging for extra bases. We let the ball roll, and it hugged the base line, hit right on third base, and stopped dead. Now I got the sign for a pitchout, which was crazy, because he had no right to be risking the tying run. We pitched out and Chacon was dead, except that he beat the throw and slid in safely. After which Kasko broke his bat swinging on a two-strike pitch and the ball blooped over the shortstop's head to tie the game.

Vada Pinson then tripled off the scoreboard, and I had myself another loss.

On my next start, I finally won a game, 1–0, pitching a one-hitter and striking out ten men. The hit was by the opposing pitcher, Benny Daniels.

Five days later, in Chicago, I came within one strike of winning again. I had a two-hitter and ten strikeouts and was leading 3–2. With two strikes on Frank Thomas, I tried to throw a fast ball by him. Thomas hit it into the seats. At the end of the thirteenth inning, I had fifteen strikeouts. In the fourteenth I walked Bouchee and Banks. Bouchee was trapped off second as Thomas missed a bunt, but made it to third base when the throw went to second. We walked Thomas to load the bases, got the next man on a short fly, and Don Zimmer, who had been traded to Chicago, singled to right field.

My losing streak extended to a game in Cincinnati on a very cold day. In the first inning the batters were colder than I was, and I struck out the side. In the second inning I walked three men and Dutch Dotterer hit a grand-slam home run, the only grand slam he ever hit in the majors. (I had formed the habit of throwing one grand slam a year, always to a catcher—Bob Schmidt of the Giants in 1958, and the Cardinals' Hal Smith in 1959.)

My record for the year was 1–8.

It was a great season. I had a little streak in August to bring the record up to 6–8, then promptly lost four in a row. At the end, my record was 8–13. The last loss was not unlike the first ones. I took a 3–2 lead into the eighth, thought I had Bob Will struck out on a 3–2 pitch, but found him being waved on to first. Zimmer bunted him along, and Santo blasted a triple off the left center-field wall to tie the score. Two walks and a double off the relief pitcher put the game out of sight, but Santo had been my responsibility.

To clear up any possible misunderstanding, I am not trying to suggest that I had bad luck. There were a couple of games I could have won if I had been lucky, but that doesn't mean I was unlucky to lose them. A good pitcher wins the close games because he comes up with the good pitch when he needs it. I had lost a long string of games because I had made a mistake at the worst possible time.

The only way you can lose a game, after all, is by letting the other team score.

When you are thirty you may well think how great it would be to be a boy of twenty-five again. When you're a twenty-five-year-old pitcher going nowhere, you do not look upon yourself as a fuzz-cheeked boy with a bright, shining future. A thirty-nine-year-old business executive can win a Junior Chamber of Commerce award as one of America's Most Promising Young Men. A thirty-nine-year-old ballplayer is a veteran, heading toward the boneyard.

I had seen the fringe players hanging on as long as possible, not primarily to put in extra time for pension benefits, but because there was nowhere else they could make anything like the same amount of money. I had no wife, no family to support. I could afford to give up a paycheck and take a chance. A couple of years later I might very well be married and have considerably less freedom of action.

I knew I wanted to stay in Los Angeles. I had just bought a home that summer. I liked the climate. I liked the people. I had already gone into business, with a partner, as a manufacturer's representative for several electrical lines. It seemed to me that I might be far better off devoting the next few years to building up that business or some other one so that I would not be starting out, at the age of thirty-five, from scratch.

After I did my two weeks up in Fort Ord at the end of the season, I began to work in the business.

It isn't that easy to walk away. To leave at the end of a successful career is one thing; the time that it's tough is when you haven't made it, when you've done nothing, when it's an admission—no matter how graciously you choose to explain it to yourself—that you've been licked.

I had to ask myself whether I had really worked as hard as I could have, absorbed as much as I should have, given myself every possible chance. Once you are thinking along those lines, the answers are probably inevitable. I decided I would give it one more year, one last, all-out effort.

As soon as I made that decision, I sold out to my partner so that I could devote all my time and energy to preparing for the baseball season. Which is a fancy way of saying that I had my tonsils out, came home, and rested.

My throat had been bothering me on and off for a couple of

years, and I had been advised to have the tonsils out. It isn't a serious operation for an adult; I was only in the hospital for two days. It's a *painful* operation, that's what it is. For two weeks I couldn't eat. I could get liquid down only by patience and perseverance. You can't even swallow your own saliva. A friend of mine's son had the operation the same day I did. Two days after I was out I paid them a visit, and there he was sitting at the table gulping down a tuna-fish sandwich and potato chips. Youth, it's wonderful.

Before I could eat again I had lost thirty pounds. By the time I reported to camp I was back up to about 184 pounds. Normally I hit camp at 205 pounds. Roger Craig saw me walking in and said, "You look like your little brother." For once I didn't have to worry about what I ate at camp. The waitresses kept forcing food on me. Eat. Eat.

Now malnutrition may not sound like the best possible prescription for a new career. But it was. The tonsillectomy turned out to be the best thing that could have happened to me. I learned something about conditioning. The notion that it's best to come to camp a little overweight so that you can work yourself into condition is one of those reversals of thinking.

What you really have to do after the winter's layoff is to take off the excess fat before you can begin to work yourself into shape to play baseball. What happens is that you have to get into condition so that you can get into shape. An overweight player will burn off eight or nine pounds in his first three days. Unfortunately, he will then turn around and put most of it back on. Exercise tears down muscle, but nourishing food and rest then build it up stronger than it had been. Muscle weighs more than fat. As the muscle builds up, the weight builds up with it.

If getting into shape puts on weight—and it does—it stands to reason that you should report to camp underweight rather than overweight. I certainly got into shape quicker than I ever had before and started the season in the best shape of my life. I have made it a point to come in underweight ever since.

Another thing I did in camp was to pay closer attention to the statistics that had been compiled by Allan Roth, the club statistician. Allan, who had been with the club since the Rickey days, kept a pitch-by-pitch chart of every game. Over the winter he would break the figures down into whatever sets of statistics seemed to be most significant for the individual player. At the very start of spring training you would always closet yourself with Allan for about an hour.

I had reason to know that these figures could be valuable. The statistic that had bothered us most over my first four years with the club was the set that showed I was consistently less effective against left-handed batters than against right-handed ones, although a left-handed pitcher is supposed to have an even greater natural advantage over a left-handed hitter than a right-handed pitcher has over a right-handed hitter.

One of the reasons, I knew, was my sheer inexperience. If left-handed hitters were unaccustomed to left-handed pitchers, I was even more unaccustomed to *them.*

Once the figures were in front of me, forcing me to think, the real reason had not been difficult to figure out. The left-hand hitter normally has trouble because the curve is breaking away from him. My breaking ball didn't. My breaking ball went straight down. I didn't come in sidearmed on my fast ball either, I came straight over the top. My stuff breaks up and down, which is the way I like it. The way I look at it, a bat is only about three inches wide, and almost three feet long. I'd rather give the batter a margin of error of perhaps one-quarter of an inch up and down than three or four inches across.

Even here, though, my fast ball, as it rises, tends to tail away from a right-hander and in to a left-hander. In other words, I was not exploiting my natural advantage against the left-handed batters at all.

By moving my fingers slightly on the ball, I was able to throw a curve that broke a little away from the lefty, as well as down. The improvement was evident at once.

As part of his orientation lecture, Allan Roth also shows you who has been hitting you the best. For the most part the names come as no surprise. There are no Mystery Guests in this category. He did not have to tell me that Ken Boyer had made me suffer in 1959, because I knew very well that Boyer had hit three home runs off me and hurt me with all of them.

It does no harm, however, to have your memory refreshed about the hitters who have been consistently getting on base in front of the big hitters.

In my first four seasons, when I was facing the Reds with some frequency, Roy McMillan had eleven hits off me in sixteen times at bat. It didn't matter what I threw or where I threw it. He blooped them, he topped them, he got bad bounces. Even when he hit it good, he got nothing except base hits.

When I sat down with Allan in the spring of 1961, he was able to show me that Hank Aaron had the best batting average against me in 1960. I had only faced him six times (partly because I had no scruples whatsoever against walking him five times) and he had four hits, including a double and home run. Henry's lifetime average against me was .475. Nineteen hits in forty tries, including five home runs. Tony Taylor had hit me good—5 for 10, which was better than I had thought. That Dick Stuart (5 for 12), Al Dark (5 for 14), and Vada Pinson (5 for 15) hit me good came as no shock at all. They had been hitting me consistently. Dark was just taking over as the non-playing manager of the Giants that spring. No one was happier to see Alvin advance in the world than I.

The list differs markedly from year to year, and I'm not sure whether it's because you bear down on the men who have been hitting you or because the law of averages bears down. Of the ten men who had hit me best in 1960, only Aaron hit me that well in 1961. All Henry had was 9 for 22, including three doubles and a triple. I talk of Aaron so often because he is the toughest hitter in the league as far as I am concerned. With Aaron, it doesn't matter whether you throw the fast ball or the curve because he has the ability to wait longer than almost any other hitter and, having waited, he has that quickness with the bat. You can pitch to Willie Mays. If you make your pitch, you've got a chance of getting Willie out. If you make a mistake, you've got a good chance of losing a baseball or a baseball game—and in the course of a ball game you're going to make mistakes.

The whole idea with Mays is to hope you make the mistake where it won't hurt you. The idea with Aaron is to hope his line drives are hit to a fielder.

For anybody who is interested in the current figures in this unequal battle, Hank had 33 hits (including 6 homers) in 74 times at bat against me through the 1962 season, a .446 average. In the last three seasons he has made only 5 hits (and no homers) in 32 times at bat, and plummeted to .358. But the figures are misleading. In the past two years he has been 0 for 8 and 1 for 9, which would lead the untrained observer to conclude that I had him well under control. Statistics, someone once observed, can lie. The last time I faced him in 1965, Hank struck out once and hit three of the hardest line drives I've ever seen, all right at somebody.

As far as the 1960 season was concerned, Allan's figures showed that my control had improved slightly, but not as much as I had thought. I was still averaging 5.14 walks per 9 innings against a league average of 3.19.

His figures showed, too, that the opposition's batting average against me had been only .207, making me the club leader in the category. (Left-handers had hit only .167 against me, which was more like it.)

All the breakdowns showed, as Allan would tell me every spring, that my only problem was control. With just average control, according to his figures, I would be a big winner.

This time there was a word of hope to go along with the pep talk. The good word was that over the last half of the 1960 season my walk average per game had been under 3.5. So how come I hadn't been a winning pitcher?

Roth had one other helpful hint for me. In 1960, he had begun to keep a completely new statistic: the count on which the decisive pitch was made; the count, in short, on which the batter either hit the ball, struck out, or was walked. We all knew that the pitcher was far better off when he was ahead on the count. Allan had set out to find out exactly how great the advantage was generally, and whether there was any significant difference from pitcher to pitcher.

The figures surprised even me. They showed that when I was ahead of the batter on the count he had hit only .146 against me. When I was behind, he had hit .286. When the count was even, the average was .267.

I had been ahead of the batter 45.7 per cent of the time and behind 21.0 per cent of the time.

When I had two strikes on the batter, regardless of the count, he had hit only .129. And I had got two strikes 53.9 per cent of the time.

Allan had been making this kind of breakdown on the Dodger hitters for some time. The statistics had shown that there is no such thing as a good two-strike hitter. Jackie Robinson had been by far the best, and his highest two-strike averages were only around .270.

The secret was quite obviously to get that first pitch over so that you would be ahead of the hitter. Except for one thing. There was another statistic that came right up out of the charts and hit you between the eyes. When the batter had hit my first pitch, his batting average had been .349. Wow. Dick Groat had led the league that year with an average of only .325.

This is, as you can see, a very tricky statistic. For one thing, it does not show how often I had got the first pitch in for a strike. If it was really that important to get ahead of the batter with the first pitch, I could afford to give up a certain number of hits.

I *wanted* the batter to hit the first pitch (even if I didn't want him to hit it for .349). I had long since come to the realization that it is far better to have the batter hit a long fly to center field on the first pitch than it is to throw five or six or seven pitches to strike him out.

The message couldn't have been clearer. My job was to throw a strike on the first pitch, while still making a good enough pitch so that the hitters would be held down to a more manageable percentage. I didn't succeed in doing it that first year. The average on the first pitch in 1961 went down to only

.312. In the two subsequent years, the only other years that Allan kept that statistic, it went down to .243 and .263.

I made one mechanical adjustment on my delivery. I finally tightened up my wind-up. Joe Becker had been after me to do it from the beginning but, as I say so often, nothing works until you believe it yourself. I thought a smaller wind-up would help my control. I also thought it would help me hide my pitches. When Wally Moon joined us in 1959, he told me the Cardinals had been reading me with men on bases. In going into my stretch, he said, I had been bringing my hands up higher for the fast ball than for the curve. That kind of thing can eliminate the guessing game pretty effectively.

It is impossible for a pitcher to throw his fast ball and his curve ball the same way, because they are two different pitches. If you studied every pitcher hard enough and long enough you would find some giveaway at some point in his delivery. When my arm is at the bottom of my delivery, my hand is exposed. If you look quickly enough and sharply enough, you will see more finger for the fast ball than for the curve, since the curve is held a little farther back into the hand. But the batter can't see my hand, only the coach. By the time the coach transmitted the signal and the batter absorbed it, it would be too late.

The real lesson was driven home to me in a B-squad game against the Minnesota Twins. The regulars were playing the Detroit Tigers at Lakehurst the same day, and I was happy to see myself listed for the trip to Orlando. In spring training, work is where you can find it.

Gil Hodges was the only regular on the list. I was down to pitch the first five innings, with Ed Palmquist and a couple of young pitchers from the minor-league rosters finishing up.

The plans began to unravel from the beginning. Ed missed the plane, and after a brief wait we took off without him. I said I'd try to go seven innings. In case we did need a third pitcher before the day was over, we were going to hold back the boy who had been brought along to pitch batting practice.

I was sitting with Norm Sherry, my roomie, who was going to catch me. Norm has always had a reputation for being a smart baseball man. He had, in fact, already done some managing in the winter leagues. As we sat there, on the short hop, Norm began to tell me to try to be a pitcher out there today, not just a thrower.

"All this is," he said, "is a B game. You haven't a thing to lose," he said, "because none of the brass is going to be there. If you get behind the hitters," he said, "don't try to throw hard, because when you force your fast ball you're always high with it. Just this once," he said, "try it my way like we've talked about. If you get into trouble, let up and throw the curve and try to pitch to spots."

I had heard it all before. Only, for once, it wasn't blahblah-blah. For once I was rather convinced that I didn't have anything to lose. There comes a time and place where you are ready to listen.

In batting practice something else happened. Gil Hodges was hit on the head. Gil wasn't hurt that badly but he was wobbly enough so that it was thought advisable to take him to the hospital for an X-ray. Bill Buhler, the trainer, went along with him, leaving Nobe, the clubhouse man, to give me the light rubdown with warm oil before the game. The whole thing was becoming more and more like a sandlot game.

Ron Fairly, who had been up with us as an outfielder, was playing first base, the first time I had ever seen him on first base in my life. Ron still insists that the first play of the ball game was a ground ball to the left of the mound, which I pounced upon no more than twenty feet away from him and fired at him point blank.

I pitched pretty much the way we had planned. It wasn't a question of throwing the ball up slower. I wasn't. I was trying to throw the ball as fast as, or maybe even faster than ever, but I was trying to go about it without pressing. I was still throwing hard, in other words, I was just taking the grunt out of it.

The Twins had a good hitting ball club. Killebrew and Jim Lemon and Allison and Battey and Rollins were all in the lineup. I felt very good and I had great success. For the most part I was just trying to throw strikes, but when I got ahead of the batter I went for spots. I found that I was hitting the spots with amazing regularity.

Not that it went perfectly and not that I didn't revert to old habits when I got into trouble. Somewhere around the fifth inning I walked two men and got mad at myself. Naturally I started to blow the ball in again and quickly found myself with the bases loaded and nobody out. Sherry came out to talk to me. "I'll tell you something, Sandy," he said. "It seemed to me like the ball was getting there just as fast when you weren't trying to throw it past everybody. Think about what you're doing. Pick me up. Watch my glove. Be a pitcher. Make them swing the bat, and maybe you'll get out of the inning."

Two of the batters coming up were Killebrew and Lemon. I settled down and struck out the side.

When I left the game, I had pitched a seven-inning no-hitter, striking out eight and walking five.

There is nothing like instantaneous success to convince you that you are on the right course.

The story even has a low-comedy ending. When we got back to Vero I was full of my new-found knowledge. Larry Sherry had gone nine innings a day earlier, so he was in a happy frame of mind too. Now there is not very much that can be done at Vero Beach by way of celebration and/or relaxation, except to go to a movie. When the movie let out we were hungry, so we drove twenty miles down the road to a pizza place, discussed the art and craft of pitching over a hot pizza and a couple of beers, and came back to camp about an hour past the 12:30 curfew. Nobody would have known or cared, in all probability, if we hadn't been boisterous enough to attract Walt Alston's ear as we passed his door.

When I heard Walt's door open, I grabbed my own door, tugged hard, and found that it was locked. Larry ran to his room, though, slipped in, and locked the door behind him. Walt ran down the hall to Larry's room and began to pound on the door. Meanwhile, Stan Williams, my roommate, had opened the door and I had slipped in.

In the morning I was informed that I had been fined $100

for breaking the curfew, which of course I had. In one day I had pitched a no-hitter and broken a curfew at Vero Beach. It was hard to say which was the more impressive feat. The rest of the players thought it was hilarious. If Larry or I had been quick enough to dream up a suitably picturesque story, we could have become legends in our own time.

Walt might have found it funny himself if he hadn't broken his diamond-studded World Series ring while he was banging on Larry's door. We were all riding the bus to Miami the next day. I was sitting in back and Larry was up front. "Hey, Larry," I yelled, "have you had your door appraised for diamonds yet?"

There was laughter from the groundlings, but none at all from the manager's box. It seemed like a good subject to drop.

That day in Orlando was the beginning of a whole new era for me. I came home a different pitcher from the one who had left. Before that game, it had been almost all bad. Afterward, it was almost all good.

The language of baseball makes it very difficult to explain what I was doing differently. Expressions like "reaching back to find something extra" and "never letting up" lead people to think that a pitcher takes a deep breath, closes his eyes, and challenges the batter to a contest of muscle. That isn't it at all. It is desire that is being talked about when they use those expressions. Determination. The trouble comes when the desire and determination are uncontrolled.

The only way I can explain it is to say that the most you can give to anything you are doing is 100 per cent. If you use up that 100 per cent in sheer physical effort, there is nothing left over for thinking. You must therefore apportion some minimum percentage—5 per cent or 10 per cent are good arbitrary, meaningless figures—to thinking about what you are doing. By concentrating on where you want the ball to go, you seem to take the stress out of throwing. You are not pressing, you are not forcing the ball. You are taking nothing out of the physical effort, in other words, except—again—the grunt.

It was not a total revelation. I had been given a few clues from time to time. In 1959 I was pitching in the tenth inning of a Sunday game in Pittsburgh. We had scored a run to go ahead in the top of the tenth. There used to be a Sunday curfew law in Pennsylvania, and the curfew was going to sound in twelve minutes. If we did not retire the Pirates inside those twelve minutes, our half of the inning would be wiped out, and the win would be wiped out with it. In those circumstances I could hardly afford to let the batter run out the count, and so, without thinking too much about it, I had to concentrate on throwing strikes rather than throwing hard. Bill Virdon went to a 1–2 count, fouled a pitch off, and then struck out. R. C. Stevens went to 1–2 also and then he struck out. There wasn't much sense in Dick Groat trying to work a count down any more. He took one ball, and flied to left field. The whole thing had taken only eleven pitches and five minutes.

Nor do I wish to testify under oath that I have not forgotten, do not—and will not—forget from time to time and revert to the wayward ways of my youth. It's usually when I'm mad or tired, but dumbness is not to be completely discounted either.

In the 1965 All-Star Game I was terribly wild. I came into the game in the sixth inning and immediately threw seven straight balls. Although I got out of the inning, it was a struggle with every batter. When I got back to the dugout, Gene Mauch told me he was going to pinch-hit for me. "When you can't throw strikes," he said, "there's probably something wrong with your arm."

There was not a thing wrong with my arm. My arm was fine. My head was something else again. Knowing that I was only going to pitch an inning or two, I had thought, "Well, hell, I'll just go in and throw as hard as I can." And there I was, right back where I'd been ten years ago, wild high.

In 1960 I had made the transition from thrower to pitcher and had not understood that in making the transition I had made a beginning, not an end. You become a pitcher before you become a *good* pitcher.

In 1961 a whole new world opened up for me. It was as if I had achieved the first rung of a ladder and was eager to climb the ladder rung by rung to find out what was at the top. It is very difficult to work hard when there's nothing coming back, when you see no progress. When you finally put your foot on the ladder and begin the climb, it becomes easier and easier to work harder and harder.

In 1961 I got the first April win of my career by beating Cincinnati 5–2. From mid-May to mid-June I had my first solid winning streak, completing and winning six straight games.

The streak came to an end when Lew Burdette came to town and won his ninth consecutive game in the Coliseum. Lew helped himself by hitting a home run for the first run of the game. I hurt myself by forgetting everything I had learned. With one out in the seventh, I walked Cimoli and Bolling to put men on in front of Mathews and Aaron. I had begun to stamp around when I couldn't get the ball over to Bolling. With Mathews, I went right back to brute strength and walked him too. With Aaron coming up, Walt yanked me. Larry Sherry got what looked like the big out when Aaron flied to shallow center, then walked Adcock on a 3–2 pitch.

We got a run right back on Charlie Neal's home run, but the second run beat us. I had lost the game, and given myself a valuable lesson, by becoming the Old Koufax.

The next time out I pitched a two-hit shutout against the Cubs, striking out fourteen. After sixty-four games I had a 10–3 record and a place on the All-Star team. I looked like I might win twenty games. I didn't. My record, at the end, was only 18–13. My last win came on our last home game, the last game to be played at the Coliseum. Come 1962, we were going to bid a fond farewell to one screen and 93,000 seats and move on to the promised land at Chavez Ravine.

For a while it looked as if we'd never leave. The game went 13 innings, and I went all the way, throwing 205 pitches, striking out 15 and walking only 3. Over the last five innings, I gave up no hits at all. I may not have been a better pitcher in those days, but I sure was younger.

There were nine road games left to be played, which meant that I still had a chance to win twenty games. The Cardinals weren't very cooperative, bombing me out in three innings. Having been knocked out that early, I still had a chance. I could start again in two days, easily and—if I won—pitch with two days' rest again on the final day of the year.

If I won . . . Two days later, in Philadelphia, the Dodgers got me a run in the first inning. In the third, a single, and error, a sacrifice, and a strikeout, and there were men on second and third with two out. Tony Taylor knocked them both home with a double. Technically, the runs were unearned. Actually, Taylor had earned them very nicely with his double. That was the way the game ended, 2–1.

Oh, yeah. I gone into the game needing six strikeouts to break the National League strikeout record set by Christy Mathewson in 1903. I got seven.

10

The Year of the Finger

This is the year I can bring my lifetime record to .500. Six bad years and six good ones. Six years of drought and six years of plenty. The excitement of having success come early, without undue effort, is something I will never know. When you are successful immediately, the success seems to come as a gift, as a message from the heavens that you are one of the favored children, one of the beautiful people. Your worth is what you *are*.

Late success is quieter. No fireworks go off. No pinwheels spin. Late success is not necessarily more satisfying—I'm sure the satisfaction in immediate success is great—but it is certainly more rewarding. You have the warm, steady glow of accomplishment, which is worth whatever it is worth. The excitement of an early success comes from the outside; the gratification of a late success, from the inside. Your worth is what you have made yourself.

Although I may have started with the gift of an arm, it was a gift that required a lot of work on the part of a lot of people. As I said much earlier, my greatest satisfaction comes in pitching a good game when I don't have a thing. That one I earned.

Those years as a loser may even be of help to me when I'm struggling. I'm not talking about technical skills here; I'm talking about attitude. I don't expect things to be always good —I don't say easy, it's *never* easy. I know there will be rough days, inside baseball or out. If it was bad once, it can be bad again.

I also know that I came this close to leaving baseball before I had achieved anything. I know, as all baseball players know, that the end is never very far out of sight. If I am left with only this little time in between, to achieve whatever goals I am after, I had better make the most of every chance I get, hadn't I? Whether I have my stuff or not. The late winner carries the early loser inside him, and losers are the worst critics of all.

Records are important to you, because you are paid according to your record of the previous year. I have never thought in terms of numbers, though. Twenty wins is a standard only because it is a nice round number. The pitcher who won nineteen has probably pitched just as well and may even have pitched better. But I'm not interested in just winning twenty games. I'd like to win them all.

The only goal you can have is to win the game you are pitching that day. I'm trying to pitch a no-hitter every time out, which means that I am trying to get every batter. That doesn't mean I expect to pitch a no-hitter. If I expected to pitch a no-hitter every time out, I'd also expect a visit from a select committee appointed by the Board of Psychiatrists.

There are pitchers who say their goal is to give up no more than two runs a game. If they can do that, they say, they know they will win a good percentage of their games. But you're not pitching a good percentage of your games; you're pitching *this* game. The only way you can be sure of winning *this* game is by giving up no runs. In *this* game you can give up two runs and go out for a pinch-hitter in the seventh inning.

I have been pointing to records here with great frequency, I know, but that's only because it is the nature of an autobiography to pause over the milestones. I have become accustomed to having sportswriters—and very good ones—sit down beside me and ask, "How does it feel to know that you're in the books as the guy who broke Mathewson's record and Feller's record. Do you think, 'Gee, Mathewson, Feller and me'?"

I can only tell them that I have never given it a second thought, and they can only make it clear that they don't believe me.

I have never felt that I was in competition with Mathewson or Feller or Cy Young. The eras are different, the game is different, the ball is different, the bat is different. The strike zone itself is different. I cannot get myself worked up because I struck out two more men in 1961 than Mathewson struck out in 1903. I had no control over anything Mathewson did in 1903. If he had struck out four hundred men, he'd have the record and I still would not have struck out one man less.

All records mean, really, is that there is somebody out there counting.

You do what you do on the field today. The paper work all comes after the fact. The game you pitched or the season you pitched doesn't change. How can they be made better or worse by what other men did at other times on other fields?

It is conceivable that if I had followed baseball more closely as a kid, I'd have a sense of the history of the game that I seem to lack. It may be, too, that I failed so consistently in my first attempts at all the established landmarks that I told myself they weren't that important anyway. Because if there is one record I know I have, it is for not succeeding in anything until the second time around.

I lost my first World Series game. I missed the twenty-game season the first time I had a chance for it. And I lost my first crack at the major-league strikeout record when I was laid low by a finger. When I tied the single-game strikeout record they said the lights were bad. When I pitched my first no-hitter they said, "Yeah, but look who he pitched it against. The Mets."

And I've had a positive genius for losing the games in which I passed another milepost on the Strikeout Trail. As we know, I lost the game in which I broke Mathewson's record. Four years later, when I broke my own record, the Pirates beat me, 3–2, in eleven innings. In 1959 I set a major-league record for most strikeouts (41) in three consecutive games by striking out ten Cubs in ten innings. Ernie Banks hit a home run in the tenth to beat me 3–0.

In 1964 I set a record by striking out ten men for the fifty-fifth time in my career. In that one I went out for a pinch-hitter in the tenth inning with the score tied 1–1. We lost in thirteen innings.

In 1962, in the game where I struck out my 1000th man, I lost 3–1. In 1964 I struck out my 1500th man and lost 3–2.

Those records will kill you!

Just to fill out the record, I struck out my 2000th man in 1965, in a one-inning relief stint against the Phillies. Jim Brewer's arm had been bothering him, and since it was my day to work out anyway, I went to the bullpen late in the game in case Jim's arm stiffened up on him. We won that one 8–4.

There was one honor I really did go after. In 1962, in my eighth year in the big leagues, I wanted to pitch the opening game, the first game that was ever going to be played in Chavez Ravine. I had worked hard and been unusually effective through spring training, and assumed I had nailed it down. A day or two before the season opened I read in the paper that Alston had said he wasn't going to open with me because I was too nervous.

The second night of the season was Chinatown Night, and my nerves and I were carted in from the bullpen by ricksha. Eddie Kasko led off the first inning with a soft fly that was lost in the lights. That was the only hit until the ninth, when the Reds got three more.

I haven't felt one way or another about the opening-game assignment since. I'd like to pitch the first game, but only because it might give me an extra start over the full season.

I still think Chavez Ravine is the prettiest park in the league. From the beginning, strangely enough for a new park, there was an easy, friendly atmosphere about it. Friendly? We have a long dressing room, with a hallway alongside, and you have to go out into the hall to get to the shower and to the trainer's room and to the Coke machine in the meeting room. The hallway has to remain open to foot traffic because of the fire laws or something, and there are strangers, lost in the labyrinth, wandering in almost every night. My locker is right by the

163

door. If no one is around a passer-by will occasionally leave a friendly reminder of his visit by walking off with a sweatshirt or a glove.

It is a good park to pitch in because there is a lot of room up the middle and no short porch along either foul line. Basically, you try to keep the ball away from the batter so that if he hits it well he'll hit it out to center field. You have to come inside now and then, of course, to keep the hitter honest, but the over-all pattern is to pitch so that you'll be making your mistakes outside.

In Cincinnati, where the ball can fly out anywhere, you have to work with the idea of never letting anybody hit the ball hard.

Pittsburgh is like Yankee Stadium. If you can keep the left-handers from pulling the ball right down the line, you've got a great big park doing the rest of the work for you.

In Candlestick Park you're playing the wind more than the shape of the park. The wind is generally whipping out to right field and in from left field. You take the club batter by batter. Cepeda had an alley in right center, and when he was there he would ride the ball right along the jetstream. Cepeda is also strong enough that he can hit the ball through the wind and over the left-field fence. Basically, you had to pitch Cepeda to try to get him to hit the ball on the ground. The Giants can worry about that when he comes back to Candlestick now.

With McCovey, you're concentrating solely on not letting him pull. He's strong enough to hit a ball out in left occasionally, but with that wind blowing in, the percentages are very much with you.

Although Chavez Ravine is a pitcher's park, the team that came in there in 1962 was a strong hitting ball club, probably the best-balanced team we've had since we moved to Los Angeles. That 1962 team won more games than the pennant-winning clubs of 1963 and 1965. Only the Giants scored more runs than we did, and they were playing half their games in a hitter's park.

Tommy Davis, Maury Wills, Frank Howard, and Willie Davis all had the best year of their lives.

Tommy Davis had an absolutely incredible year. Look at these figures: Tommy led the majors in hitting (.346), base hits (230), and runs batted in (153), the kind of figures that hadn't been seen since the thirties. He also had 27 home runs. It seemed that every time there was a man on base, he'd knock him in, and every time there were two men on base, he'd hit a double and knock them both in.

Frank Howard had 31 home runs and 119 RBIs. Willie Davis had 21 home runs and 85 runs batted in.

Maury Wills stole 104 bases, broke Ty Cobb's unbreakable record, and won the MVP award. All by himself he stole more bases than any club in baseball did. And if you eliminated Maury's steals, the rest of the Dodgers still stole more bases than any other club in baseball.

As for pitching, Don Drysdale, having his best year too, won the Cy Young Award, leading the league in games won (25) and strikeouts (232).

I had my best year too, as far as it went, leading the league in earned run average (2.54).

Everything that there was to win, we won. Except the pennant.

I had started even better than the year before. In April, when I normally struggle, I had won four games. Toward the middle of May, though, a numbness began to develop in the index finger of my pitching hand. Well, loss of circulation in a finger is not unusual in the life of a pitcher.

The finger didn't seem to get any better during the next two weeks. It became numb and cold. It had a white, dead look about it. I could press the fingernail of my thumb into it, and instead of having the flesh spring back out, the impression would remain there, almost as if it had been made in wax. I'd show the finger to the trainers and to Walt, and we'd all look at it and shake our heads. We'd all say that it sure was a nasty-looking one, all right. And we all assumed that it would go away.

I had spent too much of my life *not* pitching to think about missing any turns. Johnny Podres was having trouble with his elbow, which left me the only left-handed starter on the club.

And most of all, I had never pitched better in my life.

All the index finger really does is hold the ball. My curve spins off the middle finger, and, for that matter, my fast ball leaves off the middle finger too. My control had been quite good. From the time the finger began to go numb, I had pitched four complete games, striking out 10, 16, 10, 13, and walking a total of 8 batters.

And then, with the finger growing steadily number, I went off into the hottest streak I had ever had. It started when I beat Milwaukee, 2–1, but that isn't what I want to talk about. Roseboro struck out to open the fifth inning of a scoreless game, giving the 14,913 fans no forewarning that history was about to be made. Warren Spahn wound up to throw me his first pitch. It was a day like all days. He threw me a screwball like any other screwball. All things the same. I swung my slightly disheveled, somewhat apologetic swing. All things as always. The ball came rocketing off my bat in a rising line drive that disappeared into the left-field stands.

It is a tossup who was the most amazed person in the park, Spahn or me. There's no doubt at all who was the loudest. As I hit first base I could hear someone screaming at me. As I looked around, while taking the good home-run trot between first and second, I saw that it was Spahnnie. He was standing there on the mound, a study in disgust, and he kept turning with me all around the bases, calling me every name he could think of. As I rounded third base, Eddie Mathews got into the act. "What are you trying to do," he asked me, "make a joke out of the game?"

The only other home run I've ever hit was also in Milwaukee. That one was against Denny Lemaster, a 3-run 390-foot—sure, let's say blast, that put us out front 3–1. This time they couldn't say they hadn't been warned. I can't say I won, either. I couldn't get past the sixth inning.

In the next start after I had hit my first home run, I pitched a 1–0 game against St. Louis, and it was the first game in which I didn't give up a base on balls. Tommy Davis won it with a home run in the eighth off Bob Gibson, and back in the clubhouse Tommy and I danced around, chortling, "Us Brooklyn boys, we've got to stick together."

The last time I had won a 1–0 game had been in 1961, when a fellow named Tommy Davis hit a home run off a fellow named Bob Gibson. The next time I pitched a 1–0 game was in 1963, against the Mets. Tommy knocked that one in with a long fly.

New York had come back into the National League in 1962. There was a special feeling about returning to the Polo Grounds because there *should* be a team in New York. It would have been more fun if we could have gone back to Ebbets Field, needless to say, but I understand there's a housing development where Ebbets Field once stood.

We were coming back for the first time on Memorial Day, a fitting date. We old Brooklyn players weren't really certain whether we were going to be greeted as old friends returning or as traitors coming back to face the music.

All fears were disposed of very quickly. The old Brooklyn players were given tremendous hands as we were introduced in the pregame celebration.

Through the luck of the draw, I was pitching the first game. Having been the last player to throw a baseball for the old Dodgers, before we left, I was the first to throw a baseball for the new Dodgers upon our return. It was not one of my better games. With a 10–0 lead after four innings, it didn't have to be. Before the long day was over, I had given up thirteen hits, the most I have ever given up in a ball game and, quite probably, the most I ever will; you don't usually remain around long enough to give up fourteen.

Four of the hits came in the ninth inning, and Walt came out to ask me if I wanted somebody to pick me up. "No," I said. "I want to finish it." I had left as a hanger-on; I was returning, presumably, as a pitcher. It was important to me that I go the route.

The second time I faced the Mets I gave up fewer hits than I had ever given up before: none. The first inning of that game has to be the best inning I have ever pitched: three strikeouts on nine pitches. Every pitch went exactly where I wanted it to. I remember the second batter, Rod Kanehl, clearest of all, because I threw my entire repertoire at him: the fast ball, the change of pace, and the curve.

As the game went on, my stuff held up well but my control was spotty. In addition to giving up five walks, I went to three balls on eight other batters.

After a no-hitter you are always asked whether you knew that you had it all along. You know. Those big o's are up there on the scoreboard in living neon, and as the innings go by they become bigger and brighter and closer. In the Met game they could have torn the scoreboard down and I still would have known. Solly Hemus had appointed himself my personal score-keeper.

As I was walking back off the mound after the first inning, Solly, who was coaching at third for the Mets, passed me going the other way. "You know something?" he said, just kidding. "You've got a no-hitter."

Halfway through the game, as we were passing each other again, he said in a sort of disbelief, "You know something? You *still* got a no-hitter."

"Hell," I said, "I've had 'em later than this and lost them." So, of course, has everybody else. If all the five-inning no-hitters were laid end to end and covered with concrete you'd have a six-lane highway running between Bangkok and St. Louis.

Solly kept reminding me of it every inning after that, just to give me something to think about. As I walked off after the game, with an honest-to-God nine-inning no-hitter, he trotted by me and under his breath he whispered, "Congratulations."

The last two hitters were Rod Kanehl and Felix Mantilla, who gave me as much trouble as anybody on that club. I had played with Felix in Puerto Rico. When he was with Milwaukee he had hit me very well. With good power too. I have never pitched well to Felix. Kanehl was just a tough out for me. He was another of those guys who didn't hit the ball that hard but always seemed to come out of the game with one or two base hits.

In spring training that year, in my first attempt to go the full distance, Kanehl and Mantilla had come up back to back with two outs in the ninth. Trying to check his swing on a curve, Kanehl had hit a ground ball that followed the first-base line as if it had eyes. That tied the score. Mantilla then hit a line single to left field to win it.

Better then than now. Kanehl grounded to third, Mantilla hit a high hopper to short, and I had the no-hitter.

The finger was getting no better. I was perfectly aware that after six weeks it should have cleared up; still, I had no concern that I might be in any real danger. With that finger, I had hit my first home run, pitched my first no-walk game, and pitched my first no-hitter, all in the space of seventeen days. To keep complaining seemed ridiculous.

Before we left LA we swept a four-game series against the Phillies to go into first place, one-half game ahead of the Giants. I had won the first game of the July 4 double-header, 16–1. That's what I like—a safe and sane Fourth.

Our first stop was in San Francisco. I was down to pitch the final game in the series and then fly to Washington for the All-Star game.

By the time I was warming up in San Francisco the finger had turned reddish and was beginning to feel sore and tender. When I pressed my finger against the ball in throwing the curve, it was as if a knife were cutting into it. If I didn't rest the finger against the ball, I had no feel on the curve ball.

Alvin Dark noticed that I kept looking down at the finger while I was warming up. Once the game started, it took him about two innings to figure out that I was throwing nothing but fast balls.

I had a good fast ball, though, and I was putting it where I wanted. I actually had a no-hitter until the seventh inning, when a ground ball caromed off the second baseman's arm.

Until Bob Nieman lined a single to open the ninth, the official scorer was getting some very dirty looks from the Los Angeles writers.

By the ninth inning my hand had gone numb through the webbing between the thumb and finger. With a two-ball count on Mays, I had to come out of the game. Don Drysdale came in and got the final two outs.

The players who had been picked for the All-Star team were flying back to Los Angeles with the rest of the team and connecting with a plane for Washington.

I made arrangements, instead, to see Dr. Robert Kerlan, the club doctor, in his office, and catch a later plane out. Dr. Kerlan wanted to take me to a vascular specialist, since only a specialist would have the proper equipment for testing the blood flow through my arm. The club put in a quick call to league headquarters to try to get me excused. The league turned them down. When a pitcher on a contending club comes up with a "disabling" injury on the eve of the All-Star game, there is always the suspicion that the club is trying to protect its rotation.

Walt did ask Fred Hutchinson not to use me, so the only purpose my cross-country flight served was to prevent me from having the finger examined.

I don't want to leave the impression that I resented having to go. There is an atmosphere about the All-Star game, a combination of excitement and relaxation, that is like nothing else in the world. It is a trade convention, of course, but there is more to it than that. There is something pleasant and relaxing in not only playing alongside the greatest players in the world, but in being able to root for Mays and Aaron and White and Boyer and all the other great hitters you have been trying to get out all year. Part of it is "Okay, let the other side worry now," but the real pleasure is in being permitted to sit back and enjoy the ability of players who, through the necessities of competition, were your bitterest enemies the last time you met and will be your bitterest enemies when you meet again.

I'm sure the other players feel the same way about it. Kenny

Boyer and I had adjoining lockers in Washington. As we sat alongside each other after the game, Kenny just wanted to talk about Maury Wills, who had run wild on the bases, accounting for the final run by going from first to third when the left fielder threw behind him and then scoring on a short foul fly to right.

The only unpleasant thing about it was that my finger seemed to be turning redder all the time.

From Washington I went to New York to rejoin the club. Since there is a three-day break for the All-Star game, Walt was able to start me right away. The finger was beginning to turn blue now, and was more tender than ever. To complete the color ensemble, a blood blister formed on the tip of the finger during the game, dead blood which had apparently seeped down and collected. I still couldn't throw a curve. After seven scoreless innings, I lost all feel of the ball and had to come out of the game.

Put down like this, flatly and after the fact, it seems ridiculous to have kept pitching with that kind of finger. And yet, you have to look at the scores. I had just won four games by scores of 5–0, 16–1, 2–0, and 3–0. (The run was a home run by Ted Savage.) Over the full eight games, I had allowed 4 earned runs for an ERA of 0.53. In those 67⅓ innings I had struck out 77 men and walked 20. I could look at the finger and think "What's going on here?" but how unhappy could I be when I was pitching the best ball of my life?

My uncle, Sam Lichtenstein, visited me at the hotel while we were in New York. By then the color had become a sort of deep reddish-blue and the finger was all swollen up. He took one look at it and said, "Sandy, your finger looks like a grape. How can you pitch with that? Are you crazy?"

I have another uncle in New York, who is an osteopath, and Sam insisted that we have him look at it. He diagnosed it as a loss of circulation, probably caused by a blood clot. He warned me that I had better get it treated at once.

I stayed with the club through Philadelphia and into Cincinnati.

While I warmed up to pitch in Cincinnati, the finger was so sore that I could barely hold the ball. One of the players came over to me and said, "Forget it, Sandy. Don't even try it. Nobody will thank you for it."

Well, I pitched an inning and the damn thing split open. There was no blood to come spurting out; it was just a raw, open wound. The finger had split across the blood blister, though, and the dried blood, mixing perhaps with the sweat, was staining the ball as I threw.

The Reds had made three hits and scored two runs. When I came back to the dugout at the end of the inning I told Walt I didn't think I could make it. Bill Buhler, our trainer, called Buzzie Bavasi for me. Buzzie was in New York with Dr. Kerlan. They told Bill to have me fly right back to Los Angeles to see Dr. Robert Woods, the other club doctor. Dr. Woods took me to Dr. Travis Winsor, a cardiovascular specialist.

They were able to follow the flow of blood with a machine that takes a reading from point to point, like a cardiogram. It is, in fact, called an arteriogram. A cup was placed on the finger, and a sort of rubber band was placed around my arm at various places, almost as if they were taking my blood pressure—which, I suppose, is exactly what they were doing. The readings showed that the blood was flowing through the elbow, through the forearm, through the wrist, and continued to flow freely until it went into the palm of my hand. Below the palm, in the finger itself, my circulation was about 15 per cent of normal.

The perplexing thing to the doctors was that there was no evidence of any bruise on my palm. Nor could I recall one. The problem seemed to be that clots in the artery are rare under any circumstance. Most blood clots are formed in the veins, because the veins are closer to the surface of the skin and because the blood is returning to the heart (and therefore moving sluggishly), while arterial blood is being pumped from the heart and therefore moving at a relatively swift rate.

Given my symptoms—the gradual closing-off of the artery—an injury would have had to occur deep enough to have caused an irritation to the inner lining of the artery, which, being un-even, would have begun to catch an occasional blood cell here and there until it built up a large enough obstruction to cause a clot and begin to close the artery off. The worrisome thing was that, if I did not have the clot in the artery, the next best diagnosis was Raynaud's Phenomenon, which has exactly the same symptoms.

If it was the result of a bruise, the trouble would disappear completely when the clot was dissolved. If it was Raynaud's Phenomenon, I had a rare and incurable disease.

The doctors naturally kept after me. Had I tried to stop a batted ball with my bare hand? Had I been hit by a pitched ball? Finally I remembered.

In spring training I had decided to be real smart and bat left-handed, not because I had any great hope of hitting any better but because I had figured that in batting right-handed I was presenting my left arm to the pitcher. Since I wasn't going to terrorize the pitcher either way, I decided that I might as well hit left-handed and at least protect my pitching arm.

Back at the end of April, in the game immediately after the eighteen strikeouts against the Cubs, I had pitched a 2–1 victory over the Pirates. Leading off in the third inning, I was jammed by Earl Francis. People don't always understand what jammed means. The ball hadn't hit my hand. I had hit the ball off the handle of the bat and through the pitcher's box. Dick Groat made a good play behind second base, but I beat his throw to first. As I hit the ball the heel of the bat had sort of pinched into the palm of the hand. Once I recalled the incident, I could even remember that there had been a painful bruise on the palm, so painful that I had kept looking at the palm through the rest of the game because I had expected it to turn black and blue.

The press picked up Raynaud's Phenomenon because it is such a catchy name—it sounds like a French bonus boy—but I haven't got it and I never had it. If I did have it, I probably wouldn't be pitching any more.

By the time I remembered the jamming against Pittsburgh,

Dr. Winsor had pretty much started me on the road to recovery through various medication, injections, and pills designed to widen the artery, thin out the blood, and dissolve the clot. One of them was an experimental—and very expensive—drug which was fed to me intra-arterially for a couple of hours every day. Some time later I heard the drug had been taken off the market because some people had reacted badly to it.

Once the blood started to flow in, the skin sloughed off and the whole fingertip was raw. As the blood came back in an infection developed all around the cuticle. When Dr. Winsor released me, I had to go right to a hand specialist to get the infection treated.

A couple of weeks after I had flown back to Cincinnati, Bob Kerlan told me that everything had cleared up nicely. "You're very lucky," he said. "You don't know how close you came to losing the finger." The bluish color on the finger had been a pre-gangrenous condition; that is, an indication that gangrene was getting ready to set in. That's what gangrene is, a lack of circulation to any area of the body. With no blood to feed it, the tissue dies.

Some of the nerve endings at the tip of the finger apparently did atrophy, but only enough so that it hurts a little in cold weather.

There was something else, too. I had assumed that the infection was a natural part of the recovery process, that the infection had been sort of sitting there, waiting for the blood to bring it out. I couldn't have been wronger. Blood circulation is the body's natural defense against infection, since it is the blood that carries it away. Without circulation, an infection can spread very quickly. The doctors had been quite worried that, with my diminished circulation, the infection would spread to the bone and cause osteomyelitis. A bone infection would have brought on precisely the same result as gangrene. They'd have had to amputate.

In short, the blood circulation had to come back quickly and completely in order both to feed the tissue and to carry away the infection.

"It worked out just beautifully," Dr. Kerlan told me. "It was like a car and a train racing to a crossing, and you don't know which is going to get there first. Only in your case there were trains coming from both directions, and you had to squirt right through the middle."

When I left the ball club we were in first place by one game. To show how much they needed me, the Dodgers won seventeen of their next twenty-one games to take a five-and-a-half-game lead.

With the finger getting better, I accompanied the club on the next road trip so that I would be able to stay in shape in the event the finger healed quickly enough to allow me to pitch at the end of the year.

With the season coming down to the last couple of weeks, I began to pitch batting practice. The finger was a little tender, which necessitated a slight change in the way I held the ball. Other than that, there seemed to be no difficulty at all.

The Dodger pitching was getting so thin at the end that Drysdale had volunteered to go with two days' rest. I told Walt I'd like to give it a try.

When I made my first start, against St. Louis, the Dodgers were four games ahead with only nine games left to go. Nobody on the club had a thought that we could possibly lose. I was pitching the 154th game, the game which would have ended the season in any previous year. We were in the first year of expansion, though, the first 162-game season. Those eight extra games killed us.

In the first inning I loaded the bases with walks. There were two men out. Charlie James was at bat. It was like pitching for the first time in spring training. I had good stuff, but my control was off. I still think that if I had been able to get Charlie James I might have been able to settle down and pitch a fair game.

After fouling off an interminable number of 2–2 pitches, James caught a high outside fast ball and hit it on top of the right-field pavilion. The high outside fast ball isn't a bad pitch if the batter is trying to pull. It's a terrible pitch if he's going with it, especially in that old St. Louis ball park with its short right-field fence. It wasn't a particularly long drive, but it didn't have to be. It was plenty long enough to put four runs on the board for the Cardinals. I walked the next man too, and I was through for the day.

Two days later Walt gave me some extra work by letting me mop up in a lost game. The key game of the season for us may well have been my next start, against Houston. We were still two games ahead, with three to go, which meant that a win would clinch at least a tie. I had great stuff for four innings. The first eleven batters went down in a row, four of them on strikes. In the fifth the bottom fell out, just the way—again—it does at a comparable stage in spring training. We were still leading, 4–2, at the end of the inning, but they decided to take me out because they thought I was tiring. We lost the game anyway. We lost the final two games too. The Giants won two of the last three, and we were suddenly on a plane to San Francisco to start a three-game playoff.

Our pitching staff was in terrible shape. Podres had pitched that afternoon and lost a tough 1–0 game. Don had gone the day before and lost 2–0. During the trip to San Francisco, Walt Alston and Joe Becker called me over to their seat to ask me if I thought I could go the next day. The message was clear enough. There wasn't anybody else. If I could give them four or five good innings, they could send the bullpen in to finish up.

I had nothing at all. The infuriating part of it was that I knew just where I was, as far as my conditioning went. I was at the low point of the training drought. I know it sounds like an alibi, but that doesn't make it any less true. One more start, and I'd probably have been ready to come around.

One of the papers said the next day that I had tried to decoy the Giants by serving up slow stuff. I wish I had. That wasn't a decoy, that was my fast ball.

The mind is a funny thing. My memory insists that I got knocked out in the first inning, after Willie Mays hit a home run, without getting a man out. The record book insists that the first two Giants went out before Alou lined a double down the line and Willie hit the home run. The record book also maintains stoutly that I went out for the second inning and threw a home-run ball to Jim Davenport and a single to Ed Bailey before I was taken out.

We had lost seven of our last eight games during the regular season. We lost two out of three in the playoff, and the cry of "Choke" was heard in the land. "Choke" is a word that comes very easy to a fan's lips and lands very harshly on a player's ear. I don't think any established big-league player chokes. Anybody who chokes under pressure did his choking in the minors and choked himself right out of any chance to play in the majors.

Baseball, over the long season, is a game of momentum and cycles. You lose seven out of eight in May and you're in a losing streak. You lose seven out of eight at the end of September and you've choked.

The difference, I suspect, is that the fans and the writers have this highly romantic belief that in crucial games, when everything is on the line, it becomes a test of character as well as of ability; that there is something about the challenge of a pressure game that brings out the best in the true champion and the worst in the born loser. The only trouble with the theory is that the Giants and Dodgers have swapped years when one club came while the other faded. The Cardinals faded in the stretch one year and came charging down the stretch the next.

The word is used, though, and it isn't easy to live with. There was, then, a special gratification—and maybe even vindication —in coming back to win the pennant in 1963, when we were faced with a fairly similar situation.

On August 30, having just put the Giants away in a head-to-head confrontation, we had a seven-game lead. On the morning of September 16, we were one game ahead of St. Louis. "There go the Dodgers," they said, "choking again." The 1962 collapse was brought up pointedly. The historians in the crowd went all the way back to 1951. Nobody bothered to mention that we had been playing excellent ball. The Cardinals had picked up those six games by winning nineteen out of twenty while we were winning eleven out of sixteen. If you win eleven out of every sixteen games you play, you will find it exceedingly difficult not to win a pennant.

The attitude in the Dodger locker room through it all was something to see. We welcomed the Cardinal challenge. We were almost rooting for them to keep winning until we could get at them. I think everybody on the team was looking forward to the chance of vindicating ourselves.

The Cardinals drew to within one game of us just at the point where we were coming into St. Louis for a three-game series with only a dozen games left in the season.

Our attitude was that if these are the guys we're gonna have to beat, let's go out and beat 'em and get it over with.

Johnny Podres won the opening game of the series 3–1. I was pitching the second game against Curt Simmons.

Curt was having a great year. The last time the two teams had met, Curt and I had faced each other in a real good one. At the end of nine innings the score was 1–1. At the end of twelve innings Alston pinch-hit for me. Curt went sixteen innings before he lost 2–1. He had not lost since. He had not even been scored on in twenty-seven innings.

As for me, I was going after my twenty-fourth win. I had pitched ten shutouts during the season, including the no-hitter against the Giants. During the month of July I had pitched three straight shutouts and thirty-three consecutive scoreless innings. The more conservative journals were calling it this year's Game of the Century.

It was, in certain respects, the easiest game I have ever pitched—one certain respect being that I made only eighty-seven pitches, fewer pitches than I have thrown in any ball game in my life.

We scored a run in the first inning and, as it turned out, that was all we needed. To me, the key play came in the third inning. St. Louis had men on second and third with one out, and both runners could thank me personally. I had hit Tim McCarver and thrown Simmons' bunt into center field.

Javier hit a ground ball toward second base, and my

thoughts went immediately to the 1959 World Series when Maury had gone for the double play with men on first and third and nobody out on an almost identical ball.

It's a tough play when the tag has to be made, no doubt about it, but I was praying that he would try to cut off the run. Maury went to the plate, and his throw was up the line. But that's a play Roseboro makes as well as anybody I've ever seen. John blocked the plate while he was reaching for the ball, and made the tag on McCarver.

For six innings I had a no-hitter. Stan Musial was leading off the seventh. Stan had come to the plate in a similar spot the night before and hit the ball out of the park to tie the ball game 1–1. The only thing I could think of was that I had to keep him from pulling the ball. Musial will hit the ball where it's pitched, but I wasn't worried about a no-hitter. I was worried about staying ahead.

Musial has a favorite expression: "Ten thousand pitchers went to war," he'll chant, "and all the left-handers came back." But I'll tell you something. I had the feeling Stan didn't care whether you were left-handed, right-handed, or bowlegged. He knew he was going to hit you. At this stage of his career you had the feeling that Stan was getting to the age where you could maybe throw the fast ball by him, a dangerous misconception which Stan himself did not a thing to discourage. When you'd try to throw the ball past him with the game on the bases, that bat would come whipping around as quick as ever. Either Stan's reflexes were as quick as ever or he was using a very youthful bat.

I pitched Stan outside, and he just went with the pitch and lined it nicely into left center. (If all the line singles Musial has hit to left center were laid end to end, they would run from St. Louis to Cooperstown, which is exactly where they are headed.)

Frank Howard hit a three-run homer in the eighth, and we were home free.

In order to throw only eighty-seven pitches in a game, you must have certain conditions. To begin with, your stuff cannot be too good. If you are too fast and if the ball is really moving, you are going to strike out too many batters. You are going to have to make four to four and a half pitches per strikeout and if you strike out, say, ten batters—well, that doesn't leave you very many more pitches to work with, does it?

Your control must be very good, too, because you can't afford to walk more than one man. And even he is a luxury. Walks cost you five to six pitches.

Your stuff must be just good enough so that, with your good control, the hitters are reluctant to let you get ahead of them in the count, but not good enough so that they'll foul a lot of pitches off. When they swing at the first pitch, you want them to get enough of it to fly out to shallow center field.

You also, quite obviously, can't allow an awful lot of hits. The Cardinals had four singles, four strikeouts, and no walks. I probably had the best control of my life.

In the last four innings, nobody had more than one ball in the count.

On the last fourteen batters, there was a grand total of only two balls. In that same stretch, nine of ten batters swung at the first pitch.

Out of twelve consecutive batters between the sixth and the ninth innings there was a grand total of only one ball.

After the first couple of innings, the Cardinal batters seemed to be up there to swing. From the time Javier hit the ground ball to Wills with one out in the third, the Cardinals took only thirteen pitches, and the pitcher took three of them. In the last three innings, they took only five pitches.

To give you a more dramatic picture of how it went, here is the complete rundown of the last three innings.

7th inning:

Musial took a called strike and singled.

Boyer flied to right on the first pitch.

White flied to center on the first pitch.

Flood missed the first pitch and grounded out on the second.

8th inning:

James popped the first pitch to second.

McCarver hit the first pitch into left center for a single.

Shannon flied to center on the first pitch.

Javier took a called strike, took a ball, and singled through the hole.

Groat fouled off the first pitch and lined out to center.

9th inning:

Musial missed the first pitch and grounded out on the second.

Boyer fouled off the first pitch and grounded out on the second.

White took a called strike, took a ball, missed, hit two fouls, and hit a ground single to right.

Flood took a called strike and lined to left field.

The following night Dick Nen, playing in his first big-league game, tied the game with a pinch-hit home run in the ninth. We won the game in the thirteenth to sweep the series.

I didn't know anything about Nen's home run until I read about it in the papers the next day. I had left for Los Angeles immediately after the game to spend Yom Kippur at home.

In the no-hitter I didn't have overpowering stuff either. The first batter, Harvey Kuenn, hit a hard line drive to center field that went right to Willie Davis. Twenty feet in either direction and the no-hitter would have been gone before I had out number one. A certain amount of luck is necessary in any no-hitter, something I discovered while watching Don Larsen's perfect game against us in the 1956 Series. Leading off in the second inning, Jackie Robinson hit a line shot toward third base that caromed off Andy Carey's glove and bounced right to Gil McDougald, who threw Jackie out.

Tommy Davis was playing third for the Dodgers when I went out to face the San Francisco Giants on May 11, 1963, my sixth start of the season, and only the second start since I had torn an adhesion in my shoulder. As I walked out to the mound at the start of the game, I yelled over to Tommy, "Hang loose," a warning that he could expect to have balls rocketing at him all day. Actually, I was only kidding. My stuff hadn't been great warming up, but it had been good enough.

And that's how it remained. In the three other no-hitters, I had exceptional stuff through most of the game. In the San Francisco no-hitter, it was good but not great. The strikeouts always tell the story. I had a strikeout in the third inning (Pagan), another in the fourth (F. Alou) and two in the sixth (Pagan, Marichal). That's all.

There wasn't another really worrisome moment, though, until Alou hit a long fly down the left-field line in the seventh inning. As the ball left the bat, I thought, "Oh God, it's a home run." It wasn't quite that long, though, and Tommy Davis—who had been moved out to left field—made the catch in front of the railing of the stands.

I had winced when the ball was hit, not so much because the no-hitter seemed to be going but because I was under the impression that a home run would tie the score. Actually, we had scored 3 runs in the last of the sixth inning, and we were really ahead 4-0.

That happens. You will sometimes get so used to a score that you will not completely adjust to a big inning late in the game. Or maybe it's self-protection. You are a better pitcher in all probability under the tension of a 1–0 game than in the comparative looseness of a 10–0 lead. A big lead works both ways. I have never heard of a pitcher tiring with a 10-run lead. No, you only tire in close ball games. On the other hand, the sheer luxury of all those runs can make you lazy. It's hot, you don't really want to work any harder than you have to and, with all those runs in the bank, the temptation to try to do it the easy way can get to be overwhelming. Before you quite know what has happened, you've walked a couple of men, given up a couple of hits, and the lead is going fast. Once you've lost that total concentration it does not come back on command.

So whatever the lead, once that first man gets on base you had better shake yourself and bear down. It's too easy to get beaten by the other team, without going out of your way to beat yourself.

There may even be an advantage in pitching for a team that

doesn't score many runs. It doesn't harm you a bit to become conditioned to the idea that you do not have the luxury of ever throwing a thoughtless or a careless pitch.

The first twenty-two batters had gone down in a row before I went to 3–0 on Ed Bailey, the only left-handed batter in the starting lineup. Bailey took two called strikes, fouled off a fast ball, then took a fast ball low to break up the perfect game. Jim Davenport hit into a double play right behind him, so it was still only twenty-four batters in eight innings, the absolute minimum.

With two out in the ninth, and the score 8–0, the Giants sent up another left-hander, McCovey, to pinch-hit for the pitcher. I walked him on four straight pitches. That meant I had to face Harvey Kuenn again. Kuenn took a strike, then hit a fast ball back to me on one hop. I ran halfway to first to make sure I didn't throw the ball away, flipped the ball under-handed to Ron Fairly, and went leaping up into the air.

11

The 1963 Series:
Getting There Is Half the Fun

I have been involved in a few World Series—thank good-
ness—sometimes as an interested observer and sometimes as
an active combatant. I think most baseball fans have a misconception about what a Series means to a player.

The World Series is a time of excitement. It is not a time of
any particular pressure.

The pennant race, now—ah, there you have pressure. Accumulated pressure. Pressure-cooker pressure. The pressure of
the pennant race is the pressure of separating the winner from
the losers. From April to October you play 162 games in order
to try to win one more game than anybody else. When the race
is close and the games dwindle down to a precious few,
September . . . October . . . the perspiration flows freely and
the saliva runs dry. But we're big-leaguers, you say? We don't
feel pressure. Don't kid yourself. Being big-leaguers only means
that maybe we can stand up under the pressure. That's one of
the differences between making it and not making it.

Team games have more built-in pressure than individual
games, anyway, because you are placed in a situation where you
have to win for both yourself and the team, which is a way of
saying that if you lose, you have lost for twenty-four other men
too. If you aren't really taking bread out of the mouths of their
children, you may very well be taking mink coats off the backs
of their wives.

The World Series has a much more relaxed atmosphere. In

the World Series, everyone is a winner. Both tear
that they could stand up in the pressure cooker.
ing the ball park in triumph, like a team of mat
everything except bowing left and right to the cheer
While it would be unfair to call the Series an exhib
the All-Star Game, it is a sort of national showcase. V
really is an exhibition on a grand scale. This is par
true if the pennant races have been tight, for there is the feeling,
for the first time in weeks, that you have the luxury of being
able to lose a game, since, what the heck, there are still six
more to go.

That mood disappears after the first day. The pressure of the
World Series, once it gets under way, is the pressure of wanting
to win because you know the whole world is watching and
listening.

The World Series is really two things. It is what it is to the
country and what it is on the field. It has become a standing
joke for the players to say, "It's just another game to me," and
for the writers to say, "Oh yeah?" Both of them are right.
The writer is aware that it's not just another game because, for
one thing, his paper is picking up a heavy expense account to
send him there, because the radio and television rights have
been sold for some unbelievable sum, and because more people
are tuned in, on both radio and TV, than will be tuned in on
any other program, any other event throughout the year.

The viewer himself is aware of the special quality of what he
is watching, because the commercials seem to come more
frequently and are by Gillette (which has very cleverly made
its name synonymous with the really big event), because the
announcing teams have a national rather than local character,
and because he is being constantly *reminded*, vocally as well as
visually, of what he is watching. And also, I suppose, because
his own imagination makes it bigger than life, grander, more
colorful.

The ballplayer feels it too. In that week this country grinds
to a halt as everybody seems to tune himself in on the World
Series. All of a sudden everybody is a fan. There is a *cachet* to

.eing a fan. People relay the latest score, inning by inning, in the elevators or in the drugstore. Strangers talk to each other. It would not really be exaggerating to say that, in some odd way, the World Series ties the country together.

It would be misleading to try to say that this sense of excitement and importance does not lap over onto the field. It does. Normally when you walk out onto the field your first impression is of a huge expanse of grass. In the Series you come out to take batting practice, and the grass has been obliterated by the horde of writers. *Better Homes & Gardens* has suddenly come up with a sports editor who finds it essential to cover the Series, which is probably just as well because it gives the sports editor of the *Ladies' Home Journal* someone to talk to.

But a funny thing happens. Once "The Star-Spangled Banner" has been sung and the pageantry has ended, you take one swing around the batting order and it does become, in truth, just a ball game. The special quality of the World Series lasts for only that length of time—one time at bat.

Sure, there is a full house. But there are full houses when we play the Giants too.

One swing around the order, and we in the park find the game closing in on us. The fences are the same distances away as always, the bases are 90 feet apart, the batter is 60 feet 6 inches from the pitching mound.

On television you are watching a World Series game. In the park you are seeing a ball game, no different from any game played all year. There is even a sense of disappointment that it is only this, another ball game, and I have always had the feeling that after the first couple of innings the fans in the park have something of this sense of deflation themselves.

For me, then, a World Series is a privilege and a reward. It is something to be won, of course, but it is also something to be enjoyed. Any player who gets himself into a controversy by either downgrading the opposition or criticizing an umpire is off his head.

There's something else I should add to that. I do not believe in getting myself up for any ball game. Baseball is not an emotional experience, it is a craft. It is, as I have said, a job of work. I can see where a football or basketball player would benefit from building himself up emotionally so that when he goes out onto the field or court he has built up a store of nervous energy that is ready to explode. Baseball is not that explosive a game. Baseball is a game of the trained reflex and the refined skills. It is a game where one mistake may be one too many.

I have always felt that if you go out there so charged up that you are giving off sparks, you'll be throwing mortar shells up there in the first inning—maybe even for three or four innings—but by the fifth inning or so the nervous energy will have completely dissipated and the mortar shells will start coming the other way.

You don't need the nervous energy early, anyway. You need it late. Conditioning will get you through the first half of the game. The trick is to let your emotional energy build up gradually so that it will be there to be tapped when you need it at the end.

Besides, I have never felt that you can win a ball game by playing it over in your head the night before. You're far better off getting a good night's sleep.

I like to come to the park feeling almost lax and lackadaisical. I don't even begin to think of the other team's lineup until I go out to warm up. By thinking about the hitters that late I am forced to concentrate upon them completely. I don't want my juices bubbling at the start of the game; I want my mind fastened on my work.

I have gone into such detail about the World Series and about the calm, reasonable approach to pitching so that I can now state, with proper dramatic emphasis, that almost nothing of what I have been saying applied to the opening game of the 1963 World Series. That one turned out to be different.

The first game was important to us because we were opening in New York against the Yankees, and in 1963 the Yankees were still THE YANKEES. There are those who still feel that a World Series is something less than a World Series if the

Yankees aren't in it. I'd like to be able to say that I didn't agree with them, but I'm not that sure I didn't. The Yankees had become a sort of permanent entry, the King of the Hill, and the game was to try to knock them off. To be perfectly honest, knocking off the White Sox and knocking off the Twins wasn't quite the same thing as knocking off the Yankees. But, then, neither was my own career the same in 1959 and 1965 as it was in 1963.

I hadn't had time to build myself up for that Series even if I had wanted to. A couple of weeks before the end of the season my father had suffered a coronary, a pretty bad jolt, and he was still in the hospital convalescing.

It did become necessary to think a little about the Yankee hitters beforehand, for the very good reason that we were gathered together, upon our arrival in New York, for Al Campanis's scouting report.

Scouting reports never thrill me particularly, because they have a basic built-in flaw. They tell what other pitchers have found to be effective. It's really information twice removed. It's somebody telling you how he has seen another pitcher get them out. Even if you believe it, it is not easy to make yourself want to pitch with another man's head. I'm not any other pitcher; I'm me. I have to look at the way they stand at the plate and see how they react to my pitches before I can truly believe that yes, this is the best way to pitch them.

Campanis does good work, though. If a scout comes in and tells you to pitch somebody high inside and low outside, he is telling you nothing. He is wasting everybody's time. Generally speaking, you are pitching everybody high inside and low out-side because those are the two toughest spots for the batter to handle.

All I want to know from a scouting report, really, is who can hit the breaking ball. I am willing to assume that anybody who is in the big leagues, let alone with a pennant-winning team, can hit a fast ball reasonably well. I want to know who hits the breaking ball particularly well, particularly if they are power hitters. You know that the long-ball hitters are strong fast-ball hitters. When you get a Mays or an Aaron or—in his day—a Sievers, each of whom is also a very good breaking-ball hitter, you have a problem. My solution, such as it is, is to give them very, very few breaking balls to hit. The breaking ball is slower, and it is more difficult to control. I'd much rather challenge them with speed and control. (If the real good hitter is in a position to cost me the ball game, I'd really rather pitch around him—that is, give him the choice of swinging at a bad pitch or accepting a base on balls.)

With the Yankees, your first concern has to be Mantle. More to the point, as far as I am concerned, Mantle batting right-handed. Mickey, we were told, had become two completely different hitters, left-handed and right-handed, which is most unusual. Tom Tresh, the Yankees' other switch-hitter, was exactly the same hitter, left-handed and right-handed. He hit the fast ball good and had trouble with off-speed breaking pitches. (I am talking about 1963, remember. Hitters change as they find it necessary to adjust to the way they are being pitched to.)

Mantle, as everyone knows, had always been a much better hitter right-handed than left-handed. That was true even when the Dodgers faced the Yankees in 1955 and 1956. I had not been aware that the difference had become so marked. Mickey not only went from right to left when he switch-hit now, he practically turned upside down.

Right-handed, he was supposed to be a good low-ball hitter; left-handed, a good high-ball hitter. Left-handed, he liked the fast ball; right-handed, he liked the curve ball and murdered change-ups. When he was batting left-handed, you just kept jamming him. Mickey's knee appeared to buckle when he was batting left-handed, which made it very difficult for him to move around on the inside pitch, but apparently he'd hit that pitch very well while Campanis was watching him.

Maris is exactly the opposite, as far as a left-hander is concerned. You throw the fast ball high and inside on Maris, but try to keep changing speeds on him and try to set him up for the breaking stuff, low and away.

All I digested about the rest of the lineup was that Elston Howard liked the curve, particularly from a left-hander. Pepitone was supposed to be strong on fast balls, weak on the breaking ball. Boyer was supposed to be weak on the curve. Richardson liked the fast ball better than the curve, particularly the high fast ball, and particularly the high fast ball on the first pitch.

Looking back, I can see that I began to get a little worked up when, upon arriving in New York, I found that the game was being written up, in the pre-game publicity, not as the Los Angeles Dodgers versus the New York Yankees, but as Sandy Koufax (25-5) versus Whitey Ford (24-7).

There was also a tremendous amount of publicity about what was being called the Yankees' two-million-dollar infield (or was it three million dollars?), while our little band of ragamuffins was being written off as worth about fifty cents.

I wasn't particularly indignant on behalf of our infield, because they would be out there taking care of themselves, but I felt an unexpected surge of loyalty to the old Dodger infield of my youth, Cox-Reese-Robinson-Hodges, plus Campanella. *There* was a two-million-dollar infield. Not only were they all exceptional fielders, but all of them could hit, and all of them could run the bases.

There was, I think, another thing working on me too. My arm had grown very tired at the end of the season, and somewhat sorer than usual, and so I had asked Alston to rest me. Instead of the two starts that would have kept me in the proper physical routine for the Series, I had gone only five innings in a 1-0 victory over the Mets, then skipped my last start completely.

I was second-guessing myself a little on that. You need that steady work to stay sharp—the story of my first five years in the majors. When you get too much rest, your arm seems strong at the beginning, but your control tends to be haphazard and the bottom falls out on you in the middle of the game. That's the kind of worrying I'd just as soon do without, because it is the kind of worry that builds up the nervous energy I want to avoid.

I had been phoning home daily to find out how my father was coming along, but that day, since we had to catch the bus for the stadium at ten in the morning (which is seven a.m. out on the Coast), it was obviously too early.

I was in a good easy humor on the way to the park, just the way I like to be. About three-quarters of an hour before the game I went back to the trainer's room to have Capsolin (a hot, reddish oil) rubbed on my arm. Let me make it clear that I do not have a rubdown before I pitch. The Capsolin is rubbed *on* the arm. What it does is to irritate the skin to increase circulation.

And then I went out to warm up. I had felt from the time we came to New York that this first game was of unusual importance. The pre-series reports, especially in New York, had become a tribute to the Yankee dynasty, and if you weren't careful, you might begin to feel that you were about to go up against a team of superhumans. I felt that I had to show myself and my team, and the Yankees too, that they were just a team of baseball players, not a pride of supermen.

When I went out to warm up, all these things that had been percolating inside me just seemed to boil up to the surface and hit me. Say what you want, there is something about Yankee Stadium. Ball parks have their own personality. Ebbets Field was a ramshackle, friendly park, perfect for the Bums, and Chavez Ravine is a friendly park in the colorful, casual Los Angeles way.

Yankee Stadium stands forth as a monument of a ball park, big and green and aristocratic. Even those three memorial tablets out in center field at the far end of the greenspread make you think somehow of the Arlington National Cemetery —of something, you know, official, something with the Presidential Seal upon it. There is the feeling, as I have already said, that an occasional wildcat World Series may be played somewhere else, but the official World Series is played in Yankee Stadium.

I threw nice and easy, and I knew I had great stuff. Not good stuff, *great* stuff. You can never be sure until you see how it carries over into the game, of course, but it's an indication. When your stuff is as good as that, it's a very strong indication. Five or six times a year you have real good stuff and perfect control and it lasts over the full nine innings. Those are the five or six great games you pitch during the year. It seemed to me from the beginning that this could be one of those days.

The home-park advantage is undeniable, and yet there is something to be said, as far as pitching is concerned, about pitching on the road. When you are at home you stand at attention for the National Anthem just at the point where you are ready to pitch, and during that brief wait it is possible for your concentration to be somewhere up there in the rockets' red glare. On the road you can spend a full half-inning sitting in the dugout getting *involved* in the game before you walk out onto the mound.

I didn't get too much time to get involved in anything, because Ford retired us easily in the first half of the inning.

In my first two years of sitting on the bench with the Dodgers, we had met the Yankees in two World Series. I had seen Johnny Podres shut them out in the final game of the 1955 World Series, the game that will live forever in the halls of Flatbush and on the shores of Brighton Beach. I had seen Don Larsen pitch his perfect game. I had seen Don Newcombe walk off the mound in utter frustration. And now, after eight full years with the club, the wheel had finally turned to me.

The batter was Tony Kubek. You're supposed to jam him. . . .

The most important thing that happened in the first inning, in the game, maybe—maybe even in the Series—was the strike-out of Bobby Richardson. During the off season at least one Yankee player told me—I wish I could remember who—that when he saw Richardson go down swinging on a high fast ball he had a feeling that they were in trouble. The question he was asking, I knew, was whether I had deliberately fired the ball into Richardson's strength because I felt that if I could get Bobby, who is very important to the Yankees as a person, a leader, and a ballplayer, I had a chance of demoralizing them.

I wish I were that smart. The answer is no, I had no thought of the effect on the Yankees. Hell, all I was doing was trying to get twenty-seven outs, one by one. But the answer is also yes, I did deliberately throw the ball where I threw it.

I should make a note right here. When I say "I," I really mean, "we." The catcher calls the pitches. But John Roseboro and I have been together for so long and can fall into such a complete rapport that we can go batter after batter, inning after inning, as if there were only one man, one mind involved. I will get the ball back and think, Now I want to hit the outside corner, low with a fast ball—and I'll look down and see the sign for a fast ball, low on the outside corner. When you see me out there shaking off a sign it is, more often than not, solely for the benefit of the batter. We want him to think we are in disagreement every once in a while, to make it more difficult for him to find whatever pattern we may have developed.

I had started Kubek off with a fast ball on the inside corner, a swinging strike, and a fast ball on the outside corner for a called strike. Then I jammed him inside and came back with a good curve that dropped down and over, as Kubek swung and missed.

With one out and nobody on, I was only trying to get Richardson to hit the ball. Bobby is a man who doesn't strike out often (twenty-two times all year) or walk often (twenty-five times). Bobby is up there to hit the ball, and I was out there to have him hit it, preferably on the first pitch. I wanted to start him off with a fast ball anywhere in the strike zone. With the stuff I knew I had I was betting that I would be difficult to pull, and I was willing to let Richardson hit it as far into that vast centerfield wasteland as he wanted to. I didn't intend to get it up across the letters, but I wasn't particularly bothered at that stage of the game either.

I had started him off with precisely what the scouting report had said not to, a high fast ball on the first pitch. He swung and he missed. That told me something. It told me I had a real live fast ball. How live? I don't know. The only thing I *am* sure of is that it doesn't rise anywhere near as much as the batters say it does. How much, after all, does a ball have to rise? If the batter hits the ball one-half inch above the center of the bat, he's going to pop it up. If the ball is two inches above the center, he's missed it completely. And that, as far as I can see, is all it does rise—maybe one or two inches. The big hop the batters moan about is an optical illusion.

On the other hand, the hitter is making his adjustments according to what his eye has told him to be true. If my fast ball *looks* to him as if it is coming up about four inches, he is looking for it to rise that much by the second and third times at bat, and he is making a wholly false adjustment to compensate for a wholly false vision. It is like two errors canceling each other out.

All right, we've pretty well established that I had good stuff. Let's establish something else here. You get ahead of the hitter, and you can make good pitches. That's what pitching is all about. I've got a strike on Richardson, I can try a big curve on him. He fouled it back. Now I've got two strikes and I can make two more good pitches. That's when I began to think about that first strike. You don't deliberately throw into a batter's strength when you have him down 0-2, and I didn't. Still, I had a thought out there. When you get ahead of a batter, you will sometimes pitch *bad* to his strength in the hope of getting him to chase a bad ball. (Obviously nobody is going to swing at a bad pitch to their weakness; they're set to lay off that pitch.)

So I threw a high fast ball and threw it bad, somewhere up around his chin. Bobby swung and he missed.

We pitched Tresh according to the book, curving him on a 2–2 count for the called third strike. I had struck out the side. Now, normally three strikeouts count for no more than three long flies to center field. But I had thrown only twelve pitches, far fewer than it usually takes to strike out three men, and, most important of all, the strikeouts drove home the point that we were not up against a team of supermen.

In our half of the second, we scored four runs.

The rally started when Ford threw a chest-high fast ball to Frank Howard. The Yankees' own scouting report would have told them that Frank (1) chased low outside pitches and (2) could destroy a ball up over the plate.

Frank swung and hit what may have been the hardest line drive I have seen in my life. The ball flew over Mantle's head, over the statuary in center field, and rattled off the center-field wall, 460 feet away.

Bill Skowron, who had come to us from the Yankees in an interleague trade, knocked him in with a single to center. Dick Tracewski, who was playing only because Ken McMullen was hurt, singled too. That brought up John Roseboro, who had had a particularly good batting average against left-handers in 1963, although he does not normally hit for power against them. John gets his days off during the season when lefties are pitching. But John got himself a hanging curve ball and hit a long drive down the line and into the right-field stands, 350 feet away, the first home run he had hit against a left-hander all year.

We had scored four quick runs off Whitey Ford, the man who didn't give up runs in the World Series.

The difference between pitching with a four-run lead and a one-run lead is no more than the difference between walking into Tiffany's with a twenty-dollar bill and a thousand-dollar bill. When you are one run ahead, everybody who walks up to the plate is the tying run, and that means you have to try to keep the ball in the park. With two runs, you have a little more leeway. Just as soon as a man gets on, though, there you are with the tying run at the plate again. It's not uncomfortable— two runs are two runs—but it's not enough security to make a Goldwater man out of you either. Three runs are great. You really have a cushion now. Still, it is the fourth run that always seems to be the big one, because it puts you in the wonderful position of knowing that, even if you get yourself in trouble, it will still take a grand-slam home run to tie you. Through the course of an entire year there aren't too many grand-slam home runs.

With a four-run lead, you are more concerned with keeping men off base than with keeping the ball in the park. You will not try to hit a corner when you're behind on the count; you'll just throw the ball in there and challenge the batter to hit it. The longer the lead holds up, the truer this becomes. If the four runs hold up to the last couple of innings, you'll throw the ball in underhanded rather than give up a base on balls.

Mantle led off in the second inning. We started him off with a curve, low and outside, hoping, again, that if he hit it, it would be straightaway to center. Let him look at the curve right away with nobody on base, because he wasn't going to see it too many times again. He swung and he missed. After that I stuck to the fast ball and with a 1–2 count just caught the inside corner up above the waist, a good pitch. Mantle had an idea of going after it, but he held back and took it for a called third strike.

Several newspapermen wrote that Mickey had pulled away from the plate because he thought I had thrown a curve ball that was breaking in to him. The only way my fast ball could look like a curve ball would be if my fast ball wasn't very fast. The two pitches don't look anything alike. They come up to the plate at entirely different speeds (*any* breaking pitch is an off-speed pitch), and they break in opposite directions; my fast ball goes up, and my curve ball—especially to a right-hander—goes straight down.

It was just one of those situations where the pitcher feels he has caught a corner, and the batter doesn't. That leaves it up to the umpire, who is the only one who counts, anyway. In this instance, Paparella agreed with me, for which I wish him a long and happy and useful life.

It was four up and four strikeouts. The crowd was yelling, and I was not entirely indifferent to what was going on either.

I was glaring down now at Roger Maris. Baseball is a form

of warfare. I have never believed in fraternizing with the players on other teams, because the guys in the other uniforms are your enemies and I see no reason to get to know an enemy well enough to have any feeling other than sheer hostility toward him.

Somehow, however, you feel a little easier about making friends with guys in the other league. The obvious reason is that you know you're not going to have to pitch against them. The less obvious reason is that you generally meet them either on the banquet circuit, where everything is relaxed and friendly, or on the golf course, where it may not be quite so relaxed but is probably even friendlier. When you hit the banquet circuit you are always going to bump into a few Yankees, and I had become friendly with quite a few of them. The one I had got to know best, although I had met him very infrequently, had been Roger Maris. Roger and I just seemed to be on the same wave length, possibly because neither of us is that comfortable at these affairs.

We had bumped into each other again at Yankee Stadium the previous day and had even talked about going out to dinner that night. We realized very quickly, however, that it might not look very good for the Dodger pitcher and the Yankee slugger to be seen dining pleasantly together before they faced each other in mortal combat. It's not only a matter of discretion; it's a matter of competition. We are enemies until the Series is over, and for our own best efforts we should keep it that way.

Maris fouled off a couple of off-speed curves, and with a 2–2 count he swung at a curve ball and struck out.

Five out of five.

Elston Howard was number six. Howard swung at the first pitch, a high inside fast ball, and sent a high foul which Roseboro caught at the edge of the Yankee dugout.

The strikeout streak had ended, but that was all right. I wanted them up there swinging at the first pitch, and if I could get them out on one pitch, so much the better. That's the advantage a pitcher with good stuff has, especially when he finds himself with this kind of lead. Once they see you've got good stuff and good control, they want to make sure they get their three swings. If they take a couple of quick strikes, I can then try for the good pitch, the pitch right on the corner, and they may end up with no good swings at all.

In the top of the third, Skowron knocked in another run with a single, and now it was 5–0. I could throw a grand-slam home run and still have a lead. Happiness is a pitcher with a five-run lead.

Pepitone led off the third. He fouled off a fast ball, and you could see just by the way he swung that he was a real good fast-ball hitter. I missed on the next two pitches, though, and with the count at 2–1 he became the first batter I had fallen behind. With a 2–1 count, he could guess what the pitch was going to be. Or, more likely, *where* it was going to be. Most hitters, when they guess, are looking for a spot rather than for a pitch. I would suppose that Pepitone would be looking for an inside pitch he could pull for the short porch in right. I threw him a fast ball outside and got a called strike, then came back with the fast ball inside. Pepitone couldn't be guessing now; he had to be protecting the whole strike zone. He swung, missed, and that was six strikeouts out of seven.

Boyer and Ford might seem to be the easiest strikeouts in the lineup. The scouting report had said that Boyer didn't like to be jammed (who does?). The right-handers had been advised to jam him with the first pitch and then curve him outside. I couldn't break a curve away from him. I just wanted to set him up so that I could come back with a high outside fast ball and have him hit it to center. I didn't want him to feel free to step into the ball, because he sometimes has fair power to right field. So I threw a fast ball inside, and he liked it well enough to swing. He was expecting to be jammed, no doubt about that. On the second pitch, we went outside, and he sent a ground ball down to Tracewski.

Whitey was just going to get fast balls in the strike zone. He popped the first one up to Gilliam at third.

Three pitches and two outs: that beats striking a man out on seven pitches any time. Believe me, I'll take those two outs on three pitches and let the strikeouts go all day. Well, maybe not all day, but certainly in the third inning.

The second time around the order brings up the question of whether you're going to follow the same pattern, reverse it, or modify it. We began by going the same way with Kubek, starting him with the fast ball and getting him on a big curve on the 1–2 count.

Having established, we hoped, that we were going the same way, we then turned it completely over. We started Richardson off with the fast ball, high, the same pitch he'd struck out on the first time, just to show it to him again. He laid it off, so we came back with a curve ball around the knees for a swinging strike. Instead of going in and out on Richardson, we were pitching him up and down. With a 1–2 count, I went with the curve this time instead of the fast ball. Richardson swung and missed.

Tresh had taken the curve ball the first time on a 2–2 count. This time he looked at the fast ball on the 1–2 count and got called out again.

This all sounds as if I'm letting the world know that John and I are pretty bright. The real bright thing is to have such good control going for you that you keep getting those 1–2 counts. Let me emphasize once again that if you can stay ahead of the batter you are going to make him hit your pitch. I know you have been hearing all your lives that it is important to stay ahead of the batter, but I doubt whether anybody except a big-league ballplayer really appreciates how important it is.

To appreciate how effective I had been in the early innings, you have to look not just at the strikeouts, but at the command I had. In those first four innings I had thrown just forty-two pitches, and only eleven of them were balls. Only twice had I been behind at any part of the count, and at no point had I been behind on the key pitch; that is, on the pitch that got the man out.

In the fifth inning I still had it. Mantle was leading off again, and I went the reverse way with him too, starting him off inside instead of outside, and then going to the high fast ball on the outside of the plate. With an 0–2 count, I wanted to shave the inside corner again, just above the waist, the same pitch he had taken for a called third strike. If I missed, I was pushing him back and would be in a position to do almost anything.

I got the fast ball above the waist all right, but I also got it about three or four inches in over the plate. Mickey's bat jumped at it, and the strains of the chorus of "Downtown" started playing around in my head. The ball didn't end up downtown, though. Mickey fouled it back against the screen and stared down at his bat grimly as if he would have been happy to break it in half.

That happens. I don't want to leave the impression that I had made a terrible pitch. I hadn't thrown the ball right down the middle. But I had made a bad pitch when I was in a position to make a good one, and I had gotten away with it.

The point is this. When a pitcher reads that he "made only one bad pitch," he chortles to himself softly. If every mistake ended up out of the park, we'd all be walking around glazed and shellshocked. A bad pitch can be missed, fouled, popped up, topped, lined to the outfield, or caught against the fence. Anything. There's nothing automatic about it. The bad pitch that is caught four hundred feet away from the plate is quickly forgotten; the perfect pitch that is golfed into the stands is marked against you for life. But you get away with far fewer bad pitches on the top hitters than on anybody else. That should be obvious.

When Mantle swung I'd have settled just to have the ball stay in the park. Who knows why he didn't hit it out? Maybe the pitch had enough action on it to throw Mantle that much off. Maybe Mickey's timing was off that day. Batters can have bad days too, you know—the one thing that makes life worth living.

I threw Mickey a couple of high inside fast balls, just missing with both, then got a good curve over the outside corner for a swinging strikeout.

Maris had struck out on a 2–2 curve the first time. This time he fouled out on a 2–2 fast ball.

Two down, fourteen batters in a row. There are times when this game is easy. And then all of a sudden it wasn't.

Elston Howard was the fifteenth batter. Elston, I knew, likes the ball away from him.

One of the things Al Campanis does in scouting our World Series opposition is to make out a chart on each hitter, showing exactly where he hits every ball. In other words, if the batter has hit the ball forty-seven times while Campanis was watching him, there are forty-seven lines drawn to forty-seven spots. Howard's sheet showed an equal shading between left center and right center, with the heaviest concentration in right center. This meant that, although Howard is a right-handed hitter, we were giving him the left-field line, as well as the right-field line, and shading both outfielders pretty good toward center.

Just watching Howard swing against you shows you why. Howard stands with his feet wide apart, takes almost no stride, and obviously shoots down the middle.

That does not mean that I don't necessarily want to throw him outside pitches. We've got him defensed toward the middle, and when you defense a man that radically it is the pitcher's duty to try to get him to hit into your defense, not away from it. I'm willing to throw the ball away from him, but I want it low and away, not high and away. The high outside fast ball can be a good pitch if the man is trying to pull, because he will not get around that much. It is the worst possible pitch for a man who is going the other way—as Howard so frequently does— because it is up there where he has a very good look at it, and where, by the very nature of the human body, he can take a good natural swing. I'm going to pitch him right by the book; up and in, so that he won't feel free to step into the outside pitch with complete confidence, and low and away. And I'm not going to throw him anything slow.

I wanted to start him off with a fast ball, low and outside, but I got it up and out, just where he likes it. Elston rifled the ball into right field. Well, they were going to get a few hits, no doubt about that. What better time than with nobody on and two out?

Pepitone took a curve, fouled off another curve, and I was safely ahead of him. Then I missed on two fast balls, and I wasn't. So I came back with another curve. He didn't hit it that good, but he hit it good enough. He hit a ground ball that just scooted through between Skowron and Tracewski, and there were men on first and second. There's the luck of pitching too. Someone hits a ball right on the nose and it's an out; the next guy gets a piece of it and he has a hit.

The batter is Boyer. We're going to pitch him the same way as before. Jam him with the first pitch, and then come back with the fast ball outside.

Boyer, jammed again, swings again. The ball comes off the handle of his bat in a sort of looping line drive that passes over me to the second-base side. But Tracewski, I can see, has got a good jump on it and although the ball is curving away from him I can see that he is going to catch up to it. For one moment, as I watch, I am sure he is going to make a tremendous diving catch behind second base. I have the best seat in the house for this, and I can see as he dives that he has actually *over-reached* the ball. The ball hits at the heel of his glove and rolls away. Dick has kept the ball in the infield, though, and kept the run from scoring. A real good play. (In the locker room after the game, Dick told me he was sure he had it too. The thing that fooled him, he said, was that he had thought it was hit a little harder than it actually was.)

The one thing I had wanted to do above all others was keep men off the bases. So here I am with the bases loaded. I can't really blame myself, though. I haven't walked anybody or even got behind anyone on the count. I made a bad pitch to Howard. So what? I'm going to make more bad pitches before this day is over. The idea is not to make the bad pitch when it can cost you the ball game. That's what separates a winner from a loser.

Hector Lopez has been sent in to bat for Whitey Ford. This

is a man I would do very well to get out. Lopez has a closed stance, and he generally is striding into the ball. He'll hit to right field if he can. You don't have to be a genius to see that he is least able to handle an inside pitch and best able to handle an outside pitch. Unless, of course, he outguesses you and is looking for a ball he can pull.

A pinch-hitter comes in cold off the bench. If it's late in the game, especially on a cold night, I like to fire a couple of fast balls at him before he can loosen up. (This does not apply to Smoky Burgess and Jerry Lynch, because if Santa Claus woke them up for Christmas morning and handed them a bat, they would line a single to center.) I may not necessarily throw a fast ball on the first pitch, but you can bet that two of the first three pitches are going to be fast balls and—hopefully—strikes.

I got a fast ball in for a swinging strike, missed with another one, then tried to jam him. Lopez fouled it off. With a count of 1–2 now, I tried for a breaking ball a little more over the plate but below the knee. If he hit it, he had a good chance of hitting it on the ground. If he took it I could come back with a high inside fast ball. He took the curve and struck out swinging at the fast ball, up and in.

It had been a tough inning, but I had been throwing well.

In the sixth inning I came back out and my rhythm was gone.

Where does your rhythm go when it goes? Anybody who can find the answer to that can bottle it and make himself a fortune.

When does it go? Invariably at the beginning of the inning. Which is a clue. You know it as soon as you start to warm up. You know it because all of a sudden you feel kind of awkward and edgy. You may not know exactly what's wrong, but you most certainly know that it isn't right. Have you ever picked up a loose ball at the beach and thrown it back, hoping to look smooth and athletic but feeling instead kind of stiff and foolish? That's pretty much the way it is.

Why does it go? I've given this a great deal of thought these past few years and I have pretty much come to the conclusion that your body has tired just enough so that it is no longer tooling along at the pace you have set for it. Your body is functioning one beat below the tempo you have become accustomed to, but your effort, your will to function at the top of your power, remains constant. As a result, the two parts of your physical effort, the mechanical part and the fuel that drives it, are out of synchronization. It is like feeding high-octane gasoline into an engine that can no longer support it.

What can you do? Well, there isn't much you *can* do except call upon all your knowledge, experience, and instinct, so that you can stay alive until the body makes the necessary adjustments. Because it will. That's the most remarkable thing of all. You will end up with a different rhythm from the one you started with, but who cares about that?

It is not unusual to have to change rhythms in the second half of a game, although it does come as something of a shock when you have had such exceptional stuff in the early innings. I think there were special reasons for it this time. I would suspect that the emotional buildup at the beginning of the game—so unusual for me—had just about played itself out. What happened was what I always feared would happen. When the nervous energy goes, you flatten out completely.

Compounding that, I think, was the lack of work I'd had in the week before the Series, since lack of work (which really means lack of condition) will have precisely that effect on you at just about this stage of the game.

In short, the emotional and physical drains hit me at just about the same time.

The great problems when you lose your rhythm are that your fast ball becomes much less fast, your control becomes much less sharp, and your curve usually disappears from sight. All you can do is try to get the ball over the plate in a pretty good spot, so that it will look good enough to be swung at and not really be good enough to be hit out of the park.

I did get two quick strikes on Kubek, and then he grounded out to third base. Richardson wasn't swinging, though. Richardson took three straight balls, the first time I'd gone three balls on anybody all day. With his team five runs behind, you knew he was going to take the next two pitches. I did manage to get them both in for strikes, but I missed on the 3–2 pitch, and he became my first base on balls.

Tresh immediately became my second.

The one thing I didn't want to do with a five-run lead was walk anybody, and here I had walked two men in a row with Mantle and Maris coming up.

I pitched with great care to both of them and got them both on high fast balls on the outside part of the plate. Mantle popped up to second on a 2–2 pitch, and Maris popped to short on the 1–1 pitch. They were both good pitches, with something on them, and they were the only two good pitches I threw in the entire inning.

In the seventh inning I felt no better and maybe even a little worse, but, as I keep pointing out, there are no rules about pitching. Since you can't throw fast, you obviously can't throw faster. That leaves you with only one alternative: to throw slower. You can't bear down, so you ease up. You're not really throwing change-ups, in the usual sense of the word, since you're not throwing a slow pitch off a fast one. What you're doing is varying the speed from pitch to pitch in the hope of keeping the batter somewhat off balance.

Elston Howard had been swinging at the first pitch all day, and I could hope that he'd be swinging still. He was. He swung at the first *two* pitches, missing them both. With an 0–2 count, we could try to do something. Howard hadn't seen a curve yet today, so we pushed him back with another fast ball, then curved him, low and away. He went down swinging.

By throwing slower, and by constantly and consciously varying your speed, you are helping yourself in another way. You are gradually easing your body into the new rhythm it must find.

Pepitone took a strike, took a ball, and fouled a curve ball back to John Roseboro.

Well, the curve didn't seem too good to me, but there's no reason to argue with success. I didn't want to pitch Boyer inside on the first pitch this time anyway, because he seemed to be looking for it. I wanted to curve him low and outside. I looked down, and there was John signaling for a curve ball, low and outside. It must have looked good enough, because he went after it and popped up to Wills. In what had figured to be a struggling inning, I had thrown only eight pitches.

To me, none of the curves had been particularly good, however, an opinion which Roseboro confirmed. One of the writers asked me afterward why I had thrown change-ups to Pepitone. That wasn't my change-up, that was my curve ball.

In the eighth, Linz came up to pinch-hit for the pitcher, and we started him off with a curve anyway, just to see if we could stay lucky. He took it for a ball. From there on in, Mr. Linz was going to get the fast-ball treatment especially reserved for pinch-hitters. Your rhythm usually returns under the same conditions in which it disappears, at the beginning of an inning. I had felt a little better warming up, but you don't really know until you put the body to that little extra strain of pitching to a hitter. Linz took a fast ball, missed one, fouled one, and went down swinging. Although I still didn't have anything like the stuff I'd had at the beginning of the game, the fast ball was moving and I was putting it pretty much where I wanted to.

Now that I felt so much better, I got into trouble again. My own fault, too. After Kubek fouled off two fast balls, I got the 0–2 pitch up too high on the outside part of the plate. Tony went right with the pitch and hit a ground ball into the hole. Wills made a fine backhand stop, but he didn't even bother to make the throw.

I was still throwing fast balls to Richardson, and trying to make them all strikes. I played high ball with him again, going up . . . up . . . up, and he swung and missed all three.

Tresh, as we know, hits the fast ball better than the breaking ball. And at this stage of the game, he was going to get it. No fooling around, just fast balls that he would either hit or he wouldn't. The first pitch was waist high, catching a good hunk of the inside of the plate, pretty much where I wanted it. Tresh couldn't have been particularly unhappy about it either, since he drove it into the left center-field bleachers, a good 350 feet away. The score was 5–2.

Well, that's the risk you take. As long as I didn't walk him.

I wanted to start Mantle off with a fast ball on the inside corner. Instead, I got it in over the plate again, the same pitch Tresh had hit out of the ball park—and the same pitch Mickey had fouled off earlier in the game. He fouled this one back too. I had got away with two bad pitches on Mantle in one game, which is all the luck you can decently expect.

I had thrown twelve straight strikes, but you can see how misleading that kind of statistic can be. I wasn't trying to pitch as fine to the corners any more; I was shooting for a good hunk of the plate. Strikes aren't necessarily good pitches, anyway. The "wildest" pitch isn't necessarily the one that goes back to the screen. It can also be the one that goes right down the middle.

I didn't throw one down the middle to Mantle. I did something even worse. I threw four straight balls to him. This is known, in the pitcher's union, as beating yourself.

By walking Mantle, I had brought on the most crucial point in the game. If Roger Maris hit a home run, the score would be 5–4 and the Yankees would be right back in the game. For the first time since the opening inning I was not in a position where I could afford to throw the ball in and challenge him to hit it.

Rog is a fast-ball hitter, and I'm a fast-ball pitcher. In a spot like this, he was going to have to hit my best pitch.

Rog took a fast ball for a ball, took another for a strike, and hit a low fast ball right at Tracewski, who threw him out.

In the seventh inning, with my coordination shaky, I'd got by easily. In the eighth, with my rhythm coming back so nicely, I had barely managed to stagger through. Baseball, as some sage has said, is a funny game.

I had known all along that I had a lot of strikeouts, of course. It's difficult to keep that kind of secret from a pitcher. The way the crowd was screaming at each new strikeout, I knew I had to be close to the record. As I walked off the mound at the end of the eighth, another cheer went up. Looking back at the scoreboard, I saw they had flashed the message that I had tied Carl Erskine's World Series record of fourteen strikeouts.

Records are all right in their place. My main concern was to win the game. When you go into the ninth inning with a three-run lead, the game has been reduced to simple arithmetic. Not higher mathematics, simple arithmetic.

You have to get three men out (1-2-3) before they get two men on base (1-2). Until they get two men on base, they cannot bring the tying run to the plate, and if they cannot bring the tying run to the plate they are not in the game. Under these conditions a home run hurts you not a whit more than a base on balls. If it comes down to it, I am going to throw the ball right down the middle.

Elston Howard led off, and I was hoping he was still up there swinging at the first pitch. We gave him the outside fast ball again, about waist high, and he sent a liner to second base. An excellent beginning.

Joe Pepitone had been tough. He isn't supposed to hit a left-hander's curve too well, but he had hung in there very well against mine. He hung in there again, going to the 2–2 count before he fouled back a fast ball that just got back onto the screen. As Roseboro was giving it a good run, the fans behind the screen, rooting for the strikeout record, were yelling, "No, no . . ."

I was a few feet in front of the mound—for some reason you automatically start moving in the direction of the ball—and I was thinking: Yes, yes . . .

I tried a curve on him, and he leveled off on it nicely and lined it down the right-field line for a single.

Boyer, like Howard, had been up there swinging. Clete, in fact, hadn't let a pitch go by all day. We went back to the original pattern we had used on him, jamming a fast ball on the fists. When he swung and missed, we went to a curve outside, taking a little off it. Clete hit it pretty good, but it was just a fly ball to Willie Davis in center field. (It was not until I went over this game just now that I realized it was the only fly ball hit to an outfielder all day.)

So that brought it down to Harry Bright, pinch-hitting for

the pitcher. Alston came out to find out if I knew anything about him. "I remember him from Pittsburgh," I told Walt. "He likes the off-speed pitch."

Walt nodded and walked back to the dugout. I set myself to throw Mr. Bright as many outside fast balls as he cared to look at. He took a strike, he took two balls, he took another strike. With the count down to 2–2, he swung at an outside fast ball and topped it down the third-base line. The play was mine if it stayed fair. It drifted foul, down the turtleback of the infield, and Harry and I returned to our appointed spots.

Whenever a World Series is played in Yankee Stadium you hear about "the lengthening shadows" that move down over home plate and creep out slow toward the mound. You read how difficult it is for the hitter to try to follow the ball as it moves from light into darkness. And there is no doubt that they do give the pitcher a definite advantage, particularly on the fast ball.

Bright swung and missed at another fast ball on the outside of the plate, and it was strike three, ball game, and record.

Harry said later that he had dreamed all his life of being in a World Series, and here, late in his career, he had finally made it, only to find 69,000 hometown fans rooting for him to strike out.

Carl Erskine came down to the dressing room to congratulate me on breaking his record. As the photographers were posing us together, Carl said, "I suppose I should thank you for letting me hold it four more years."

It took me a while to understand what he meant. This wasn't the first World Series game I had ever pitched. I had pitched against the White Sox in 1959 and started in a blaze of glory by striking out two men in the first inning. Carl, who had retired only that season, came down afterward and told me that he had turned to his wife, Betty, at the end of the inning and said, "You don't mind losing that record today, do you?"

I'd just as soon we held it together. But how can you tell that to a man without sounding phony? "When it got to fourteen," I told him, "I thought that it was enough. But you saw how it was, I had to get the last man." Like I say, no matter how you put it, it comes out sounding phony.

The next day Maury Wills opened the game with a single and was promptly picked off base by Al Downing. Maury took off for second, a dead duck all the way. But Pepitone's throw was bad. It came to Richardson high, pulling him away over toward the infield, and Maury dove into the open side of the base. The team that didn't beat itself had handed us another opening.

They kept on doing it. Wills held up at third on Gilliam's line single to right, and when Maris's throw came in to the plate too high for the cut-off man to handle, Gilliam went on to second.

To finish everything off, Maris slipped as he turned on Willie Davis's well-hit line drive. Willie had a double and we had two runs. That was all Johnny Podres needed.

Back in Los Angeles for the third game, Don Drysdale pitched one of the best games I have ever seen, as he beat the Yankees and Bouton, 1–0. The run came in when Bobby Richardson got a bad hop on a ground ball. You can't blame a man for not handling bad hops.

As I went out for my second start, we had a chance to win in four straight. I have spoken just a little about the self-hypnosis of pitching. In the first game I'd had another little example. Somewhere during the first game I had apparently torn off a soft corn between my first and second toes. And I hadn't even been aware of it until the game was over. It had bothered me just a little when I worked out between starts, and I was afraid that if I unconsciously began to favor it during the game I just might begin to throw unnaturally. Before I went out to warm up, I asked Dr. Kerlan, the club physician, to give me a shot of Novocain. That was all. Dr. Kerlan froze it, and I didn't feel a thing through the entire game.

I had drawn Whitey Ford again, and this time Whitey Ford pitched like Whitey Ford. This may surprise you a little, but Whitey pitches pretty much the same as I do, except that he uses the curve as his bread-and-butter pitch and I use the fast ball. Whitey would like to have you believe that his fast ball isn't fast enough to knock a bird off its perch. Don't believe it. Warren Spahn played that same game for years. Spahn kept talking screwball, screwball, screwball until everybody came to think that he just kept nibbling, nibbling, nibbling at the corners. He nibbled all right. And when he had the batter leaning to the outside corner, he'd blow the high inside fast ball through there. Poor Spahnnie, he probably didn't get more than 40 per cent of his outs with his fast ball.

Ford really pitched a great game. He had everything going for him except luck. In the fifth inning, he threw a perfect pitch to Frank Howard, a fast ball low on the outside corner. Frank goes so far out after those pitches that he sometimes ends up swinging the bat with one hand.

Frank fished for this one too and ended up swinging with one hand. The ball ended up in the second deck of the left-field bleachers, where no ball had ever been hit before.

So much for perfect pitches.

Meanwhile, I was pitching well enough. You can pretty well tell how good my stuff is by my strikeouts. I had four strikeouts in the first three innings, and only one in the next three innings. My stuff was good enough, though, and I was putting the ball where I wanted to. The Yankees had only two hits. Richardson got a double when his blooper was lost in the sun. Elston Howard, who continued to be tough, had a single to center.

And then the sins of my past caught up with me. Mantle came to bat in the seventh inning, and for the third—and maybe even the fourth—time in the Series I got that fast ball out a few inches too much over the plate. This time Mantle didn't foul it back. This time he hit it deep into the left-field stands to tie up the baseball game.

Fair enough. It's not right to get away with that many mistakes on a hitter like Mantle. Understand what I am saying, now. I am not saying that it is ever a joy to have a home run hit off you; I am only saying I can sometimes recognize the justice of it. Baseball is a game of instant rewards and punishments. To err is human; to get away with it forever is impossible.

It is also, in a larger sense, sloppy and unrewarding. If you didn't have to pay some kind of reasonable price for doing your job badly, what would the reward be for doing it well?

It may not even have been a case of the law of averages straightening things out. I had thrown so many pitches to that spot that Mantle may very well have been under the impression that I was doing it deliberately. In other words, he just might have been waiting for that pitch all day.

We got the run right back on one of the weird plays of World Series history. Gilliam, leading off for us, hit a high bouncer over third base. Our home dugout is on the third-base side of the field, so I had a perfect view of Boyer's fine leaping play. I didn't have any angle on Pepitone at all and, frankly, I couldn't have cared less, since it was obviously a routine play. There was no indication whatsoever that Pepitone had lost sight of the ball until all of a sudden it was bouncing off his hand and rolling down the right-field line. Pitchers are supposed to sit back and play it cool. We are supposed to conserve every ounce of strength. But I was up and yelling with everyone else because it was important for Gilliam to get to third. If Junior had reached only second, it would have taken a bunt and a long fly to bring him in. This way, we had two chances at the fly.

Willie Davis delivered the long fly immediately—a low line drive, actually, to right center—and that sent me out to the ninth inning with a one-run lead.

Over the winter everybody kept asking me whether any first basemen had trouble with a reflection like that during the season. I could only answer that we didn't play enough day games at Chavez Ravine to know. But there's no doubt that it was a freak thing. In the split second that Pepitone turned to pick up the ball, the sun had reflected off someone's shirt or belt buckle and blinded him. For all anybody will ever know, some woman may have pulled out her mirror to fix her lipstick between innings and lowered it suddenly as she saw a play developing. It was the moment and the angle, a split-second freak of timing. Luck, as I keep saying, is a factor in this business.

I still had to get the Yankees out in the ninth. In the first game, where I had gone into the ninth with a three-run lead, I was willing to challenge the man to hit a home run before I would walk him. With a one-run lead, your strategy is reversed. Now you have to keep the ball in the park and still try to keep the winning run from coming to the plate.

That was the situation I had in front of me as the inning started. If I could get the first two batters, I'd be able to pitch to Mantle with nobody on.

So Richardson opened the inning with a single to right center field, and that changed everything. It meant that Mantle was going to come to the plate as the winning run unless I got lucky enough to have Tresh hit into a double play.

Tresh went down on a called third strike. It was described the next day as a particularly explosive curve, probably because Tresh was walking away before the umpire called him out. But it wasn't a big curve at all. Quite the contrary, it wasn't even a particularly good one. In that spot, I wanted to break the curve all the way down to his knees so that if he hit it he'd have a good chance of hitting it on the ground. Instead, the ball just did catch the top of the strike zone.

Mantle had to be pitched to, and this was no time to make another mistake with him. Roseboro called for a fast ball, high and inside. Good. That's what we'd been doing with him basically in both games, crowding him. Mantle fouled it off. We came right back with another fast ball, high and inside, crowding him even more. Mickey swung and missed.

And then came my most vivid memory of the entire Series.

As I got the ball back and began to look in for the sign, I thought to myself: I'd like to take something off my curve ball. . . .

Now why does a thought like that come to you? A change-up curve is exactly what you don't throw Mantle, particularly in a spot where it can cost you a ball game. Change-up curves are what Mantle hits out of ball parks. I hadn't thrown a change-up in the entire game, as far as I could remember. And at the same moment that the thought came into my mind, there flickered the answering thought: But how will I explain why I threw it if he hits it out of here?

I know it isn't brave, noble, or professional to worry about being second-guessed. It's just human.

And while the thought was still half formed in my mind, I was looking down toward the plate, and John Roseboro was putting down two fingers, the sign for the curve. He was putting them down hesitantly, though, so hesitantly that I had the feeling there was something more he wanted to tell me, something that couldn't be communicated by means of a sign. Normally he'd pull the fingers right back. This time he left the fingers there for a couple of seconds and then, slowly, still hesitantly, he began to wiggle them, the sign to take something off it. (Yes, the signs are that simple with nobody on second base. One for the fast ball, two for the curve, just like in high school.)

As soon as I saw the fingers wiggle, I began to nod my head emphatically. I could see John begin to smile behind the mask, and then the fingers began to wiggle faster, as if he were saying to me, "Sandy baby, you don't know how glad I am that you see it this way too."

As for Mantle, Lord only knows what he was thinking when he saw my head bobbing up and down so vigorously. The one thing he should have been thinking was: They're not going to give me anything to pull—which would mean that the last thing in the world he'd be expecting would be a change-up curve.

And maybe that was one of the reasons the change-up curve didn't bother me. As far as I'm concerned I don't think it makes any difference whether you let Mickey pull the ball or not. If he hits it right, he's going to hit it out of the park, regardless. Inside, outside, up, or down. He's so strong that if he hits an outside fast ball right—and he hits the ball away from him real well—he'll send it out of the park in right center.

As it was, I copped out just a little. I did take something off my normal curve, but I didn't throw it real slow. It was a good pitch, though. It broke right down in there for a called third strike.

As soon as we hit the clubhouse, I grabbed Roseboro. "What was the matter, John?" I said. "You seemed a little hesitant about wiggling the fingers on Mantle." And he grinned back and said, "I wanted to call it, but I was thinking: How are we ever going to explain a change-curve if he hits it out?"

That's how close the rapport between us can get. Not only did we have the same idea at the same moment, we even had the same thoughts about what could happen back in the clubhouse.

We weren't in the clubhouse yet after Mantle went down. Richardson was still on first base, and we were still an out away. As a matter of fact, the game ended twice. It ended the first time, it seemed, when Howard hit the ball into the hole, not too hard. Wills grabbed it with his bare hand and made the throw to Tracewski on second. As the umpire's hand started to shoot upward, I went into my victory leap. When I came back down again, there were men on first and second and we still were in a ball game. Even while I was in the air I could see that Dick didn't have the ball, that he had never had control of the ball at all.

A hit would tie it now. An extra-base hit would probably put them ahead.

My father, having just been released from the hospital, had been following the game by a sort of indirect pickup. The doctors didn't want him to sweat out the game, pitch by pitch, but they didn't want him to suffer the anxiety of waiting until the game was over either. So, while he wasn't permitted to actually watch the game, the results were relayed to him, batter by batter. With the game almost over, he hadn't been able to stand it. He had turned on the television just in time to see Howard hit the ball to Wills, to see the out call—and then to see it changed. "And then I turned it off," he told me. "I didn't think I could survive another play like that."

Hector Lopez was the batter. We threw him a low fast ball in tight. Lopez tried to check his swing, couldn't, and hit a little nubber off his fists. Wills came in quickly, flipped the ball to Tracewski, and it was like a rerun for the West Coast, only this time we did it right.

I was happy then that the umpire had reversed that first call, because if the game had ended on a disputed play everybody would always have said that we had won because we'd got a lucky call just when the Yankees were beginning to get to me. This way, it was sharp and clean.

Looking back, I am also very happy that Lopez hit the first pitch. If you think the game has ended, and then find yourself still in trouble and falling behind on the count, there is the danger that you'll begin to think: Dammit, this thing should have been over! Once you begin to think in terms of what should have happened, instead of concentrating entirely upon the situation that confronts you, you're in terrible danger of letting down.

Concentration. Con-cen-tra-tion. You must forget the last game and the last inning and the last batter, because there is not a thing that you can do about them. The only batter you can get is the one standing up there at the plate with the bat in his hand. You can have the strongest arm in the world, but without total concentration you will never be a winning pitcher. Nobody knows that better than I, because it was not a lesson that came to me easy.

12

The Weeping Hinge

When the Good Lord created man, he gave him a prehensile hand and a hinged arm to enable him, among other things, to fling a few rocks between the ears of a rabbit. This wasn't known as pitching; it was known as eating. There are some batters who still insist that pitchers are headhunters. A word of advice: never believe anything a batter says. They are a most untrustworthy and treacherous lot.

Nowhere is there any indication that the arm was constructed with any thought that its proprietor would throw anywhere from 200 to 250 pitches (counting warm-ups) just as hard as he could. Pitching, as any pitcher can tell you, is an unnatural act. Pitchers you can believe. They are among the noblest creatures on earth.

When a man throws a curve he is performing an even more unnatural act. To throw a curve you tuck your wrist inside your elbow and snap it down hard just before the arm is fully extended. This puts a strain on everything: shoulder, elbow, wrist. Which is why a pitcher can throw all fast balls but can't throw all curve balls.

When you perform this unnatural act every fourth day, your arm is going to rebel. As we say in the technical jargon of the dugout, it hurts. There is an occasional wonder—almost always named Warren Spahn—whose arm *was* constructed to throw a baseball. Spahn, they tell me, could go out on the first day of spring training and play catch with an outfielder two hundred feet away. In twenty-five years, he had one sore arm.

After you have pitched a ball game, you expect the arm to hurt. The morning after a game you can have a very gritty time combing your hair and brushing your teeth.

Am I saying, then, that all pitchers have arm trouble all the time? No, I am not. What I am saying is that all pitchers have sore arms some of the time. The difference is this: if you can't pitch when your number comes up, you're having arm trouble. If you can pitch, you just have an arm that hurts. All pitchers feel that way about it. If they didn't, the clubs would have to import new shifts of pitchers monthly.

I don't want to overstate this or make it look as if I'm alibiing for pitchers. I'm just trying to explain how ballplayers react. You are forever reading that baseball players go off in a corner and sulk whenever they have a hangnail, while hockey and football players can't wait to have their heads stitched up and their bones reset so that they can go racing back into the game. It just isn't true. A ballplayer hangs in there for as long as he can function effectively. There's nothing brave or noble about it, any more than it is brave or noble for a coal miner to go back down the shaft with a hacking cough. These are the occupational hazards of the job. They become so much a part of your life that you automatically discount them.

Most of the injuries are minor. A full season of pitching stretches the muscles of the arm. Over the winter the muscles relax back into place, and whatever little injuries may have occurred in either the stretching or the relaxing develop scar tissue or, as they are more commonly called, adhesions. (It is possible for the adhesions to form during the season but not, as a rule, when you are pitching with any regularity.)

When you begin to stretch the muscles again during spring training, the adhesions—which do not stretch—are torn away. Take a rubber band, spread some mucilage over it, let the mucilage dry, then stretch the rubber band. The mucilage will crack and break loose. Same thing. The difference is that we are dealing with living tissue. When the scar tissue tears away, a certain amount of bleeding and swelling will take place and the pitcher may be out of action for ten days to two weeks.

In 1964 my adhesions did not tear loose during spring training. I got to pitch the opening game, finally, but it was more off my previous year's record than any particular showing in spring training. I won it, too, shutting out the Cardinals.

In my third start, in St. Louis, I had a man on, two out, and a two-strike count on Bill White. As I came over the top to throw a curve ball, I could feel something tear in my forearm. The ball went slipping out of my hand and bounced far in front of the plate. White, thinking fast, swung at the wild pitch, striking out and going to first as the ball went to the backstop. Charley James hit the next pitch out of the park. I stayed in there and got the third out, but that was all the pitching I did for the next twelve days.

By May 27 my record was only 4–4, but it had nothing to do with the forearm. I didn't feel right, even when I seemed to be pitching good ball. My rhythm was off. I felt off balance. I was working too hard. Something had to be wrong, anyway, because my fast ball was sinking and tailing away from the right-handed hitter. Now a fast ball that is also a sinker and a screwball is not a thing to be scorned. I'll take it over a hanging curve any time. The only thing wrong with it as far as I was concerned was that it wasn't my fast ball and I didn't know what in the world to do with it. When I throw my fast ball I expect it to rise.

Joe Becker and I figured out that I was throwing across my body, which simply means that I was stepping to the left of where I normally step and blocking myself off. In other words, I was pitching against my body instead of with it.

I opened way up, stepping far off to the right, and tried to work my way back in until I could find the old feeling of the smooth, even flow. From time to time, I'd think I had it in practice, but somehow it was never quite right in the game.

Even when I brought my record up to 5–4 by getting a win in Pittsburgh, I was hit very hard and knocked out of the box in the eighth inning. Roberto Clemente hit an outside fast ball that was still rising when it hit against the light tower in left center field, 450 feet away from home plate. And on a 1–2 pitch at that.

But there is no such thing as a good pitch to Clemente. Ask me how to pitch to Clemente, and I will tell you with complete confidence, "How do I know?" Roberto can hit any pitch, anywhere, at any time. He'll hit pitchouts, he'll hit brush-back pitches. He'll hit high inside pitches deep to the opposite field, which would be ridiculous even if he didn't do it with both feet off the ground.

I had been looking through magazines for pictures of myself so that I could find out where my foot had been landing when I was striding correctly. I came across a lot of pictures of myself with my foot up in the air. But I never came across the right shot taken at the right angle.

In the visitors' locker room in Philadelphia there is usually a pile of old dog-eared magazines. I was browsing through a back issue of *Sport Magazine* the day we arrived, when I suddenly came across a shot Dave Sutton had taken from behind home plate during the no-hitter against the Giants. I knew I had been throwing right *that* night. Studying the picture carefully, I could see that I had to open up a little.

It being my day to throw anyway, Joe and I went right out to try it. Suddenly I was throwing easy, the rhythm was right, and the fast ball was moving the way I had become accustomed to having it move.

Warming up two nights later, I had tremendous stuff. Plus good control. When you've got everything working, you almost can't wait to get started. With two out in the fourth inning, I threw three balls to Richie Allen. The count went to 3–2, he fouled off another pitch, and then I walked him. Danny Cater went to a 2–2 count. The next pitch was outside, but Richie Allen was running and Roseboro threw him out. When Cater came back up as lead-off man in the fifth, he went to 2–2 again before he went down swinging. On that one go-round, as you can see, I threw seventeen pitches to Allen and Cater. The other twenty-five outs came on only eighty pitches. Eliminating the first pitch, I was behind only two other hitters all day, and both of them eventually struck out.

Since Richie Allen, the only man to reach base, went out stealing, I had faced only twenty-seven men, the absolute minimum. On the other hand, I had really got only twenty-six men out myself, hadn't I? When you're talking about a no-hitter, that's cheating a little, isn't it? But I'll take it.

The other important factor, never to be ignored, was the score. For six innings the game was scoreless, which meant that I wasn't thinking about anything except not giving up a run. Frank Howard hit a three-run home run in the seventh, and once we had those three big runs, I did concentrate on the no-hitter. Actually, I got even stronger as I went along. Four of the last five batters went down on strikes.

It ended with a sort of dramatic wait. With two out in the ninth, Bobby Wine came up to bat for Chris Short. Wine fouled the first pitch right back off umpire Ed Vargo's leg, and the game had to be held up for a few minutes while the other umpires and both trainers gathered around Ed.

If something like that happened in the middle of a routine ball game, there might be some danger that your concentration would go. But hardly on the last batter of a no-hitter.

Vargo was also behind the plate when I pitched the perfect game against the Cubs a year later. He was hit on the throat by another foul ball in that game. All of which would seem to indicate that Vargo is luckier for me than I am for him.

We had been going very badly. I'll tell you how badly. Don Drysdale had lost, 1–0, in eleven innings the night before and had been given permission to go to Washington on business. Don's story is that his transistor radio cut out on him on the train, and he couldn't follow the game. When he got to his hotel room, he says, he turned on the radio just in time to hear the announcer talking excitedly about the no-hitter that had just been pitched. The announcer went on endlessly about the "ranks of the immortals" and "the first man to pitch three no-hitters since Bob Feller" until Don finally shouted, "I don't want to know about history. Who *won?*"

To me, as a pitcher, the real importance of Allen's being thrown out stealing in the fourth inning was that I didn't have to face Cookie Rojas, the Phillies' lead-off man, in the ninth. Rojas wears me out.

It can go the other way too. The no-hitter set me off on a winning streak that ran to eleven games before the Giants beat me 5–2. Going into the ninth inning of that game, I had a 2–1 lead. The first batter bunted and went to second when the ball was thrown away. He then went to third on a sacrifice and scored the tying run when Harvey Kuenn's short fly was dropped. The next batter popped up.

It was bad enough that the score was tied. It was even worse that I still had to pitch to another batter. Worst of all, that extra batter was Willie Mays. Willie doubled in the tie-breaking run, and Jim Ray Hart followed with a two-run homer. See what I mean?

This inning also shows, incidentally, that the earned run averages can be very kind to a pitcher. I had, after all, been racked for a double and home run in a clutch situation, and yet, officially, every run in the inning was unearned.

After the no-hitter we were in eighth place with a record of 22–25. My personal winning streak had hardly picked up the team, for when the streak ended we were still in eighth place. Obviously the Dodgers were not going to win in 1964, with me or without me. They ended without me.

On August 8 I won a tough game in Milwaukee. Tougher than I thought. We were behind 2–1 in the fifth inning when I singled off Tony Cloninger and went to second base on Maury Wills's single. Cloninger tried to pick me off, possibly on the theory that I was a stranger in that part of town. I dove back safely, but I landed hard on my elbow. It stung, as you'd expect an elbow to sting when you give it a good rap. Before the inning was over, Ron Fairly hit a bases-loaded triple and scored on Tommy Davis's single.

By the time I was back out on the mound, the pain had pretty much subsided. Dennie Menke hit a two-run homer in the seventh to make it 5–4, and that's the way it ended.

The next morning I woke up in the Schroeder Hotel with a lump on my elbow. It wasn't a bruise. There was no discoloration. It was the kind of swelling that you get when the joint fills with liquid.

I couldn't swear that the bang on the elbow brought it on. There is just the assumption that if you bang your elbow one day and it swells up the next, a reasonable cause-and-effect relationship may be drawn. At any rate, there is no indication that a rap on the elbow ever did a pitcher any good.

There is a definite routine that is followed when you are in the regular four-day rotation. On the first day after you pitch, your arm is always stiff, so I just ran some at the park. My arm felt something more than the usual soreness, so I decided against getting into a game of pepper.

The second day is the day of work. You run again, but you'll also throw, and keep throwing until you are satisfied that you have loosened the muscles. With me, that means anywhere from twenty minutes to half an hour. It has always seemed to me that if the choice lies between working too little or working too much, the safety factor is all on the side of too much. If I don't throw enough it's going to affect me at the beginning of the game, which means that I could be out of the game before I loosen up. If I've thrown too long, it isn't going to affect me until late in the game, which means I can pitch a good seven innings and either finish or get help.

When I came out for the second-day workout we were in Cincinnati. My arm was sore. So sore that I told Wayne Anderson, our co-trainer, that it seemed to be getting worse. And yet when I began to throw it loosened up very nicely. At the end of the workout it felt just fine.

Except that, as soon as the arm cooled off, the soreness began to creep back.

The third day you ease off, pointing to the game the next day. You'll run about as much as the other two days, except that even here you'll run easier. You don't throw at all. I didn't feel much like throwing. The swelling had come back again. So had the ache.

But when I warmed up for the game the next day, the same thing happened. The arm loosened up very nicely. Deron Johnson hit a home run off me, but he had been hitting home runs off me all year. Deron may not have become a star in the National League until 1965, but he was a superstar against me a year earlier. He had hit a three-run homer off me on my second start of the season, to beat me 3–0, and, having found the way to the door, he kept coming back. Of the seven runs Cincinnati had scored off me in the four previous games, he had knocked in five. He made it six out of eight. This time I had a 4–0 lead when he hit his homer in the seventh inning, so I got off easy.

I had pitched a good ball game, striking out ten and walking only one. The elbow was obviously just another of the little injuries that come and go.

The next morning the swelling and the pain were there again. We had returned to Los Angeles. I was due to face the Cards on Sunday. The arm loosened up again as I was pitching, and I pitched one of my better games of the year, striking out thirteen and again walking only one.

Anyone could see that the elbow was no problem at all. My record had come up to 19–5, and I had won fifteen of my last sixteen decisions. I was actually one full start ahead of my 1963 record.

I never won the twentieth.

When I woke up in the morning I couldn't believe it. I had to drag my arm out of bed like a log. That's what it looked like, a log. A waterlogged log. Where it had been swollen outside the joint before, it was now swollen all the way from the shoulder down to the wrist—inside, outside, everywhere. For an elbow, I had a knee; that's how thick it was.

The elbow was so swollen that the whole arm was locked in a sort of hooked position. I couldn't straighten it out and I couldn't bend it. I didn't have more than an inch's worth of movement in any direction. But, just moving it that tiny distance, I could actually hear the sound of liquid squishing around, as if I had a wet sponge in there.

Actually, I was more surprised than frightened. As I've said, you expect the arm to hurt and maybe swell up a little, even though you don't really expect it to take off and go into business for itself.

Monday was an off day. I hoped the swelling would go down to reasonable limits before I had to go to the park the next evening for my second-day workout. I'd throw a little bit, I figured, and it would feel just fine again.

Tuesday it was as waterlogged as ever. Dr. Kerlan was at the park. He took one look at the arm and drove me down to his office for treatment and X-rays.

He had taken other X-rays of my elbow through the years, so he had a basis for comparison. After you've pitched for any length of time, the X-rays show spurs and a general irregularity brought on by the accumulation of minor injuries to the protective cartilage covering the joint—all the nicks and chips and pulls and tears from the thousands upon thousands of times that the hinge has snapped, the sheer wear and tear of pitching.

Dr. Kerlan's test showed that it had passed over the line between temporary damage and permanent trouble. An arthritic change had taken place.

Briefly, there are two principal forms of arthritis: osteoarthritis, which is wear and tear on the body brought on by old age; and rheumatoid arthritis, which is an infectious disease about which little seems to be known. Traumatic arthritis ("trauma" meaning injury) is a near relative to osteoarthritis, in that it is also brought on by wear and tear. In traumatic arthritis the cartilage has been chipped away by physical wear and tear, rather than having been worn away in the passage of time.

The blow to the elbow in Milwaukee may have been the final traumatizing incident, but the condition—and I suppose it is more accurately called a condition than a disease—had been developing for as long as I had been pitching. If it had not flared up when it did, it would probably have flared up later.

It is possible that the condition was brought on solely by the stress and strain of pitching. It is also possible that there was an initial injury to the joint, which had been irritated over the years, constantly and irrevocably, by the act of pitching. Some scarcely noticed and quickly forgotten fall on a basketball court, perhaps, or a crash into one of the steel poles holding up a playground basket. It could have been anything.

Whatever the initial cause—*if* there was an initial cause—and whatever the traumatizing incident—*if* the blow to the elbow in Milwaukee was the traumatizing incident—it is fair and accurate to say that my traumatic arthritis was caused by continuing minor injuries to the joint surface of the elbow during eleven years of pitching.

All pitchers have interesting X-rays. Some of their elbows probably look even craggier than mine. Some of them may well have a mild form of arthritis. But everybody reacts differently. In my case it wasn't the joint itself that had become inflamed. It was the lining of the joint. For any interested medical students, this is called synovitis.

Every joint in the body has a lining which manufactures lubricating fluid when and as the joint needs it. When the lining becomes inflamed, it "weeps" far more fluid down into the joint than the joint wants, needs, or can handle. The lining of my elbow had produced enough fluid to blow up my whole arm.

A football player, taking blow after blow on his own vulnerable joint, the knee, develops water on the knee. What I had, quite literally, was water on the elbow, something rare and maybe even unique in a pitcher.

The first problem was to draw the fluid out of the elbow; the second was to reduce the inflammation.

The fluid was removed by aspirating—drawing it out with a needle. The inflammation was treated by injections of cortisone plus oral medication. Or, as we say in English, they gave me some pills.

After that it was a matter of waiting for the swelling to go down and then finding out whether the elbow was going to weep every time I subjected it to the strain of pitching.

It was made clear to me at that time, although we did not announce it publicly, that I had arthritis. It was also made clear to me that, while arthritis can be controlled, it cannot be cured. Arthritis is a degenerative condition, which means it gets progressively worse. In my case, since I would be contributing further wear and tear to the joint every time I pitched, the outlook was far from bright.

Two weeks later the team was going out on the road. I went with them. The swelling had gone down. The arm felt fine again. In St. Louis, our first stop, I decided that the time had come for the test.

I threw three or four pitches to Joe Becker. It felt pretty good. And then the elbow began to hurt. I could feel it start to swell up. Looking down, I could *see* it blow up. When I tried to find out how much movement I had in my arm, it sounded again as if I were squeezing a soggy sponge.

That will shake you up a little. It will also end your pitching for the day. It will, in fact, put you on a plane back to Los Angeles. We were back to the aspirating and the cortisone and the pills again.

This had to be the most discouraging time of all, the one time when it did seem as if my pitching career might be at an end. Two weeks later, with the Dodgers home, I went out to the park to throw batting practice. The idea was to find out whether I was still an active pitcher. During the first workout there was no swelling. Again the soreness pretty much disappeared in the course of the pitching. The next morning the arm was stiff, but no stiffer than one would expect after the first workout in two weeks. I could still throw good when I went back out the next evening, although the soreness had not completely disappeared. After the third day my elbow did swell up more than usual, but even then it was no worse than it had been after the Milwaukee game.

By this time there were only about ten games left in the season, and we were fourteen or fifteen games behind. The best thing to do, we felt, was to rest it over the winter.

And that's all I did over the winter. There was no treatment, no further medication. Just the healing touch of nature.

In the spring I had no trouble at all. In fact, I came along much faster than usual, pitching a full nine innings earlier than I ever had before.

On March 30, a full week before we were to break camp, I pitched another complete game, this time against the Chicago White Sox at Sarasota. As far as I was concerned, the arthritis might flare up from time to time, but the water on the elbow was a thing of the past, a freak one-time reaction.

I woke up in the morning, and the arm was blown up again. It was not quite as bad as it had been the year before. This time I could move it as much as three inches in either direction, and without any accompanying sound effects.

Dick Tracewski, my roommate, was up and shaving. I just showed it to him, and all he did was shake his head.

It was a blow, no question about that. Still, there was no sense going off half-cocked. If the arm had felt so good all spring and had blown up so suddenly, there had to be a reason. I must have been doing something different against the White Sox, I felt, something I hadn't done all spring. And, thinking about it, I realized that I had. The White Sox had presented an unusual number of lefties in the lineup, and I will sometimes throw sidearmed to lefties, almost without thinking. Sometimes as many as twelve or fourteen times during the course of a game. Thinking back to the St. Louis game in 1964, I remembered that I had thrown an unusual number of sidearmed pitches to their left-handers too.

There. That was it.

Okay, I would throw no sidearmed pitches ever again. Not ever. While I was about it, I mentally scratched the slider from my repertoire too. Giving up the slider was no great sacrifice, because I had thrown it rarely and not very well.

Before I went to Doc Anderson's room to let him look at it, I put on a heavy sweater. I didn't want to walk around with my arm ballooning out at everybody. Nor did I want any fuss made in the press, for I still felt that the swelling had a good chance of going down in another day.

Doc Anderson called Buzzie Bavasi to let him know about it. Beyond that, there was nothing to be done except to wait for tomorrow.

The next day it was swollen at least as much and maybe a little more.

The club was leaving for Clearwater to play the Phils. After they left, I went to find Buzzie. I found him in the empty dining room, nursing a cup of coffee. "It looks like I'm in trouble," I told him. "There's no way I'm going to be able to pitch with this for a while."

Buzzie just looked at it grimly and agreed that I should go right back to Los Angeles. "I'll make the plane reservations, and I'll call Bob Kerlan and set up an appointment for you in the morning. You just better pack what you need and get ready to leave."

The Dodgers were opening the season in New York, which meant that they would not be returning to Los Angeles. The extra stuff goes back to Los Angeles via truck anyway. I left a note for Dick, telling him that I'd either get back to Vero before we broke camp or let him know where to ship my stuff. "I just don't know what's going to happen," I wrote.

Dr. Kerlan's first impression was that it would be a miracle if I got back by opening day. I wasn't concerned about opening day. I just wanted to get back as soon as possible.

When it was first determined that I had arthritis, back in 1964, we had decided not to make any announcement until we had some idea of the long-range effect. We decided that we might as well make the announcement now, although we were perfectly aware that, no matter how fully it was explained, most people would hear the word "arthritis" and draw their own conclusions.

Dr. Kerlan treated it with cortisone for a couple of days, and little by little the swelling began to go down. There was no way, however, of telling whether the cortisone was doing it or just the passage of time. Finally he injected the cortisone right into the joint. The next morning the swelling was almost gone. The day after that the elbow was perfectly normal.

The question before the house was how long we could expect it to stay that way. On the medical evidence, we had to assume that it was going to swell up every time I pitched.

That changed the question to how fast we could get the swelling down to where I could take my turn again.

I was not as pessimistic as I might have been. The last cortisone treatment had encouraged me. If the elbow blew up again, he could always lay the needle right into the joint again and knock the swelling down.

Dr. Kerlan was not that optimistic. Looking at it practically, he didn't feel that we could function on an emergency basis two times a week. I gathered that, as a doctor, he didn't like the idea of shooting me up and sending me back out to pitch. He didn't seem to feel that the arm could stand up to that kind of crash treatment, anyway. As far as Dr. Kerlan was concerned, I'd be lucky if I could pitch once a week.

The prospect of becoming a Sunday pitcher didn't entrance me at all. Baseball is a game of the long season, of the long haul, of the whole career. If you're a big-league pitcher you go out there when your number comes up, every fourth day.

Doc Kerlan and I went over the schedule together to find out how many times I would start if I pitched every sixth day or even every fifth day. It was really amazing to me. The difference between starting every fourth day and every fifth day was the difference between forty-one starts and thirty-four starts. We were talking, he made clear, of only seven starts.

But, once again, I had spent too many years of my life *not* pitching to become a part-time pitcher voluntarily.

"Doc," I said, "before I give up any starts, let's see whether I can just give up everything else. I won't throw on the second day. I won't pitch any batting practice. I won't pick up a baseball at all between the time I finish one game and the time I begin to warm up for the next one." If that didn't work, I said, we could try every fifth day; and, if that didn't work, every sixth. If everything else failed, we could consider the bit about the Sunday pitcher.

That's the way we left it. Our goal was to keep the arm in good enough shape so that I could pitch seven or eight times before it blew up so bad that I'd have to miss a turn. That was the best we hoped for at that point, though—that I could get away with missing only one turn every month.

The season, to put it mildly, was a surprise to us all.

The Dodgers were going to New York by way of Jacksonville and Washington. Instead of joining the team in Washington, as I had planned, I decided to go back to Vero and pack my own stuff. I had been gone only six days.

We arrived in Washington on Friday, leaving an open day before our weekend series with the Senators. It was cold, it had been raining, the worst kind of weather for arthritis. After a week's layoff, though, I really needed to get some running in. It also seemed to me that I did have to throw a ball sometime before I pitched my first game. Jim Brewer was going out to the park. I went with him. I didn't need a catcher because I wasn't going to be throwing that hard. Jim and I ran, played a little pepper, and went out to the bullpen. The mound was so muddy out there that I couldn't have thrown hard even if I had wanted to.

My arm felt good enough so that I decided I would like to pitch a couple of innings on Sunday. Walt and I agreed that I would go down to the bullpen during the game and, if my arm still felt all right, I'd pitch two innings.

As happens so often after a layoff, I had great stuff warming up, the best stuff I'd had all spring.

You can't tell anything about an arm, though, until you test it in a game. You can throw batting practice for an hour, bearing down all the way, and you won't even be stiff the next day. Pitch two or three innings in relief and, believe me, you will be. The act of throwing does not become an act of violence until you are trying to get a hitter out. Competition brings forth that much more effort. Or perhaps the competition gets the adrenalin flowing and gives you the ability to get that much more out of your body.

I came into the game and struck out the first two batters. After two innings I still felt so good that I asked to go another inning. When it was over I had faced ten men, striking out five. There are a dozen ex-Dodgers on the Washington squad, starting with the manager, Gil Hodges. My old friends Joe Pignatano and Rube Walker are coaches. My old roomie, Doug Camilli, who had caught the no-hitter against the Phils, had been sold to the Senators over the winter. In other words, they gave it to me pretty good.

Doug Camilli, the last batter I pitched to, popped up. As he was trotting down the base line he yelled over to me, "Sore arm, my eye!"

After opening the season in New York, we were going to Pittsburgh for two night games, with a day off on either side, before we played Philadelphia. The plan was for Drysdale to open in New York and for Osteen and me to pitch in Pittsburgh. The first game in Pittsburgh was rained out, however, which put me off until Philadelphia.

As it turned out, we were in Pittsburgh for four full days because the Dodger plane, on which we travel, had been sent back to Vero to transport the minor-league players to their assigned clubs. If I had ever doubted that I had arthritis, my doubts were dispelled during those four cold, wet days in Pittsburgh.

Since we were down to one game in Pittsburgh, I asked to go to the bullpen in case a left-hander was needed in relief.

Osteen needed no help from anybody. He pitched a one-hitter.

My first start was pushed back to Sunday afternoon, to keep Drysdale in rotation on Saturday night and give me, hopefully, a warm Sunday afternoon. It turned out to be a cold, miserable Sunday afternoon. I pitched the kind of ragged game you might expect when you consider that I had worked only three innings in the preceding eighteen days. Just the kind of rough, ragged game I needed.

If it was a workout I was looking for, I got it in the first inning, although I got out without any runs scored against me. Dick Stuart, who hits me almost as good as he says he does, let me know he was back in the National League by hitting a home run in the sixth, which is no way to greet an old arthritic friend. Still, anybody who can say, upon being asked whether he is slowing down, "I'm still fast enough to get out of the way of ground balls," is entitled to a certain amount of tolerance. Dick likes to say that he approaches a ground ball the way a smart bullfighter approaches a bull, with a decent amount of respect. A smart pitcher approaches Dick the same way.

In the ball game, which we won 6–2, I gave up five walks and six hits, and struck out seven. Late in the game, when the Phils loaded the bases with one out, I had to labor my way out of it. I threw a lot of pitches. There was no doubt that the arm had been put to the test under the best possible laboratory conditions.

In the ball game, you either do or you don't. I was worried about how the elbow was going to react *after* the game and, beyond that, how it was going to hold up over the first full month. Even there, I wasn't really worried. It would be more accurate to say that I was curious. I'd had a whole winter, after all, to accommodate myself to the idea that I might be in permanent trouble. If the elbow did blow up after every game, I felt that Dr. Kerlan could handle it. More than anything else, I simply wanted to know how I was going to go through the season, the hard way or the easy way.

The elbow was sore in the morning. It was a little puffy. That was all. I could hardly have expected anything less than that.

By the end of the first month my record was 4–2. My eighth start of the season and—incidentally—our first game under the dome turned out to be the real test. We went into extra innings, tied 1–1. The Dodgers scored four runs in the top of the eleventh, which was very good thinking because the Colts scored two runs off me in the bottom half, knocking me out. I had gone as far as I could.

In the morning, the elbow didn't feel any worse than usual. For the first time I began to feel that I just might be able to go through the season without having to take those periodic rests for emergency treatment.

What can I say about the season except that it turned out to be almost embarrassing? In the first half of the year the obligatory question was, "How does the arm feel?" By All-Star time it had changed to, "Is it possible for a pitcher to win thirty games any more?" After all the publicity about the arthritic elbow, I didn't miss a start all year. Not only did I win twenty-six games, I pitched twenty-seven complete games (seven more than I had pitched in 1963) and broke the major-league strike-out record. My 336 innings were the most pitched by any left-hander since 1906, and the most by anybody since Robin Roberts pitched 337 innings in 1954.

Mel Durslag of the Los Angeles *Herald-Examiner* called me the pin-up boy of the Arthritis and Rheumatism Foundation.

I don't want to leave the impression, however, that my arm recovered as if by magic. Every morning when I woke up, my first thought would usually be about the condition of my elbow.

It usually did puff up the morning after a game. Not always, and not always to the same degree. But most of the time. The best cure—to use the word loosely—was the act of throwing itself. It would feel better when I threw between starts, and best of all in the game itself.

Yes, I know I had decided not to pick up a ball between starts. That resolution lasted for exactly one start. Although we beat the Mets 2–1 in my second start, I didn't feel right. My rhythm was off, and I didn't have good control. Two days later I asked Hector Valle, our third-string catcher, to warm me up a bit on the sidelines.

If I had thought it through, I would have realized that I never feel right in the early weeks of the season and that I always have trouble with my control. Considering the long layoff in the spring, I had probably been pitching far better than I had any right to expect.

At any rate, I threw very easy to Valle, far easier than usual. As I threw, the arm began to feel better; the swelling seemed to go down. I had discovered, back in 1964, that the act of pitching seemed to pump the fluid out of the joint and spread it through the arm, where it could be more easily absorbed. I don't say that's the medical explanation. I just say that's what I thought.

I continued to throw easy on the second day for a while. As the season progressed, I began to work harder and harder. By the end of the year, I was throwing almost as hard as ever.

The truth of the matter is that, everything else aside, there is something psychologically comforting about following the regular routine. A pitcher works only once every four days. Those three days off are impossible unless you have something to do, unless you feel you are spending your time for some purpose, working toward some end. Complete rest is not very satisfying on either count.

Dick Sisler, the manager of the Reds, kept saying through the season, "Yeah, some sore elbow! It's sore except between the first and ninth innings."

And I had to smile because, although Sisler thought he was joking, he was absolutely right.

There's an interesting point lurking around in there somewhere. Years of pitching had brought on the traumatic arthritis, and yet the act of pitching in itself lessened the effects, even while—and there is no reason to doubt this—it was also irritating the joint further. It seemed like a nice balancing of cause and effect.

Generally speaking, my arm would be swollen the day after I had pitched, would feel better after the second-day workout, would swell a bit again the third day (although less than the first day), and would be almost normal by the time I went out to warm up for the game.

There were no rules, though, and no guarantees. There were

235

times when it didn't bother me at all between starts. There were times when it remained sore enough so that I had to believe the day had finally come when I'd have to miss a turn. There were a few times—not many—when it was still stiff and tender enough after I had warmed up so that I came very close to telling Walt to have a pitcher warming up.

Once or twice it was still painful after the first couple of innings. But usually it loosened up. There were very few times when it didn't feel all right by the middle of the game, and it never stayed so bad that I had to be removed because of it.

The worst swelling of all came after I had pitched the first game of a twi-night double-header in Pittsburgh on September 1. I had lost in eleven innings, 3–2, on a two-out double by Jim Pagliaroni. (It was the game in which I broke my old National League season record for strikeouts. But that's typical. I had also lost the game, back in 1961, when I had originally set it.)

It was also my third loss in a row, bringing my record to 21–7, and my fourth start without a win. We had started the day with a one-and-a-half game lead. When Drysdale got beat, 2–1, in the second game, we ended the long night in a virtual tie with Cincinnati.

On the road treatment was somewhat restricted. My next start was scheduled for Houston. As always, the elbow loosened up after a couple of innings. That doesn't mean I was around at the finish. I came out of the game for a pinch-hitter in the eighth inning, trailing 2–1.

Boy, I was mad. Five starts without a win, and the pennant was slipping away. I stormed into the clubhouse, more red-necked than I had been in years, sighted a couple of rubbing tables standing thoughtlessly in my line of vision, picked up one of them, and flung it against the wall.

Then I thought about my elbow. *That's all I need! To have it blow up on me again because I'm throwing rubbing tables around.*

Jim Gilliam pulled the game out for us in the ninth on a two-out triple, and all of a sudden the world became a lot brighter.

Now all I had to do was wait to see whether throwing rubbing tables was bad for an arm. But, as I have been saying, exercise seems to help. We flew back to Los Angeles that night, and when I woke up the next day, my elbow felt as good as it had felt all year. On my next start I pitched a perfect game against the Chicago Cubs. I still haven't thrown another rubbing table. I'm saving it for an emergency. Shot-putting has to wait for the ultimate crisis.

I never went in to Dr. Kerlan's office for a shot of cortisone all year. There were times when I was tempted. There were times when I'd see Bob in the locker room and tell him, "I think I'll come in to see you tomorrow." But I never did.

I was even able to cut back on the medication. When the arm blew up originally, I had been given a pill called phenylbuta-zone alka, a drug which apparently attacks the inflammation head on. The only possible exception anybody might take to the pill is that it can cause a depletion in the blood count. The only reason anyone would worry about a depleted blood count is that it can get to be fatal.

The main reason I wasn't worried was that Dr. Kerlan was taking the pill himself.

Dr. Kerlan, who was a great high-school athlete and, I believe, a basketball player at UCLA, suffers from rheumatoid arthritis of the spine. In one of those bewildering ironies of life, one of the outstanding doctors in the field of orthopedics is himself bent over from arthritis. Dr. Kerlan is forever using himself as a guinea pig. Every now and then he'll come into the locker room and tell me, "I'm taking a new one. I'll let you know how it works out—I hope."

In my case, the dosage was controlled. We kept adjusting it steadily downward until I was taking only the minimal amount that would be helpful. I also tried to take it only when there was more than the usual amount of soreness. The worst part of it, as far as I was concerned, came in the early part of the season, when they were still testing my sensitivity. Every week while I was taking the pills, they'd take a drop of blood from the end of my finger so that my blood count could be checked.

Anyone who has ever had that done—and I suppose everybody has—knows how annoying that little pin wound can be for a couple of days. Every time you reach for something, you seem to stick that finger into it.

There was also the routine physical therapy as administered by the trainers at the park. Visiting writers seemed most interested in what they took to be a hot-and-cold treatment, a rubdown with hot ointment before the game and an ice bath afterward.

As far as the Capsolin—the hot red ointment—is concerned, it isn't used for a rubdown and it doesn't have a thing to do with arthritis. I had been having Capsolin applied to my arm for years. Don Newcombe used it, among others, and I probably picked it up from him. The Capsolin is an irritant; it burns the skin almost to the point of blistering. By irritating the skin, you are whipping up the circulation underneath. I use it, as Newk used it, because I have a tendency to be stiff at the beginning of a game, even in warm weather. I also had discovered, very early in my career, that I enjoy the feeling of warmth on my arm. After all these years, a mixture that might parboil someone else's arm is no more than warm to me.

When I first began to take the ice baths, we discovered that the skin would dry out and crack until it looked as if I had suffered frostbite. To protect the skin, Bill Buhler, our co-trainer, cut a full-length sleeve from the inner tubing of a tire. In Dodger Stadium we had a little plastic tub, maybe four times the size of an ordinary ice-cube container. One of the trainers would fill it up with crushed ice and water, so that the temperature would remain around 35 or 36 degrees. The tub was just large enough so that I could soak my elbow in it, rubber sleeve and all, for thirty-five to forty minutes.

On the road we'd use the regular clubhouse sink or whatever other facilities were available. Unfortunately, I seemed to pitch on a remarkable number of getaway days. By the time I had finished the ice treatment and got dressed, everybody else would be out in the bus, waiting for me and the trainers. We would board amidst a certain amount of commentary, not necessarily complimentary but always sparkling.

There is no way, of course, of knowing whether the ice treatments helped. All I know is that if you're interested in keeping swelling down, ice sure isn't going to hurt. Since the joint never did blow up, we could say that it worked. But we don't really know what would have happened to the elbow if I hadn't packed it in ice, and I wasn't about to skip a treatment to find out.

I did have some curiosity about it myself. Before the seventh game of the World Series I told Bill Buhler that we were getting a perfect chance to conduct our own medical experiment, since the season was indisputably coming to an end. An hour or so after the game, with the excitement diminished and the writers departed, I changed my mind. I was going to Palm Springs to play in a ballplayers' golf tournament, and I didn't want to have to scratch myself because of a swollen elbow. I decided to protect my golf game, which needs all the protection it can get, and let medical science shift for itself.

The possibility still exists that the arthritis can flare up at any time and, indeed, that if I push it far enough not even Dr. Kerlan, with all his magic touch, will be able to bring it back under control. It is Dr. Kerlan's view, frankly, that the medical probabilities are not on my side.

But then, the medical probability was that I would be a Sunday pitcher in 1965.

I don't want to sound as if I'm making the speech over the Thanksgiving turkey. Still, if my pitching career came to an end tomorrow I'd be grateful for the years I've had.

If I have a weakness in my elbow, it is only reasonable to conclude that it is part of the same over-all construction that gives me the ability to throw a ball hard. It all comes, after all, in the same package. I have unusually long arms, large hands, and long fingers. The long arms give more leverage. The long fingers put an extra spin on the fast ball and the curve.

An arm is a pretty good catapult. It is a catapult with a

239

hinge, however, and pitching puts the hinge under enormous pressure. Since I have accepted all the advantages of this build without the slightest hesitation, I don't see how I can complain about the disadvantages.

At the end of 1964 Dr. Kerlan was not particularly optimistic about my prospects for anything like a complete recovery. With Johnny Podres coming off an elbow operation, Buzzie decided he had better get himself another left-handed pitcher.

He went out and made the deal for Claude Osteen, and without Claude we would never have won the pennant. Osteen's record was 15–15, but the record was misleading. He was a consistently good pitcher and, most of all, he won some big games. He won a game against the Cards in July to break a four-game losing streak, and he stopped another slide in mid-September, at our lowest point in the season. Don Drysdale and I had both been beaten in Chicago, and we had fallen into third place for the only time of the season, four and a half games off the pace. Claude shut out the Cubs, 2–0, to start us off on the thirteen-game winning streak that brought us the pennant.

All in all, 1965 was the sweetest, most satisfying season any ball club ever had. We were the team that was picked to finish sixth even before we lost our best hitter. We were the team that couldn't possibly win even while we were holding on to first place through almost the entire first four months of the season. We were the team that faded in September, just as everybody said we would.

And we were the team that came back and won.

13

Along Came Lou

The 1965 season came to an end for us on May 1 in the fourth inning of a Saturday-night game against San Francisco, when Tommy Davis broke his ankle. Nobody was even looking. Tommy was on first base after leading off with a single. I was sitting on the bench even more idly than usual, since it was the day after I had pulled a muscle in my thigh. When Ron Fairly hit a ground ball to Cepeda, my eyes swung automatically to Jim Perry, who was racing for the bag to take Cepeda's throw in what was obviously going to be a bang-bang play.

Everything routine. Except that the feeling came over you that something was wrong. Tommy was still lying on the ground at second base. You could see José Pagan, the Giants' shortstop, look down, wince, and jerk his head away as if he had seen something that had made him sick.

Tommy, undecided whether to slide, had apparently caught his spikes in the hard stadium dirt. The ankle was so badly twisted that they cut the pants and socks off him before they carried him off on a stretcher.

There was very little reaction in the locker room that night, although there was none of the happiness that you'd normally get after a win, either. Injuries are a part of the game. You could only shake your head and think, "And he didn't even have to slide. Isn't that the way it always happens?"

Or maybe it just took twenty-four hours for the enormity of the loss to sink in.

Sunday was different. For some reason you associate funerals with Sunday, and there was that funereal heaviness over the locker room. We talked softly, we dressed quietly, we moved out onto the field as quickly as possible. We played a listless, losing game on the ball field, the kind of game that told us it was going to be a long, hard season. Professionals are realists. We were beat, that's all.

And then along came a guy named Lou Johnson.

Having no chance at all, we went out and won eight of our next ten games. And, oddly enough, the left fielder—the man replacing Tommy Davis—kept delivering the winning hits. Al Ferrara started us off when he knocked in two runs in an 8–2 victory.

Two days later Derrell Griffith, who was being platooned against the right-handers, hit a home run and a single to account for three of our runs in a 4–3 win. The next day Griffith knocked in our first run and scored another in another 4–3 win.

Lou Johnson had reported a couple of days after Tommy's injury, a knockabout ballplayer identified in the prints as "the best the Dodgers could bring in as a replacement was . . ."

For the first week or so he was used only as a defensive caddy in the last couple of innings. On May 10, in his first start, he beat out an infield bounder with two out in the tenth, stole second, went to third as the throw went into center field, and scored the winning run on Ron Fairly's single. A typical Dodger run, you thought. The guy fits in, anyway.

In his second game Lou hit a home run to get me off to a lead and then was hit so hard on the helmet that you could hear the sound reverberate like a gong. The first report was that he would be out for two weeks. He was back after two days. In the interim, Ferrara played left field against the Cubs and got our only hit, a three-run homer in the eighth inning, to beat Dick Ellsworth.

Then Lou came back and kept winning games for us. He kept giving us the winning hit, stealing the key base, making the great play in the field. All of a sudden you were thinking,

"Where has *this* guy been all these years?" Lou had been in the minors forever. He had played for eighteen different clubs in thirteen years. It didn't seem possible that a player of his talents could get lost over that length of time.

One day he'd tie the game in the ninth so that Fairly could hit a home run in the extra innings. A day later he'd single in the ninth to win it. With Wills out of the game, Lou led off, scored three of our four runs, stole a base, and roamed all over the outfield. With Wills back in the lineup, Lou dropped back down in the batting order and hit two home runs to knock in four runs and beat Milwaukee all by himself. Then they did it in combo, with Lou opening the ninth inning with a single and scoring the winning run on Wills' two-out single.

He also kept getting on base the hard way, by getting hit. Lou hangs over the plate, but a lot of other players hang over the plate too. Five pitchers could throw five balls at Willie Mays, front, rear, up, down, and center, and none of them would hit him. Lou gets hit.

The fifth time he was hit—in thirty-seven games—his right thumb was bruised so badly that he was out for twelve days. So he came back against Pittsburgh, singled in the deciding run, and was hit in the left leg his next time up. A batting helmet is protection enough for most hitters; Lou Johnson needed a coat of armor.

The record book shows that Lou batted .259. Pay no attention to the record book. He hit .350 in that first month, when we needed a shot in the arm. He kept us on top when we were prepared to have the bottom fall out. I truly believe that if he had hit .259 in the first month and .400 for the rest of the season, it would have been too late.

He breathed life into the locker room too. Lou is an incredibly good-natured man, bubbly and enthusiastic. His feelings are always on the surface. He enjoys himself and he enjoys life, and he has such an infectious quality about him that you enjoy life more when he's around. If you saw him clapping his hands as he ran around the bases after hitting the home run in the seventh game of the World Series, then you saw the real Lou Johnson. He wasn't trying to show people he was happy; he was *being* happy. That's Lou.

Lou lost the top of his right ear in his first year in pro ball when the club bus blew a tire and ended up in a ditch. The local doctor cut a little pocket in Lou's stomach and attached the ear piece so that the tissue would remain alive until he could have a plastic surgeon reattach it at the end of the season. By the time Lou showed up for the plastic surgery, however, the "ear" had already begun to shrivel up.

It is still in his stomach, although it is now little more than the size of a pea. Lou, who is a great spinner of stories and a great phrasemaker, likes to tell new interviewers about it because he knows their invariable response will be, "But doesn't it bother you?"

"Why no," Lou says, feigning surprise, "it doesn't eat much." That's Lou.

When we got to Milwaukee, he was called into court to pay the $234.78 state income tax he had neglected to pay when he played for the Braves in 1962. That's Lou too.

With six games left in the season, he hit a twelfth-inning home run against Cincinnati to put us in the lead to stay. That—most of all—was Lou.

The whole ball club finished with a batting average of .245, the lowest batting average to win a pennant in history. Despite the anemic batting average, I can say with complete confidence that our run-scoring ability was even worse. (We were seventh in the league in batting average, and eighth in runs scored.) Our great ability was to stay close and to get the one run we needed. Although we were eighth in runs scored, we were only shut out six times all year.

Ron Fairly was the clutch man for the first half of the season, delivering the winning hit eleven times.

Jim Lefebvre, an ex-Dodger batboy, who wasn't even supposed to be with us at the beginning of the season, came on strong at the finish to win the Rookie of the Year Award. Lefebvre delivered the winning hit in game after game over the last two months.

Don Drysdale, who hadn't missed a start in four years, cracked a couple of ribs in the middle of the year, swore the trainer to secrecy, and kept on pitching.

Jim Gilliam started the season as a coach and was reactivated after a month. The impression that Jim was called back as an emergency measure isn't correct. None of us doubted for a moment that Junior would be put back on the roster shortly after the cutdown date. The ball club had a lot of young infielders to protect, and Junior was made a coach only so that the others could be tested, sorted out, and distributed. Junior is a winning player. He is solid. He does all the things that don't get into the report of the ball game.

After you have been around baseball for a while, you understand that nobody has a good game every time out. One man delivers the winning hit today, and another man delivers it tomorrow. You also come to understand that you lose just as many ball games on mistakes as you win on great plays and timely hits. There's one thing about Gilliam that you can count on absolutely. He may go for a week without helping you, but he is never going to hurt you.

Junior doesn't rattle. In 1959, when we ended the season in a tie with the Braves, we played our last game in Chicago and took a train up to Milwaukee. Danny McDevitt, who was going to pitch the first playoff game, was seated in front of me beside Gilliam. Halfway there, Danny turned around and pointed to Gilliam, flaked out alongside him. Junior's straw hat was pulled down over his face, and he was sound asleep. "Oh no," Danny said. "I can't pitch for a nervous ball club like this."

But most of all there was Maury Wills, who hits a .286 that sounds, looks, and feels like .386. There is no sense kidding ourselves. We cannot win without Maury Wills in the lineup, because Maury has been the key to our run-scoring, especially in Los Angeles, where the fences are off on the horizon.

Wills sets our style. They said in 1965 that we play old-fashioned baseball. I don't know what they mean by that. Our game was the bunt, the steal, and the sacrifice. It was run, run, run. Someone would beat out a hit, be sacrificed to second, steal third, and score on the overthrow. Then we would gather the wagons into a circle around the dugout.

Maury has become a dominant figure in our locker room. He has come to believe that there is nothing he cannot do if he sets his mind to it. There is something almost mystical in his belief in himself, especially when you remember that he came to us after nine full years in the minors with all the uncertainties of the fringe player hoping to hold on.

It is a curious thing that while a home-run hitter is expected to fatten up in the routs, and the pitchers are certainly not supposed to let up, the opposing team becomes furious when a base is stolen after a game is apparently out of reach. Particularly the manager. The theory seems to be that the stolen base is somehow extraneous to the game, that it is an extra effort, a thumbing of the nose. Not on *our* team it isn't. Stealing bases *is* Maury's game, and—to a sometimes alarming extent—it was the Dodgers' offense.

Maury's game is to get the other team upset, to get them into a frame of mind where they are so eager *not* to let him show them up that the catcher throws the ball too hastily and the fielder rushes his tag. Result: the hasty throw is off the mark and the infielder neglects to wait for the ball.

Maury's game is called Panic!

Maury had been made captain in the first week of spring training, a title which usually entitles its bearer to carry the lineup card to the umpires and draw an extra $500 on his salary. Maury took it seriously, and his leadership had a strong, cohesive effect.

At the All-Star break, Maury had stolen fifty-one bases in eighty-three games, twenty-three games ahead of his record pace. It took a hemorrhaging of his leg, brought on by all that sliding, to keep him from breaking the record.

Ballplayers, in the normal course of clowning around, will talk about winning the pennant, especially when their team has broken on top. Nobody takes it seriously. The pennant race doesn't heat up until you've survived the dog days of July and August. Just before the All-Star break the Reds edged ahead of us. Just after the All-Star game we went off on a five-game winning streak that pulled us back in front. The next night, against Houston, we were tied 2–2 in the ninth. I had struck out the first time and hit into double plays the next two times, a development which could only bewilder students of the game. I had come up with four hits (all bloops) in the previous two games, and I looked upon myself as a fearsome hitter. With two out in the ninth, Lefebvre walked. "Get that runner to second," I said expansively, "and I'll drive him in." Junior Gilliam walked too, and there I was with a prediction on my hands. So I swung at Ron Taylor's first pitch and lined it—*lined* it—into left field to win the game.

Maury Wills' locker is across from mine. As we were dressing he turned to me and said, in complete seriousness, "We're going to win it."

I'm not superstitious about these things, of course. That's why I put my fingers to my lips and looked around to make sure nobody had overheard him. "Let's wait awhile," I said.

"We're going to win it," he said. Maury believes in the power of positive thinking. Maury believes in believing.

Early in September we were hanging on to first place, a game or so in front. This time Maury and I found ourselves almost alone in the locker room in Houston. "Don't forget what I said," he told me. "We're going to win this."

I looked at him, thought for a second, and said, "You know something? You're right."

So we immediately went into a losing streak and dropped into second place. I guess I should have kept my voice down.

By the end of the year most teams were defensing Wills by bringing the third baseman in close to guard against the bunt and playing the left fielder so shallow that there was a minimum amount of space for a fly ball to drop in. That gave the pitcher the option of pitching Maury outside and challenging him to do his best with that packed defense or pitching him inside and daring him to pull. Maury doesn't pull that well. Most managers, I would assume, feel he is doing them a favor when he tries.

The day after Lou Johnson put us back into the lead, I was pitching against Cincinnati. There were five games left in the season. We were leading, 1–0, in the seventh, a typical Dodger squeaker. The last three games I had won had all been 1–0. With men on first and second, I was supposed to bunt, but I kept fouling off the pitches and ended up walking. The pitcher was Jim Maloney, who is very fast and therefore difficult to pull. Maloney pitched Wills inside, and Maury lined the ball down the right-field line. The ball came right over my left shoulder, and I had to turn my head to make sure it went through. By the time I started running, Maury was halfway to first. By the time I got to third, he was practically behind me. I had to keep running, and while I scored without any trouble I managed to slip on the grass on the far side of the plate and dig up a good-sized divot. If I hadn't been on first, Wills might have had an inside-the-park home run.

The best thing that happened to Maury Wills in the World Series was Zoilo Versalles. Wills, by himself, is not as talented a ballplayer as Versalles. The only thing he can do better is run the bases, and even there Versalles runs a very close second. In the first two games of the Series, when everything was going the Twins' way, everybody was writing that Versalles was rising to the challenge of Wills. It was really the other way around. Versalles was the challenge to Wills. Maury is at the stage where he is roaming the world, looking for challenges so that he can overcome them. Maury believes in himself, and he has just about made a believer out of everybody else.

The pennant race was tight throughout the second half of the season, with first Cincinnati, and then Milwaukee, and finally San Francisco making runs at us. Our great rivalry is traditionally with the Giants. When we went from New York to California, we discovered that Los Angeles and San Francisco scowl at each other down the shoreline of the Pacific no less ferociously than Brooklyn and Manhattan scowl at each other across the Manhattan Bridge.

From my personal point of view, the rivalry has been more

intense in California. In my three years in Brooklyn the Giants weren't factors in the pennant race, and while tradition and the crosstown (or cross-state) rivalry may be the basic ingredients in any baseball feud, it takes a hot pennant race to ignite them.

There had been bad blood between the clubs all season. On August 22, a Sunday in San Francisco, it came to a boil. In the first inning Wills beat out a bunt and scored on Fairly's double. The second time up, Wills and Fairly both got knocked down.

If they're throwing at us, I've got to protect the guys on our side, and they have a right to expect me to protect them. The first batter up for the Giants was Willie Mays. I'd have waited for Willie to come to bat anyway, because if I'm going to throw at somebody, I'm going to throw at their best.

I'm sure Willie was looking for it, because he went halfway down although the ball was considerably over his head. To be truthful, I'd wanted to throw it much closer. I wanted to knock him down.

Still, the message was delivered. By the time Marichal came to bat, the whole thing seemed to be over. I threw a pitch, took Roseboro's return throw at the bottom of the mound, turned around, and walked back behind the rubber. Then I turned back to take the sign and I saw—I couldn't believe it! —I saw Marichal belt John across the head with the bat. That was my first awareness that anything had been happening. I had heard no crowd reaction, no nothing.

I went running in toward the plate, almost by reflex action. By the time I got there, they had turned completely around. John was now on my side, his back to me, and Marichal was on the other side of John, still holding the bat as if he was looking for an opening. I reached over John's shoulder a couple of times to try to grab the bat, but John himself was always in the way.

By this time players were pouring out of both dugouts to pull them apart. John was trying to break loose to charge at Marichal. Willie Mays had his arms wrapped around him and he was saying, "John, your eye . . . your eye . . ." The eye, I could see, was filled with blood. The sight of it made me sick because it looked as if it were hemorrhaging from the inside. For a few moments there, I really did think that John might have been blinded in one eye. It was not until he went to the dugout and had the blood wiped away that I could see that it had been dripping into his eye from the cut above. It's too bad for all concerned and for baseball that something like this had to happen.

When I returned to the pitching mound, one of the umpires came over, pointed to my hand, and said, "You'd better put something on that."

The whole side of my left hand was smeared with blood. It must have happened, I knew, when I was reaching over John's shoulder to try to grab the bat. "I don't think it's mine," I told the umpire.

I didn't have a cut, but I didn't have my concentration either. I didn't know how badly John had been hurt and I couldn't get the idea out of my head that I should have been able to do something to prevent it, which was clearly ridiculous, since I was sixty feet away and since John had been hit before I knew what was happening.

While I was trying to rewrite the scene to make it all come out different, I was walking two batters. With Willie Mays coming up, I knew I had to forget everything else and concentrate on my pitching. The first pitch went just where I didn't want it, a high fast ball over the plate. Willie hit it out of the park.

The home run made the score 4–2. We scored another run in the ninth but lost, 4–3.

It was getaway day. John had been taken to the hospital for X-rays and stitching, and we had no idea whether he'd be coming back with us or not. When we boarded the plane, there he was, with a patch over his eye and a San Francisco Giant cap on his head. That's John.

I was so upset at the time because I feel very strongly about John Roseboro. This is one of the nicest guys I know, an honest, solid guy. John is one of those rare persons who never learned how to say anything except the exact truth. If he is being interviewed in the postgame show, and the announcer says, "Sandy was great today," John may very well say, "No, he didn't have a curve at all. I thought he was lucky."

The man doesn't know how to let up, either. During our early years in Los Angeles, a promotional stunt was arranged through the Art Linkletter show with a man around town who was working with a college squad on his special theories of hitting. He had trained one kid to hit against Drysdale. We were to put our team on the field, and if the kid was able to get a hit off Don he was going to win himself a pretty fair hunk of money.

Don was in an off-day on his rotation. It was my day to throw between games, and so they tapped me to pitch to the kid in his place, which, to be perfectly fair, upset the whole theory. (Although, between you and me, the kid, who was a right-handed hitter, was far better off hitting against me than having Don come wheeling in from the side.)

I wasn't going to have my best stuff two days after I'd pitched, but I was throwing pretty good. The first pitch was a fast ball, which he took for a strike. And then John signaled for a curve. I mean, John was going to give the kid two curves in a row. I didn't have any intention of letting up on him, but it wouldn't have broken my heart to see him collect the money, either. I shook John off and threw a fast ball. The kid fouled it off.

Now John put the two fingers down, and you could see that he meant it. There was going to be no more fooling around here. If you pitched to somebody, you gave him your best shot. I threw a curve that broke pretty good and struck him out.

When John is your catcher, you know you are getting 100 per cent of what John Roseboro can give you. Any day. Any opposition. Pitching is a lonely business. When John is catching I have a feeling that I have someone on my side.

When I am having a real good day—those five or six times

a year when everything is going right—I have a mental picture of myself in action. Even while I am winding up, I have a picture of exactly what the ball is going to do and exactly where the catcher is going to catch it. I've pitched to John Roseboro for so long that, no matter who the catcher may actually be, my mental picture is of John Roseboro catching the ball. (When I pitch, I pitch to a target. The target may be the glove; it may also be the shoulder or some other part of the anatomy since batters have been known to peek behind them to see where the catcher is holding his glove.)

The Marichal-Roseboro incident was supposed to affect him, me, them, and us in varying order and degree. That kind of thing doesn't really affect a ball club for more than a day. We come to the park to put in a day's work. For a pitcher, who doesn't go again for four days, the last game is almost ancient history.

We did go into a slump, no question about that. I went into my own little bad streak, which seems inevitable once a year, and Maury was playing on a bad leg.

When San Francisco beat us twice in Los Angeles two weeks later, the pennant race had become a four-team event. We were tied with the Giants, Cincinnati was half a game behind, and Milwaukee was one full game back.

The next day we were open, and Willie Mays hit his forty-fourth and forty-fifth home runs, to put the Giants in the lead. Cincinnati won too, and we were tied for second place, one-half game behind.

Chicago was coming in to play us only one game, an odd bit of scheduling. It was hardly worth the trip.

I was pitching, and I didn't have any particular stuff at the beginning of the game. Just average. I was throwing mostly curves through the early innings. In the last half of the game, though, my fast ball really came alive, as good a fast ball as I'd had all year.

Bob Hendley, pitching for the Cubs, was great. But luck, as I say so often, is a factor in pitching. Hendley, pitching a one-hitter, ran into a perfect game. There are only a few times in any season when a pitcher finds everything working perfectly. Those are the games he should win. It didn't matter to Hendley whether his team scored eight runs the day before and eight runs the day after. The law of averages doesn't go for the pitcher, because he isn't working every day. A pitcher can find that over the full season he's the lucky guy who works the days when his team isn't scoring runs.

The one hit Hendley allowed didn't even figure in the run. The way we scored the run, and won the game, was typical of the way we scored all year. Lou Johnson walked, was sacrificed to second, stole third, and scored when the catcher's throw went into left field.

We didn't have our hit until Johnson blooped a double down the right-field line with two out in the seventh.

I, of course, sympathized with Hendley mightily. Since we already had the run, I, needless to say, rooted for him to get his no-hitter so that we could walk into the record books hand in hand. Like heck I did. I was sitting there rooting for us to score six more times and knock him out of the box.

I sympathized with him only as a fellow pitcher, only in retrospect, and—most of all—only when we were in the locker room with the game safely won.

The Giants won fourteen in a row to take their four-and-a-half-game lead. We won it, in the end, by winning thirteen straight games with the pressure piling higher and higher. The key game was undoubtedly the sixth in the streak, the last game the Braves were playing in Milwaukee's County Stadium. I had been the last pitcher for the Brooklyn Dodgers, I had pitched the last game in the Coliseum, so naturally I was getting the chance to bury County Stadium too.

While I was about it, I did everything except bury us along with it. I had nothing. Frank Bolling hit a grand-slam home run in the third inning, and I left the game, trailing 5–1. Gene Oliver must have been sad to see me depart, but he greeted Howie Reed with an inside-the-park home run to make it 6–1. The Giants were in a scoreless tie with the Reds, and with Marichal pitching they looked awfully strong.

But we came back to win in eleven innings, 7–6, and the Giants lost 7–1. Instead of being four games behind with ten games to play, we were only two games behind, all the difference in the world.

We really had the feeling as we flew back to LA to finish out the season that we had not only pulled out a ball game but turned the pennant race around.

I didn't realize that our winning streak was that long until an interviewer told me, after the 5–0 victory over the Reds—the game of Wills's bases-loaded triple—that we had won twelve in a row. I couldn't believe it. If someone had asked me, I'd have probably put the streak at no more than seven or eight.

In the ordinary rotation I was down to pitch the last game of the season. When the streak ended at thirteen straight, we were two games ahead, with two to go. If we won one more game, it didn't matter what the Giants did.

On Friday night, after the Braves had brought the streak to an end, Walt asked me whether I wanted to hold to the rotation or go the next afternoon with two days' rest so that Don Drysdale, who had shut the Braves out the night before, could come back, if necessary, and pitch the final.

I'll tell you, the innings had been piling up and I wasn't sure I could go with only two days' rest. The great advantage was that Don—who would also be going with two days' rest, of course—had been great against the Braves all year. His victory in the opening game of the series had been his fourth win and second shutout against them of the season.

When I came in Saturday morning, Walt said, "Well, how do you feel about it?"

"I'll give it a try and hope for the best," I told him. "If I can't do it, Don can pick us up tomorrow, and we'll at least know that we're having two shots at it."

The game that clinched the pennant pretty well summed up our whole season. We scored a Dodger run in the first when Gilliam walked, stole second, went to third on the catcher's overthrow, and scored on a wild pitch.

Gene Oliver—who else?—hit a home run to tie it in the fourth.

In the fifth inning, Lou Johnson walked and went to third on Lefebvre's single. Johnson was caught in a rundown when Willie Davis grounded to Joe Torre at first, but Lou slipped out of it and slid safely back to third. With the bases loaded, Roseboro walked to force in the go-ahead run. I then came up and got a base on balls to force in another. It took two pitchers to walk me. Tony Cloninger threw the first three balls, and Ken Johnson threw the fourth. We had scored our three runs on only one hit, which was just as well, since we had only two hits—another single by Lefebvre—in the entire game.

The game ended when Dennis Menke hit a fly ball to left, where Lou Johnson was waiting to catch it, squeeze it, and leap triumphantly into the air.

Nobody was more entitled.

14

The Seventh Game

Before a World Series begins, everybody predicts what's going to happen much in the same way everybody picks the winner of the Kentucky Derby. The attitude seems to be that if you study the form chart, making all the comparisons and reading all the portents, you can somehow come up with the inevitable winner. It isn't true. The variations during every game are infinite. The game is changed, as one instance, every time you decide to pitch around a man. That's precisely why you do pitch around a man—to change the pattern.

After it's over, the experts—which means everybody between the ages of seven and seventy—come up with a pattern that very neatly explains the winner's basic superiority or the loser's fatal flaw. But it is a pattern which has been imposed after the fact. It tells you what has happened, not necessarily why it happened and certainly not why it had to happen. Let the two teams play again next week, and the outcome might be entirely different.

In 1963, when we defeated the Yankees in four straight games, every game could have been turned around by one base hit. If the Yankees had won the fourth game, there was nothing to prevent them from winning four straight and taking the Series in seven games. It's never been done before? So what? Do you really believe it is never going to be done till the end of time?

In 1965 a pattern was uncovered very early. The only trouble was that the pattern kept shifting, as the teams themselves shifted between Minnesota and Los Angeles.

After we lost the first two games, scoring a grand total of three runs and making a grand total of four errors, those columnists who couldn't understand how we had won the pennant to begin with wrote us off as the worst team ever to represent anybody in any World Series. We were a disgrace, it seemed, not only to the National League but to the nation and maybe even to the boys fighting overseas. This may be called the Two-Day Minnesota Pattern.

We then came home to Los Angeles and became hitting, running, pitching fools, scoring eighteen runs and batting .354 while holding the Twins to two runs. We won in the manner we had won all year, with infield hits, stolen bases, and gung-ho base-running, while Minnesota infielders dropped balls, rushed tags, and failed to cover bases. This was not our home-and-away form at all, incidentally. Since we have moved into Chavez Ravine we have always scored far more runs on the road than at home. It was a freak. In the fourth game alone, we had six infield hits. In the fifth game I myself had a single with the bases loaded, an indication that a lot of hits were finding the right holes.

No matter. We now became the team that had revolutionized the game. Power was no longer desirable or even reputable. Speed had taken over baseball. The Twins, with all that unseemly power in their lineup, had become a disgrace to baseball and the winners in a pitifully weak league. Everything that had been said about us was now being said about them, with minor variations. This may be called the Three-Day Los Angeles Pattern.

We went back to Minnesota to play out the final two games. They won the first game, keeping the home-park pattern alive. We won the final game, however, which left everyone with no workable pattern at all.

There is one significant fact to be noted, beyond the day-to-day winning or losing. The Twins defeated us 8–2, 5–1, 5–1. We defeated them 4–0, 7–2, 7–0, 2–0. In every case, you will notice, the winning team got a well-pitched game. In every case, the winning pitcher finished. That's the oldest pattern in the world.

Through a whole season, pitching may be 60 or 70 per cent of the game; your figure is as good as mine. Given one game, the pitcher becomes as dominant a factor in the big leagues as he is in high school or college, where, as we all know, an overpowering pitcher is simply unbeatable. In any one game, then, pitching is possibly 95 per cent of the battle.

Despite everything that had been said about the somewhat unimpressive Los Angeles attack, we always managed to score a few runs if the opposing pitcher wasn't doing a good job. We didn't do much scoring in the first two games because Grant and Kaat kept us from scoring.

The key game for us was Osteen's shutout in the first game in Los Angeles, not because it established any pattern but because it put us back into the tournament. If Minnesota had won, they'd have been three games ahead and we would have been given the opportunity of becoming the first team to come back and win four straight.

I had already pitched and lost the second game because of the coincidence of the opening game falling on Yom Kippur, a situation which I think was played all out of proportion. I had tried to deflect questions about my intentions through the last couple of weeks of the season by saying that I was praying for rain. There was never any decision to make, though, because there was never any possibility that I would pitch.

Yom Kippur is the holiest day of the Jewish religion. The club knows that I don't work that day. When Yom Kippur falls during the season, as it usually does, it has always been a simple matter of pitching a day earlier, with two days' rest, when my turn happened to be coming up.

I had ducked a direct answer about the World Series because it seemed presumptuous to talk about it while we were still trying to get there. For all I knew, I could be home watching on television.

I knew I wouldn't be hurting the club one bit by not pitching. Don Drysdale had won twenty-three games. He had been our most effective pitcher down the stretch, ending the season with a string of twenty-three scoreless innings (and only one un-earned run in his last twenty-seven innings). If that isn't a pretty good opening-day pitcher, I've never seen one.

As it turned out, he didn't have a thing that day. The whole club was flat. That will happen. It will happen, in particular, when a club comes into the World Series after winning the pennant in a photo finish.

The surprise of the day, as far as I was concerned, came the next morning when I was reading the report of the game by Don Riley, the columnist of the St. Paul *Pioneer Press*. His column took the form of "An Open Letter to Sandy Koufax," in which he was kind enough to tell me how badly we had been beaten in the opener and warn me of the terrible things that lay in store for me.

"But, hey, Sandy," he wrote—to give you an idea of his keen wit and lucid prose—"can you beat the biggest threat outside a mortgage foreclosure? Can you back guys away from the plate who see T-bones on the dish? Can you overcome an anchor in a manager who gave up in the third inning? Can you overpower people who carry sticks in their hands and belong to a cause? Can you win with two runs? I don't believe so."

As an example of the gee-whiz, goshamighty school of sports-writing, which I thought had disappeared when Grantland Rice was still a boy, I found it vastly amusing. Until right at the end. "Spitballs dissolved Tuesday," he wrote. "And the Twins love matzoh balls on Thursdays."

I couldn't believe it. I thought that kind of thing went out with dialect comics.

I clipped the column so that I could send it back to him after we defeated the Twins with a friendly little notation that I hoped his words were as easy to eat as my matzoh balls. I didn't, of course. We were winners. Two runs had, it seemed, been ample. The winners laugh, drink champagne, and give the losers the benefit of all doubts.

What surprised me as much as anything else when I did get beat in my first start was that the accent was placed so heavily on my not winning when it should have been on Jim Kaat's pitching. Kaat pitched a better ball game than I did. It was as simple as that. I didn't feel that I'd pitched badly. When I left the game after six innings, we were trailing only 2–0. I've won games where I pitched worse. If Bob Allison hadn't made that tremendous sliding catch along the left-field foul line, we might have tied it, I might have stayed in the game, and—who knows?—we just might have won.

In my second start, at Los Angeles, my curve was my best pitch for the first seven innings. Unfortunately, I kept falling behind the hitters, two balls and no strikes (eight times in the game), and I'd have to forget the curve and rely on the fast ball. Even more unfortunately, I tired badly in the last two innings and, as happens when you tire that quickly, I lost the curve. I had something just as good to take its place though. Luck. After Allison walked in the eighth, the only walk of the game, Wills made a flashy play on Mincher's hot ground ball toward second and turned it into a double play.

When Quilici and Valdespino opened the ninth with back-to-back singles, I was not only one hit away from losing the shutout, I was one hit away from being taken out of the game. Nossek hit a solid line drive. Wills turned it into a game-ending double play.

From the time we returned to Minneapolis, we could see the situation developing where I might be tapped to pitch the seventh game.

After we lost the sixth game, Walt called Don and me over in the locker room and asked, "Are you both ready?" We both told him that we were. "Well, I don't know yet," he said. "I want you both to be ready. I'll let you know tomorrow."

I had pitched with two days' rest at the end of the season so that Don could get in an extra turn if the whole pennant race came down to the last day of the year. If I were to pitch with two days' rest again, I would be taking Don's regular turn.

I had been hoping, and I'm sure Don was too, that Osteen would win the sixth game and end the whole thing right there.

At that stage of a World Series, you're not the least concerned about who is going to be the winning pitcher. You just want to win and get it over with.

But ever since I began to win games with some regularity, people have been trying to get Don and me to say something that would indicate we were jealous of each other. I suppose that kind of thing is to be expected. Back in Brooklyn there used to be an annual spring story about Newcombe and Hodges having a fist fight, although Newk and Gil were two of the best-natured men alive.

Don and I have been together too long for that. We learned about pitching together. We lived together for six months in the army. He'd stay at my house on weekends while we were at Fort Dix. I'd spend Thanksgiving and other holidays with him and his folks after I moved to Los Angeles.

For the most part we found the stories amusing. Every once in a while one of us would even say, "Hey, shall we have a fight and make everybody happy, or shall we wait until the next time it comes up and sell tickets?"

The whole atmosphere seems to change on the seventh day of a World Series. When you wake up in the morning you know at once that this is the day it ends. It's like discharge day in the Army. Tomorrow you'll be a civilian again, a free man with the whole long winter stretching out ahead of you.

There's a finality about it that is rather comforting. We will go out this one last time, we will give it everything we have this one last time, and nobody can expect any more than that.

At breakfast the jokes are on the order of, "Do good today and you can take tomorrow off." At the park you even have a friendly word for the Minnesota players you know. "Have a good winter," you say. "See you at spring training."

There is still, however, the last game to be played. On the bus to the park, Don and I were sitting in back, kidding each other about which one of us was going to pitch it. I kept telling Don why it was going to be him. He kept telling me why it was going to be me.

We were still taking off our street clothes when Walt called us over to his locker again. Lefty Phillips, the pitching coach, was there with him, but Walt did all the talking.

"I haven't made any announcement yet," he said. "But it's going to be the left-hander." Walt is not a man given to long speeches. He didn't have to explain his thinking to us, but he did. "First of all," he said, "I want to start a left-hander against this club. Second, if I have to make a change I want it to be left-right-left. If Don has to come in he'll catch their right-handed lineup. If they go to their left-handed lineup against him and we have to take Don out later, they'll be locked in with their lefties against our left-hander."

He didn't have to tell us that the final left-hander was Ron Perranoski, any more than he had to have Ron over there with us. For Ron it was a routine day. He's always in the bullpen ready to come in if he is needed over the last half of the game.

Walt had another reason for starting me, too. If I came up in the third or fourth inning with, say, the bases loaded and one out, Don, as our number one right-handed pinch-hitter, could bat against Kaat and stay in the game.

There was no doubt that it was the sound way of doing it.

"I'll do my best," I said. And then I told Don, "But it's good to know that you're out there."

"I'll be there," Don said. "But you're not going to need me."

Before I left the locker room for the final time to go out and warm up, Walt told me, "If you feel like you haven't got it any more, let me know right away. We've got Don ready. We'll get him in there quick."

He undoubtedly told John Roseboro the same thing. "If he's beginning to lose it, let me know quick."

In one way, it was like spring training. We were set, if necessary, to have three men go three innings each. In another way, it wasn't. I didn't go out with the intention of pitching three innings. I went out with the idea that I was going to try to do a good job for nine innings.

In the first inning I had a curve, even though it wasn't a very good one. All I can say for it is that it was a better curve than I had for the rest of the day. I even got Earl Battey looking at a curve to end the inning after two men had walked, the best curve I threw all day.

Roseboro led off our half of the third with a double and remained on base throughout the inning, which meant that I had no chance to talk things over with him. After the last half of the third inning, I walked over to him in the dugout and told him, "John . . . *bad* curve ball."

John looked at me and said, "Well, there's one thing about it. It's . . . got . . . to . . . get . . . better. There's just no other way for it to go."

After six innings I walked over to him again, stared at him accusingly, and said, "You *lied* to me."

The game was played in something remarkably close to absolute silence. When Versalles struck out to lead off the Minnesota first, there had been no reaction at all. Leading off for us in the fourth inning, Lou Johnson hit a high fly along the left-field foul line. You could see it had plenty of distance; the only question was whether it was going to stay fair. On the bench, everybody leaped up, cutting off my vision. I was sitting back the way a pitcher is supposed to, conserving my energy, but I could tell by the reaction from the guys in front of me that it was a home run. From the stands there was still that absolute silence. Lou, rounding first base, held up for just a second. The ball was on the field, which meant that it had to have hit the screen on the inside of the foul line. There was no way for the ball to be on the field unless it was a home run. Still, the roar of the crowd is such an accepted part of a home run that Lou had to reassure himself by looking to the umpire for a sign.

Up in the press box, they tell me, some of the writers closed their typewriters and said, "One run, that's enough." Not from where I was sitting. From where I sat, I'd have liked about ten more runs before the inning ended. We got one more.

The fifth inning was the one I had to survive. Don Mincher led off. Mincher was the only batter I changed styles on during the Series. The report on him was that he was a good fast-ball hitter. Facing him in the first game, I had the feeling that he was looking for the curve. In my second start, I went to the fast ball on him. In this final game I'd probably have stayed with the fast ball under any circumstances. The fast ball was my best pitch, and I'd have to be willing to put my best against his best. Having no curve ball at all, I had no choice. Mincher fouled out to third base on the first pitch.

Frank Quilici followed with a double to the base of the wall in left center. Rich Rollins pinch-hit for Kaat. The count went to 2–2. We threw him a curve ball on the outside corner, a little higher than I might have wanted, but, I thought, a strike. The kind of pitch that every pitcher wants and every hitter wants too. The kind of pitch a hitter has to have all the guts in the world to take with two strikes on him. No matter which way the umpire calls it, he is going to get a dirty look from someone.

Ed Hurley called it a ball. You are not allowed to question a ball-and-strike call, on penalty of swift expulsion. You *are* allowed to stroll in and ask the umpire where the pitch was, purely in the spirit of scientific inquiry. "It was close," Hurley told me, meaning close to the strike zone, not close to the batter.

Although neither Hurley nor I was aware of it, he was umpiring his last game. He called such a good game that I hate to think that I was the guy who gave him his last beef. Not that it was much of a beef. "At this time of the year," I said, "I might want a close pitch."

For the only time in the game the crowd was up and screaming. Roseboro called out something to me as I returned to the mound, and I couldn't make out what he was saying. I came back a few steps toward him, and I still couldn't make it out. I was pretty sure it had something to do with the signs. When Quilici doubled we had gone from the simple one-finger signs to a more complex series of signs, something that is done automatically when a man is on second base, where he can see the signs being flashed.

To make it as difficult as possible for the base-runner to break the code, you keep switching to a different set of signs after every two or three pitches, according to signs agreed upon before the game. We had already switched once with Rollins at bat, and I knew it was time to switch again.

I also knew I wasn't going to throw another pitch until I was sure I was reading the same signs John was giving. In my last start of the season, against Milwaukee, there had been a mix-up on one of the switches. Well, not really a mix-up. John was sure he knew which set of signs we were going to, and I was sure I knew. The idea isn't to be sure separately; it's to be sure together. I had switched to the wrong set, the pitch had gone to the backstop, and the Braves had ended up with men on second and third instead of first and second.

I finally walked all the way back in. All John had called to me was, "Are you sure you know which ones we're using?" I guess John remembered the Milwaukee game too.

As it turned out, it didn't matter. The 3–2 pitch was way up high, and there were men on first and second.

Versalles had been a tough hitter all during the series. He hadn't been a particularly lucky one. His luck wasn't about to get any better. With a 1–2 count he hit a shot down the third-base line for what looked like a sure two-base hit. But Gilliam made a tremendous backhand stop, fell to his knees, scrambled up, and ran to third for the forceout.

Anyone who didn't feel the game was over after Johnson's home run seemed to think it was over right there. There is a feeling that when a pitcher is pulled out of a hole by a great play he looks upon it as a sign that he is going to win. That isn't the way you think, though. Any pitcher worth his salt looks upon the great play as part of his pitching repertoire. You have to. You know that more times than not you are going to need a great play somewhere along the way to keep you in the ball game. The importance of Gilliam's play to me at the moment was that I had two outs in the inning and nobody had scored.

If there is any psychological effect at all, I suspect it is on the team at bat. When a great play is thrown at you, right where you are about to break the game open, you cannot help thinking, "What do we have to do to score a run around here?"

Important as the second out was to me, I didn't realize I had two outs immediately. I had been concentrating so completely on the situation that I had forgotten that Mincher had led off the inning. When Wills and Tracewski came in toward the mound to make sure I was settled down, I asked, "Who am I supposed to pick up?" What that means is that I wasn't sure whether Dick or Maury was going to be covering second base if the ball was hit back to me. "Dammit," Dick said, "wake up. There's two out. You throw to first."

Nossek grounded out to Wills. Rollins was the last batter to reach base until the ninth inning.

In the last two innings I had my best stuff and my best control of the game. I had made no conscious adjustment; I had never been able to figure out what I was doing wrong. It happened the way it usually happens. Everything had fallen into place, slowly, during the game.

The weather helped too. It had rained during the night, and the temperature was in the low sixties, perfect for pitching at that stage of the season. In that last game against Milwaukee, when the temperature had been up in the nineties, I had felt physically drained over the last couple of innings.

By now you should know exactly what I was thinking as I came out to pitch the ninth. I'm not going to walk a man if I can possibly help it, right? I'd just as soon have him hit the ball out of the park as put him on—right?—because in either case I've got the tying run at the plate. I had the hitters who could hit it out, too: Oliva, Killebrew, Battey, and Allison.

According to our report, Tony Oliva almost never pulled the ball, possibly because he was playing with a bad finger. We had been giving him right field, and—there's no other way to put this—he had been having a very bad Series. His best moment had come against me in the first game I'd pitched. I had given him the outside pitch he wanted, on a two-strike count, and he had gone to left field for two bases to knock in the first run. He was going to have to hit an inside pitch off me in this spot. He went to left field anyway, grounding out to the third baseman.

Harmon Killebrew is a good hitter. He had been hitting me well all along. The pitch I didn't want to throw him was a low inside fast ball. I had thrown him exactly that pitch in my first start, right after Oliva's double, and he had rifled it into left field to knock in the second run. I had made the same mistake in the second game I pitched, and he had lined to left field.

When you make a mistake on a hitter like Killebrew and the ball stays in the park, you feel you've got away with it. Darned if I didn't throw him the same pitch again, on a 2–1 count. He rifled it into left field for another single. That changed everything. With the tying run at the plate, you could be sure I was going to throw nothing except outside fast balls to Earl Battey and Bob Allison.

It changed things in another way too. With Killebrew on first base, I had to pitch off a stretch. There are times when you feel you might be a better pitcher off the stretch, especially when your timing is off. But in the late innings, when you are tired, you are bound to have better stuff from the wind-up, because you are pitching, as it were, off a running start. This late in the game I could have used the running start.

Hitters change. I had been facing Battey in spring training for years, and he had always been a pull hitter. The scouting report said that he had turned completely around all of a sudden and now looked to hit everything into right and center. There was no reason not to believe it. Looking back to my first two years with the Dodgers, I could remember that between the 1955 and 1956 World Series Gil McDougald of the Yankees had changed from a hitter who pulled everything to left to a hitter who stroked everything to right.

In this spot, though, Battey figured to be swinging for the home run, and when you swing for the home run you're going to be pulling. If he went with the outside fast ball and hit it to right—well, that's where we were playing him.

He swung at the first two pitches and took the third one on the corner for a called strike.

Bob Allison fouled the first pitch back and took a ball just off the corner. I had thrown five straight pitches to the same spot. Well, you have to give the hitter credit for thinking too. Especially since Allison is strong enough to hit the ball out of the park in right field if he decided to go that way. To vary the pattern, I threw the 1–1 pitch up under his chin. That should keep him honest. On the next two pitches, we went right back to the fast ball on the outside of the plate. Allison swung at them both and missed them both.

15

I Was Ready
to Walk Out the Door

One of baseball's proudest boasts is that it is the one profession where a man can earn what he is worth. That isn't
necessarily so. It would be far more accurate to say that a
ballplayer's salary is limited only by what his boss is willing
to pay him. Contract negotiations have always been "nego-
tiation by ultimatum," which is, of course, a complete contradiction in terms.

Once you sign your first baseball contract, you are owned by
the club, a condition that is never completely absent from the
bargaining table. Management will talk to you and they'll let
you make your points and, if you are patient enough, they'll
come up to their maximum figure. But the threatening under-
tone is always there, the hidden clamp. The owner can always
say, "All right, we've talked enough. You will now accept what
we are offering or you are no longer in the business of playing
baseball."

As a ballplayer, you have only one alternative to signing
at the owner's figure: *not* signing. There, that doesn't sound
so revolutionary, does it? You can say to him, right out in
the open, "No, I will not sign at that price, even if it means
I cannot play baseball for a living any more."

That has the secondary value of adding to the humor—and
therefore the health—of the nation, since it never fails to
bring forth gales of laughter from the sports pages. *Nobody*
ever quits. The scene always drawn—the sports page carica-

ture—is of the country boy threatening to sit out the season on his farm, where he is presumably working for little more than his keep. The caricature doesn't happen to be true any more. The ballplayer has changed. All athletes have changed. The football player can even play out his option and take his services over to the other side of the field.

A ballplayer can negotiate in the true meaning of the word only if he is prepared to set the minimum figure he will take and walk out the door if he doesn't get it. If you are not prepared to walk out the door and never come back, you can sing your songs and dance your dances, but it is all wasted talk and wasted motion.

Much as it would have pained me to leave baseball, I was prepared to walk out the door. I was halfway gone when they called me back.

It may not come as a complete surprise if I reveal that Don Drysdale and I held out as a team this spring, thereby narrowing the negotiating gap and enriching the language with the tantalizing question, "Holdout or holdup?"

I would suppose we had as many supporters as detractors, and yet it was astonishing to me to learn that there were a remarkably large number of American citizens who truly did not believe we had the moral right to quit rather than work at a salary we felt—rightly or wrongly—to be less than we deserved. Which leaves you, in their eyes, with no choice at all. Just take what the nice man wants to give you, get into your uniform, and go a fast twenty-five laps around the field.

The nice man was offering me $100,000 and Drysdale $85,000, and I am perfectly aware that you can't expect any great outpouring of sympathy while you are explaining why you won't take the $100,000. One hundred thousand dollars is a lot of money, and I realize it. But I also realize that it's just a salary, not an honor. Before this season, baseball had become so successful in establishing $100,000 as the ultimate salary to which any player could decently aspire that it had become something like a plaque in the Hall of Fame. The

Giants had paid Willie Mays $105,000 because they wanted him to be the highest-paid player in baseball, but it was recognized as that—$5000 above the limit.

In an earlier era, Babe Ruth had put up two walls for future generations to shoot at: 60 home runs and $80,000.

Who said $100,000 was the limit? To begin with, a ball-player's value lies in two areas, what he does on the field and what he brings in at the gate. As a ballplayer, Ted Williams was worth $100,000 years before he got it. Toward the end of his career, when he wasn't playing that often or hitting that well, Williams may not have been worth $100,000 as a player but he was worth $500,000 at the gate. The same thing was true of Stan Musial in his last few years, and it is true of Mickey Mantle today. He is worth $100,000 if he does nothing but pinch-hit, because he is Mickey Mantle and people come to the park to see him.

When the wall came tumbling down this year, there were people who seemed offended to the marrow of their bones at the idea that a ballplayer could think he was worth more than $100,000.

I don't know what anybody is worth. I thought one of the things we believed in this country was that a man is entitled to whatever he can honestly get.

If television hadn't been invented, everybody's profits would be smaller and so would our salaries. But if television hadn't been invented, Barbra Streisand wouldn't be getting $500,000 for one show a year, would she?

Is she worth it? They're paying it, aren't they? That means she's worth it.

The big difference is this: when Streisand appears on television, she gets paid for the number of people she can draw to the set. When she sings in a concert she gets a guarantee against the option of taking a percentage of the gate. In an 1800-seat Broadway theater, the actor who can fill the seats is guaranteed $5000 a week against a percentage of the box office.

Don and I could demonstrate that we drew people into

the ball park. Nobody denied it for a second. We weren't asking for a piece of the action. We were only asking that the ball club consider the fact that we did bring people into the park as well as the fact that we had won forty-nine ball games between us. I cannot see how that's a challenge to the structure of the game.

We challenged the structure of the game, too, it seems, by asking to negotiate as a team. If we got away with it, the critics said, the next thing you knew a whole outfield or in-field would insist on bargaining as a unit.

So what? The idea that a $50,000 shortstop will refuse to sign unless a $10,000 second baseman gets what he wants is ridiculous. The $50,000 shortstop has always signed, even when he himself didn't get what he wanted. Ballplayers are not unrealistic. They know they are not going to be paid beyond their worth.

With football having elbowed baseball out of the top position—let's be honest about this—you would think baseball would be thankful for every player of sufficient status to command a huge salary. Looking at it realistically, our million-dollar holdout gave baseball its first publicity victory over football since Sonny Werblin signed Namath for $400,000 to be paid out over some long period of time.

There were some cynics who even went so far as to hint that we were influenced by the tremendous bonuses that were being thrown around by the professional footballers. Well, I'll tell you. When a player fresh out of college gets half a million dollars, it certainly does set a fellow to thinking. It sets you to thinking that there's a lot of money around these days, in baseball as well as in football.

Nor did it go completely unobserved that the football players were preceded by lawyers, most of whom took care to instruct their clients not to even talk to a representative of the club until after the deal was made.

There were other onetime admirers who hinted broadly that our formerly sound values had been corrupted by a "Hollywood-type" business manager. (And *you* know they're the worst kind.) To such contamination I must once again plead guilty, even though I must also report that Hollywood-type lawyers do not seem any more nimble than the Chicago-type and Texas-type lawyers who sent their college boy out into life with undreamed-of wealth. Much as I hate to disappoint anyone, the idea was ours. Don's and mine.

It seems exceedingly odd to me that any clubowner would object to dealing with an agent, especially since the best agent in the world couldn't alter the built-in advantage the reserve clause gives the club. I was under the impression that everybody in this country is entitled to representation. Walter O'Malley, as a lawyer, was a professional representative himself. Even the worst criminal in the world is entitled to representation (although that's not a comparison I would want to push too far, since a criminal is trying to preserve his freedom, while we are only trying to improve our finances).

Ballplayers do need agents. We need them for the same reason that writers, actors, singers, and dancers need them. We need them because *it is difficult to sell yourself when what you are selling is a talent not a product.* You are put in a position of bragging about yourself, of telling how good you are, a position which most of us find uncomfortable and just a little ridiculous.

Don and I could undoubtedly have negotiated far more effectively for each other than for ourselves. I could have sat there and spoken for hours on his ability, his personality, his over-all contribution to the team, without any of the natural inhibitions I'd feel in trying to say the same things about myself. It's impossible to say those things about yourself.

It is also difficult for a ballplayer to negotiate for himself because the man you are negotiating with holds your future completely in his hands. You have become conditioned from the beginning to courting—or at least hoping for—his good will. The marginal player cannot completely erase the fear that if he gets the general manager mad he might be dropped a year or two early. It is a wholly unrealistic fear, in all probability, and yet it has to be there in the back of his head. What's a marginal player going to do anyway? Quit over $1000? As soon as the general manager makes it clear that his patience is at an end, that the club has gone as high as it is going, negotiations—such as they are—have come to an end.

The man on the other side of the desk, being a professional at the business of negotiating, knows that he has all these advantages working for him, and he uses them.

An agent is a professional bargainer. He has no compunctions about using the tools of his trade either. He is there as your representative. His job is to sell you. He can exaggerate all your assets and he can minimize all your failings. He has no personal relationship to be preserved with the man he is bargaining with.

Management has another gambit that is almost impossible for the player himself to handle. They play you off against one another. When the Dodgers were in Brooklyn, with a small ball park and a great team, they would always sign Pee Wee Reese first. Under normal circumstances, the salary released to the press is a little high. With Reese, I suspect the figure was always a little low. Because as soon as the others saw what Reese was getting they could pretty well guess what they were going to get.

If they didn't, the front office had only to ask, "Do you really think you're worth more than [as much as, almost as much as] Pee Wee?"

If an agent were in there dealing for you, he could easily say, "Sure, I think he's worth more than Pee Wee. He did this and he did that." What does the agent care? He's just there to get the most that he can for you.

Or he can say, "Reese's dealings with this club are his own concern. I'm here to represent *my* client.

In fact, an agent just might even commit the ultimate indiscretion of saying, "If you're going to use Reese's salary as a basis for negotiating with me, then let me see Reese's signed contract so that I'll know what you *are* paying him."

When I signed the original bonus contract, I also signed, if you remember, a two-year contract calling for the minimum $6000 salary. That was all right. I was frozen to the Dodgers through those two years, and my contribution, as it turned out, was nothing to flex my muscles about.

The club won pennants in both of those years, which meant that I picked up two World Series checks to augment my salary. Augment, did I say? Double would be more like it. On the other hand, everybody was getting pay raises in those happy years except me.

In my third year, my salary went up to $6500, not as a reward for my services or a tribute to my bargaining prowess but simply because no club keeps a big-league player at the absolute minimum for three years.

I was not so young and innocent that I wasn't aware that the total salary list was budgeted or that the seating capacity of Ebbets Field limited the budget. The ball club always makes it clear that it has to take care of the older players first. The implicit promise is that you don't have to worry, young fellow, because once you've accumulated those service stripes you're going to be taken care of too.

It never occurs to you at that point in your career that a token raise of $1000 in each of the first two years would be worth $20,000 over the next ten years. It never occurs to you that when they dole out that $20,000 at the end of your career they are really turning over money they have been, in effect, holding for you.

You're not geared to think that way at all. You're young and relatively footloose, and you're happy to be in the big leagues. It is only much later that you begin to wonder whether it wouldn't be fairer if the man who is a top player in his third year were paid a top salary in his third year. By holding your money, baseball forces you to stay on past your peak.

My career as a near-minimum player would probably have lasted another year if the Dodgers hadn't moved to Los Angeles. When I rejoined the team after coming out of the Army, I had no contract. The night before the season began I signed a blank contract. I had to be signed in order to be eligible to play.

In Brooklyn I had lived with my folks. In Los Angeles I was living in an apartment house and eating in restaurants, the first time I had ever come face to face with the inflationary spiral. When you're a big-league ballplayer you have to live like a big-leaguer, dress like a big-leaguer, and tip like a big-leaguer. The waiter doesn't care whether you're only getting the minimum. After about a week, I projected what my expenses were going to come to, whistled softly, gulped twice, and put in a call to Buzzie.

He was going to have to raise my salary, I said, whether he thought I deserved a raise or not. "I just can't afford to live on what I got last year," I told him. "And it doesn't make too much sense to play big-league baseball at a loss."

"How much do you think you need?" he asked me.

"At least $10,000."

My first paycheck was based upon a salary of $10,000. Don't jump to the conclusion that I kicked myself for not asking for even more. I still felt I was lucky to be in the majors, and I was grateful for the raise.

For the first four years, then, I didn't even make a pass at negotiating. I just signed on the dotted line.

In the next two years I showed a certain amount of effectiveness. In 1958 I had one of the best won-lost percentages on the club (11–11), which demonstrates conclusively what a woeful year it was. My salary went up to $14,000 in 1959 (8–6). I could say I had something to do with the winning of a pennant. When you win the pennant in a playoff, *everybody* has something to do with it.

My salary went up to $19,000, which is not exactly a sky-rocket to the moon. I knew, however, that pitchers were paid not so much on the won-lost record as on the number of innings they had worked. If you pitched close to two hundred innings, you had to be in the regular rotation the greater part of the season. Win, lose, or draw, they still hadn't been able to find anybody better than you.

After the 1960 season I found that it wasn't necessarily so. Although I did not have a good year I had pitched 175 innings, the fourth highest on the club (Drysdale, 269; Podres, 228; Stan Williams, 207). My contract called for a cut from $19,000 to $18,500.

Wrong again.

Since I had been so dissatisfied with my performance that I had seriously considered looking for some line of work to which I was perhaps better suited, I was hardly in the proper frame of mind to fight like a tiger. I had made up my mind to give it one last all-out effort. I took the cut with scarcely a whimper.

In 1961 I had my first good year (18–13, 256 innings, 269 strikeouts). In the course of being interviewed in Los Angeles, I was asked whether I thought I was going to have any trouble over salary. I answered that I didn't see why. I felt I deserved a raise, I said, and I thought I'd get it.

When Buzzie and I got down to the real bargaining, we had no trouble at all. Except that he said, "Look, I'd rather you wouldn't negotiate your salary through the newspapers."

I hadn't been aware that I had. Still, I could see his point. If players were quoted as expecting big raises, he could, with some justification, feel they were putting pressure on him. When I told him that I wanted a raise of $10,000, he told me that I couldn't, after all, expect to make it all in one year. It was only my eighth year coming up. He raised me $9000, to $27,500.

After 1962, the year of the finger, the salary went up to $35,-000. Now, $35,000 is not a buck and a half. It's a lot of money. On the other hand, I was in my ninth year in baseball and I knew very well that there were players who had been with the club only three or four years who were making more than I was.

I had seen almost all my original teammates pass out of baseball, and each time one departs he is reminding you that you'll be walking that route soon too. Beyond that, the close call with the finger had driven home the point that it is not a bad idea to have enough money put aside so that you will have some control over what you do after you can no longer play ball.

After that first real good year in 1963, I felt I was entitled to a healthy increase in salary. Like double the $35,000 I had received the year before, plus another $5000 for good measure, good conduct, and good luck.

They could hardly say I didn't deserve it; I had just completed the best year of my career, sweeping the boards in percentage (25–5), ERA (1.88) strikeouts (306) and shutouts (11). I had won the Cy Young Award and the MVP Award. Not to mention the two victories in the World Series sweep over the Yankees.

While I was in Rochester during the winter to pick up the Hickok Belt as the Athlete of the Year, I was asked how much money I intended to ask for. Mindful of Bavasi's admonition against negotiating through the newspapers, I said, "I made $35,000 the past year, and I don't intend to ask for anything ridiculous this year."

That was non-committal enough, it seemed to me, so that Buzzie could certainly not accuse me of negotiating through the press.

To protect the reserve clause, the ball clubs have to get their contracts into the mail by January 15. Once you're in a position where the club knows it's going to have to negotiate with you personally, that first contract is meaningless. They'll either write in the previous year's salary or even the minimum salary, just to satisfy the legalities. The player has the option of sending it back with either a funny note, an indignant note, or no note at all.

About three weeks before we were due to leave for spring training, Buzzie and I had our first talk. As a matter of fact, my recollection is that I just happened to bump into him while I was picking up something at the public-relations office. I had my strategy nicely planned by then. I began by asking Buzzie about the possibility of an attendance-bonus clause. Now I knew as well as anyone that Mr. O'Malley's philosophy of operation does not include giving anybody a percentage of the attendance. I figured that if I gave Buzzie a chance to turn me down on something, I would be making it that much more difficult for him to turn me down on the salary—the only thing I *was* interested in.

I also brought up the subject of the players' participation in pay television, which was supposed to go into effect during the season, just to serve notice that the ballplayers were thinking in terms of sharing in the inevitable bonanza—as, indeed, they are. And as, indeed, they should.

As I expected, Buzzie pushed the whole pay television issue aside as a policy matter that would eventually have to be thrashed out between the league and the players' association.

Having heard him say no twice I thought the time had come where he should be ready to say yes. I saw no real reason why I shouldn't let him know exactly what I wanted. It has always seemed rather silly to me for grown men to start out by throwing absurd figures at each other so that they can proceed slowly and laboriously toward some middle area where they both know they are going to land from the beginning.

I told him I wanted $75,000. He offered me $65,000. At that moment, I suppose, I could have said, "Okay, let's split the difference," and we'd have shaken hands. If we had, my relationship with the club would have been entirely different.

Instead, I told Bavasi that, while I would *settle* for $70,000, if that was as high as he was willing to go, the club could make me happy by giving me that extra $5000, if only as a token payment for the years when I felt I had been underpaid. It was important to me—don't ask me why—to know that they agreed with me.

It was left there, with the understanding that we both would ponder upon our positions and meet again on another day.

It may seem hopelessly naïve, put down this way in black and white, to have weakened my position right at the start by telling him that I would settle for the lesser figure. I thought that complete candor on my part would call forth complete candor on his part. I thought that, after the season, we were in an era of good feeling. And, most of all, I hadn't given up any real bargaining position because in baseball you don't have any bargaining position to give up.

You're darned right I'd take the $70,000 if that was all he was going to give me. I had no other choice.

I didn't hear from him again. I didn't realize that the longer I waited, the weaker my position was becoming.

Three days before the Dodger plane was due to leave for spring training, I called Buzzie to suggest that we get together. "When the plane leaves," I said, "I'd like to be on it."

Actually, I *did* know at this point that I was in trouble. According to the morning papers, Drysdale had just signed for $72,500. I could expect Bavasi to ask me whether I really felt I was entitled to as much money, after only three good years, as Drysdale was getting after seven good, solid years. This is the negotiating gambit, as you may have gathered, that gripes me more than any other, because they are playing around with your relationship with your own teammates. You know you're going to be playing alongside the guy all year, and you don't want word to filter back to him, in garbled form, that you were downgrading him to the front office in an attempt to raise your own salary.

Neither Bavasi nor I budged from our previous positions. We parted without setting another date to talk. Either Bavasi was going to be calling me the next day, I thought, or the plane was going to be leaving without me.

The next day I picked up the paper and saw a headline; KOUFAX THREATENS DODGERS—$90,000 OR I QUIT.

WHAT!

What $90,000? *What* quit? What was I going to do if I quit, go play ball for the Little Sisters of the Poor?

The story said that I had demanded $90,000 and the Dodgers had flatly refused to pay it. When you got down into the body of the story—*if* you got down that far—you found that the $90,-000 which had been mentioned so prominently seemed to include "fringe benefits" such as an attendance bonus, a subject which had been completely dropped weeks earlier.

It went on to tell the folks about the Dodgers' "fine offer of $65,000." It quoted Bavasi as saying, "If Koufax insists on his demands we would place him on the voluntarily retired list, and add another minor-league pitcher to our roster."

Bavasi was also quoted as saying, "I have told Sandy this. I also told him that both of us have an obligation to twenty-four other players."

The story went on. "Strange as it may seem in this particular instance, both O'Malley and Bavasi are on Koufax' side, but are compelled by 'fringe' circumstances to stand their ground, even to the point of letting Sandy quit."

They were great, they were generous, they were even on my side. It was just that out of consideration for my teammates they had to turn me down reluctantly and send me on my way.

That made me picayune, selfish, and inconsiderate.

Even assuming that the $90,000 figure had been right, I had been under the incredible misconception that I had been asking the Los Angeles Dodgers, not my teammates, to pay my salary.

When a club sets a budget for salaries, it's only an arbitrary administrative decision, not a wage freeze passed down from on high. If a budget is set by administrative decision, it can be changed by administrative decision. The Dodgers, having just completed two straight years of all-time record-breaking attendance, could throw another $5000 into the pot without blinking an eye.

I'll tell you, the whole tone of the story threw me into a spin. I'd had one big year, it said, and now I wanted it all, the whole wide world with a fence around it. At best, I was Jesse James, mask and all. At worst, I was a quitter.

What threw me most of all was the deliberately created impression that we were $25,000 apart. "Koufax came down $5000 from his first figure," Bavasi was quoted as saying, "but he hasn't budged since."

No one reading that story would have dreamed that we were, at most, only $5000 apart.

I had asked for an extra $5000 as a gesture to show that maybe I had been underpaid, and this was their answer. It hadn't even come to me direct, it had come through what I could only assume to be a leaked story.

And this was the club that had told me not to negotiate through the newspapers.

I called Bavasi immediately and told him I wanted to come in again and try to get it settled. I don't know whether I was more hurt or angry. I was too stunned to have any clean, sharp reaction at all. Except disbelief. I couldn't believe they had done it.

I didn't mention the story to Bavasi at all. There was nothing to be gained, as far as I could see, by accusations or recriminations. We still didn't get off ground zero on the contract, but we didn't have an awful lot of time. I didn't arrive at the park until late in the morning and I had to leave to keep a luncheon engagement.

When I walked out into the reception room, I walked into the middle of a crowd. The place was jammed with television cameras, photographers, and newspapermen.

"How does it look, Sandy?" one of them called.

"Not too good," I said. It sure didn't. I hadn't known myself that I was going to be in the office when I got out of bed that morning, and yet the whole communications industry of southern California had magically appeared to report on whether I had signed my contract or was still doing my well-known imitation of Jesse James.

I looked at that crowd and I thought, "Sandy, you've been set up again. Two days out of two."

I went back into Bavasi's office and told him, "Don't go away. Let me make a call to say that I'm going to be late, and we'll talk some more."

I withdrew the request for the extra $5000, and we settled for the $70,000 I had been willing to settle for in the first place.

The difference between $70,000 and $75,000 is a difference only in the ego of the player. I had made that clear from the beginning.

I had spent the winter on mostly unpaid appearances, to attend sportswriters' dinners or dinners which involved kids' groups or the raising of money for charity. These were the people who had a right to expect me to appear, I felt, and they were also the affairs that baseball itself had a right to expect me to attend.

I am aware that a lot of people, including some of my best friends, thought I overreacted to what was, after all, just a routine publicity gimmick. The Dodgers had got themselves some publicity at the opening of spring training and pressured me into taking their figure in the bargain. A twin killing, as they say up in the press box.

I didn't see it that way. I had specifically put it in terms of "Look, I've never beefed. I've never given you a second's trouble. I'm conceding that you're being generous in your offer. Throw in that little extra package just because I don't think you've always been that generous in the past."

If they didn't want to make me feel happy, fine. But they were not only turning me down, they were showing me exactly what they thought of me. I was an employee, and they were my employers.

I got the message. I was never going to make the same mistake again, because I was never going to presume a relationship that did not exist. There is no law that says you have to like your boss, or that your boss has to care.

Actually, I could hardly have been accused of "overreacting" at the beginning. At the beginning, I didn't react at all.

It was only afterward that I began to get mad, not only about what had happened but about the docile way I had accepted it. I was disappointed in myself. Just because I had found myself in an unexpected fight in a strange arena didn't mean that I shouldn't have fought back. I would have thought I was a better competitor than that.

I called Buzzie at his home that night and told him, "All right, I'm signing this as we agreed. It's all over and done with. But I want you to know that I'm not happy about it. It's not that I'm not happy with the money. I'm just not happy about the way it was done."

Buzzie told me that he wasn't either.

The more I thought about it, the more I didn't like it. The only thing to do, I decided, was to confront Buzzie on the plane the next day and ask him whether it had been he who had given out the story after telling me not to talk about contract negotiations with the press.

But he wasn't on the plane. He was going to Chicago for a few days. That was funny; the newspaper story had said that I was the one who would be keeping him off the plane if I didn't sign.

By the time we put down at Vero Beach, I had worked myself up to such a pitch about not being able to straighten the record with Buzzie that I couldn't sleep. Besides, it had just occurred to me that I had not even put my side of the story on the record.

I have never been a pop-off. If the writers had any complaint about me, it was that I didn't say enough. The time had come, I decided, to pop off. The first writer to ask me anything about my famous holdout was going to get the full story.

As it turned out, I got more coverage than I could have hoped for. Milton Gross of the New York Post, Joe Reichler of the Associated Press, and Shirley Povich of the Washington Post, had driven up from Fort Lauderdale together to catch our first day at camp. They hit me as a troïka, and I told them precisely what had happened and precisely how I felt.

Even before I talked to them, I had received word that Mr. O'Malley wanted to see me. Nothing looks better, I always say, than to be missing from the opening of practice. Especially after you have been accused of being completely indifferent to the welfare of the team.

Mr. O'Malley was apparently out to pacify me. Somehow it didn't quite work out that way. The trouble with me, I discovered, was that I didn't understand negotiations. "Ask your father," Mr. O'Malley said. "He understands these things."

"You just may be right," I said. "Then you'll be willing to negotiate with a third party instead of with me the next time we have to sign a contract."

He didn't say anything.

I told Mr. O'Malley that I had been enjoying the negotiations until the club started negotiating through the newspapers after specifically instructing me not to.

Mr. O'Malley denied that the Dodgers had done any such thing, and it got just a little warm in there.

We ended on a calm and hopeful note, though. "You're still a young man. You've got a lot of time to make money. Just remember that you can't make it all in one year in this business," he said, "and you'll find that over the long run you'll be very well taken care of."

That's fine. Over the long run my career had almost come to an end a year earlier, and over the short run it almost came to an end again before the 1964 season was over.

When Buzzie finally arrived, he insisted that he had not been the man who had leaked the story. All right, I wasn't going to go any further than that. I was sick of it by then, anyway, and I had the distinct impression that everyone else was too.

The great Koufax-Drysdale holdout came about two years later because Don and I had grown weary of being played against each other on alternate years. Although we had talked about it earlier, we came to a decision, only a couple of weeks before the beginning of spring training, to pool our strength and make our salary demands as an entry. Our opening proposition, the three-year contract and the $1,000,000 package, was just that, an opening proposition. It was, from the beginning, highly negotiable.

We told the club that they could deal with us as a team by offering us a package to be divided between the two of us according to our own private agreement or, if they preferred, they could deal with us separately. We made it perfectly clear, however, that if they dealt with us separately neither of us would make any final commitment until the other one was happy too.

In short, we didn't demand that they deal with us together. Combining our strength was a tactic, not a goal. As a matter of fact, it was purely accidental—and almost funny

—that we ended up with the same representative. Don's own lawyer happened to be handling a case for Walter O'Malley, and legal ethics did not permit him to represent anyone against O'Malley at the same time. Since Don had to find another representative anyway, it became a matter of simple convenience for my lawyer, Bill Hayes, to represent us both.

What was the goal, then? Our goal was to make them believe, in the face of all their experience, that we were serious. The goal was to convince them that they would have to approach us not as indentured servants but as co-equal parties to a contract, with as much dignity and bargaining power as themselves.

To set the record straight, we were never as adamant about the means to achieving that end as everybody seems to think. The fault for any failure in communication was our own. We decided not to say too much during the holdout—and were much criticized for it—because we felt that once we began to issue communiqués we'd soon be answering each other's charges day by day. At the end of two weeks the whole thing could degenerate into a name-calling contest which would leave both sides bitter and both sides stubborn.

I even stopped reading the sports pages because I could see little to be gained from irritating myself and perhaps losing my temper. (As a result, I was probably the last person in organized baseball to be aware that Ralph Terry was holding out too. I didn't know he had been traded until the season had almost begun.)

We wanted the Dodgers to recognize our right to be represented by a third party. But we didn't demand it. When Buzzie showed little inclination to meet with Bill Hayes, we felt it would be both inconsistent and self-defeating to close off negotiations when our whole purpose was to bring the club to us so that we *could* negotiate. We simply told Buzzie that Bill was available any time he couldn't get in touch with us, and left the choice up to him.

We met Buzzie three times before the team went south.

He never budged from the position that his first offer was also the final one.

From my point of view, nothing was more negotiable than the request for a three-year no-cut contract. I told Don from the beginning that the first thing we were going to hear was that they couldn't give me a three-year contract because I had a bad arm. In our second meeting, I told Buzzie that I wasn't particularly interested in a three-year contract, and left it up to Don to go whichever way he felt best for himself.

The truth of the matter is that while the Dodgers' much-publicized policy against giving multi-year contracts may be technically true, it is also true that, to all practical purposes, Don and I were both really on three-year contracts from the year before.

When I signed my contract in 1963, Buzzie gave me two other contracts, for 1964 and 1965, at the same salary. He signed them both. I didn't sign them, but I had them both, as an insurance policy, any time I did want to sign them. I believe Don did sign his. It didn't matter one way or the other, because there was a clause in there which gave the player the right to renegotiate.

In 1965 I had a contract for $80,000, with a $5000 bonus if I pitched more than 300 innings—since the club had no guarantee that the elbow would be all right.

Teaming up together had a value we hadn't appreciated at first. We were able to give each other moral support. As the spring wore on and the pressure built up, there was a certain amount of comfort in being able to call back and forth and alternately moan about the silence of the club and exhort each other to hold on. Not only did we give each other moral support, we gave each other a golf partner, and you can't do much better than that.

For thirty days no one called. Nobody made a move. Nobody seemed to believe we wouldn't come crawling back. Believe me, the movie contract we signed was no publicity stunt. Although I had no thought of making acting a career, it was a great relief to know that I was going to make a few bucks right away, so that I could decide what I really wanted to do. Psychologically, we hoped that the fact of the job would in itself convince the club that we weren't fooling. But whatever may have been claimed on our behalf in the psychological warfare, we weren't fooling anybody, least of all ourselves, that we could make as much money outside of baseball as in it.

In that whole time there was only one, rather confusing, contact with the club. Don called to tell me that his wife, Ginger, had talked to O'Malley, and that Mr. O'Malley wanted us to call him at Vero Beach that night. We called Mr. O'Malley under the impression that we were returning his call. I found out later that someone from Vero Beach had called Ginger and told her that Mr. O'Malley wanted her to call him back.

It turned out to be a very pleasant conversation. Mr. O'Malley just wanted us to know that his offer was indeed the final one and, since we didn't seem disposed to accept it, he wanted to wish us all the luck in the world in our fascinating new careers as actors.

We wanted to wish Mr. O'Malley all the luck and success he deserved too, and we asked him to relay our best wishes for a great season to the ball club.

And on that note of mutual good will we all said good-by.

Mr. O'Malley had also let us know, in passing, that the Mets had expressed great interest in us (an interest which was apparently supposed to make our blood run cold). I told him that since I had a home in Los Angeles I'd prefer to remain there, but that if I was traded to the Mets I would, of course, be delighted to play for them.

Although we had the distinct impression that he was taking our temperature, there was no way of being sure. He also could have been giving us one last chance before writing us off.

Shortly thereafter, both Don and I received letters from Buzzie Bavasi, which seemed to indicate that, since we did not seem interested in accepting the "final" offer, it was absolutely essential to retire us according to the proper administrative procedure. We could go on the voluntary retired list, the suspended list, the ineligible list, or a hundred or so other lists. It took a whole page just to list the possible lists. We were, of course, touched to find out there were so many ways for us not to play baseball.

But it wasn't really funny. For my part, I was no longer giving us better than a 50 per cent chance of playing ball. And then, just before the Dodgers broke camp, Buzzie came back to Los Angeles and called Bill Hayes. Within eighteen hours we were signed.

But it wasn't that easy. Not by a long shot. Buzzie started by upping the ante to $100,000 for Don and $110,000 for me. This, he said, was definitely the final offer. Bill called us in to talk it over, emphasizing that we had to make this decision ourselves, without any advice from him. The reason for that was clear. What we just might be deciding, quite obviously, was whether or not we were going to remain in baseball. Still, it wasn't a hard decision to make. Neither of us considered it a reasonable advance from the original offer. Both of us turned it down.

There was one hopeful note, beyond the obvious fact that contact had been made and the talks had been resumed. Bavasi had voluntarily talked to our representative, as we had requested, which did seem to be an admission, on his part, that our position was not without merit.

Before we left the office, Don, who has always been a close friend of Bavasi's, asked me if it would be all right if he called Buzzie and asked him whether he really wanted to sit down and talk seriously.

We were both at the stage, quite truthfully, where we wanted to either settle it once and for all or forget it once and for all.

I said, "Don, if that is what you want to do, go ahead. Do anything you think is right."

There's a certain irony, of course, in having Don go in to negotiate from friendship immediately after we had established the right of dealing through a third party. But the circumstances were special and rather unique; you will rarely find the closeness between a player and a general manager that you find between Don and Buzzie.

Later in the day Don called to tell me he had made an appointment to see Buzzie in the morning. "Look," he said. "I'm going to tell him just how we feel and we'll see what happens. I'll let you know what he says as soon as I can."

And then something happened which, I think, showed the value of having a third party involved in this kind of emotional dogfight. Buzzie was quoted as having said that if only one of us signed—while the other presumably held out or quit—the player who signed would have to accept the original offer.

Bill Hayes called early in the morning to warn Buzzie that if he made that kind of proposition to Don, he had very little chance of signing either of us.

Don went out with Buzzie and gave him the minimum figure we would accept. The deal was made between them—without too much difficulty, apparently—contingent upon my acceptance.

When Don checked back with me I asked him if he was happy with the deal. "Okay, then," I said, "it's all right with me too."

Buzzie called shortly afterward, right on schedule. I drove down to the office a few hours later to smooth out a few details, and that was the end of the great Koufax-Drysdale holdout.

Part of the agreement was that neither side would make the exact figure public, and this is an agreement I must honor. Let's just say that Don and I had our own agreement not to sign anything unless we were both happy with our salaries. We both signed. There is little doubt that we got two of the biggest raises in baseball history.

It should also be said that if they gave, we gave too. We were battling for a legitimate compromise, and that's what happens in compromises: both sides have to be willing to move. The big thing to us was that somebody came and negotiated with us, even though there was no place else we could play.

We received a limitless amount of outside advice from the people who were on our side in the dispute. One of the most amazing things to me was the number of people who wanted to tell us about the California employment law, which bars any personal-service contract that runs for more than seven years (the reason for the seven-year option contracts on which the old Hollywood studios were built). In California the law is drawn so strictly that the employee is not permitted to waive his protection even if he wants to.

We were not out to break the reserve clause; we were trying to find a way to live more comfortably inside it. I think baseball needs the reserve clause; I don't see how it could remain competitive without it. Everybody concedes, however, that while the reserve clause may be necessary, it is a necessary evil.

We hadn't given a thought to a court battle at the beginning and we didn't do anything more than discuss the law academically, even at the end. And yet I would suppose that if we had been out of baseball, our perspective could have changed and we might have begun to think about the courts quite seriously.

I don't think courts are the answer, though. I do think—and have thought for a long time—that a board of arbitration should be established so that the players are not at the mercy of the management. I understand that the minor leagues do have a set-up whereby a player can appeal to the Governors' Board of the National Association.

If Don and I had not played this year, it would have been because the majors have refused to set up any independent panel, organization, or group to temper the disputes. The player is not so much helpless as frustrated. There is nobody for him to talk to. There is nowhere for him to appeal. There is nothing for him to do except swallow his pride.

It would not be difficult to set up an arbitration board. If the will is there, there's no wrong way to do it.

How an issue would get to the board is a simple matter of policy. If a player hasn't come to terms by, let us say, the middle of spring training, the dispute would be turned over to the board for binding arbitration. I don't feel ballplayers are unreasonable. With a board sitting there to arbitrate, if necessary, management would have to negotiate with its players seriously.

Neither Don nor I is trying to hold ourselves up as intrepid pioneers in this jungle. The times are changing. If we hadn't pushed it, someone else certainly would have come along within two or three years.

It's easier for the lower-paid player to point up the issue for the public, but he suffers from one slight handicap. He has no chance at all of winning. I never doubted for a minute that if Don or I had been in it alone we would have been chewed up and very thoroughly digested. I don't know whether there's any single player—except perhaps Willie Mays—who could bring a ball club to him. The Giants were perfectly willing to give Mays well above $100,000 and to have a representative negotiate for him. Before the Dodgers would have given in to me alone, they'd have traded me or let me sit it out. You can trade one player and get an approximation of value. You can't trade two of your top players. We were in a rare position to make a stand.

While Don and I might have got all the publicity, Ralph Terry's holdout was probably more pertinent. Ralph apparently believed he got a bad deal last year that was being reflected in what he was being offered this year. An impartial examination might have shown that he was mistaken. It might also have shown that he wasn't. But why should he be placed in the position of having his grievance judged by the very person he is accusing? Terry is more typical too because, when he showed that he was willing to walk out the door, they simply traded him.

Baseball is a business. That's why franchises are on the move so constantly. As businesses, the clubs do not feel they can afford to let the troops challenge the budget. If a player they can get along without holds out, they'll let him go to work somewhere else.

The real problem is to raise the minimum, which has been

$7000 now since 1958. As the top salaries go up, they make the minimum look increasingly ridiculous. And they pull the middle salaries up with them too. I think most of the players were for us. The players felt—I hope—that the more we got paid, the more they would get paid in the future.

Koufax Statistics

Compiled by Allan Roth

KEY TO PERFORMANCE RECORD

* —road game
n—night game
t—twilight game
CG—complete game
F—finished
INJ—injured
KO—knocked out
PH—left game for pinch-hitter
REM—removed
+—started next inning,
  retired no one
SV—save

Opposing Teams

C—Cincinnati
Ch—Chicago
H—Houston
M—Milwaukee
NY—New York
  (Giants, 1955-58; Mets, 1962-65)
P—Pittsburgh
Ph—Philadelphia
SF—San Francisco
SL—St. Louis

Koufax: lifetime game no.	Koufax: season game no.	Dodgers: season game no.	Date	Opposition	As starter	In relief	IP	H	R	ER	BB	SO	W	L	Score	Season W–L
1n*	1	66	6/24	M		PH	2	1	0	0	1	2				
2n	2	70	29	NY		F	1	2	0	0	1	0				
3n*	3	80	7/ 6	P	KO		4⅔	3	1	1	8	4				
4	4	95	23	M		F	2	2	2	2	2	0				
5	5	97	24	M		F	1	0	0	0	0	0				
6t	6	123	8/25	C		F	1	0	0	0	0	2				
7	7	126	27	C	CG		9	2	0	0	5	14	W		7–0	1–0
8n	8	130	31	M		KO	1+	5	4	4	0	0				
9	9	133	9/ 3	P	CG		9	5	0	0	2	6	W		4–0	2–0
10*	10	143	11	C	KO		6⅓	7[1]	4	3	6	1		L	3–5	2–1
11*	11	146	15	SL	PH		4	6	2	2	0	1				
12n*	12	153	24	P		KO	⅓	0	2	2	3	0		L	1–6	2–2

1. Allowed first home runs of career—by Musial and Repulski, successive batters.

Koufax: lifetime game no.	Koufax: season game no.	Dodgers: season game no.	Date	Opposition	As starter	In relief	IP	H	R	ER	BB	SO	W	L	Score	Season W–L
13	1	10	4/29	P		KO	⅔	5	4	3	1	1				
14n*	2	15	5/ 4	SL		PH	⅔	0	0	0	0	0				
15n	3	24	18	C		PH	3	3	1	1	0	1				
16	4	25	19	C		PH	2	2	1	1	0	0				
17n	5	28	22	M		F	1	1	0	0	2	0				
18*	6	35	30	Ph		PH	2	1	0	0	0	1				
19*	7	39	6/ 3	Ch	KO		8+	5	3	3	4	5	W[1]		4–3	1–0
20n*[2]	8	44	8	C	PH		6	7	3	3	1	1				
21n*	9	48	12	SL	KO		3+	3	1	0	3	2				
22n	10	53	19	SL	KO		2⅔	5	4	4	2	1		L	0–6	1–1
23	11	57	23	C	KO		5⅓	6	5	4	2	2				
24n*	12	81	7/17	C	KO		8	9	4	4	3	7		L	3–4	1–2
25*	13	87	22	SL	KO		8⅔	8	3	3	3	5	W		4–3	2–2
26	14	94	29	Ch	KO		2⅓	4	3	1	2	2		L	2–4	2–3
27	15	102	8/ 5	SL	KO		1+	2	1	1	2	1				
28*	16	130	9/ 2	NY	KO		4⅓	5	4	4	4	1		L	1–4	2–4

1. First road win.
2. First National League hit, single to right vs. Klippstein—16th at bat.

Koufax: lifetime game no.	Koufax: season game no.	Dodgers: season game no.	Date	Opposition	As starter	In relief	IP	H	R	ER	BB	SO	W	L	Score	Season W–L
29	1	4	4/21	P		F	3	2	2	1	0	3				
30n	2	7	24	NY	PH		4	7	2	2	1	5				
31n	3	11	30	Ch		PH	2	1	0	0	0	3				
32	4	16	5 /5	M		PH	3	2	1	1	3	5				
33n	5	17	6	M		F	1	0	0	0	0	1	W[1]		5–4	1–0
34n*	6	20	10	NY		PH	3	2	0	0	1	2				
35*	7	21	11	NY		PH	2	0	0	0	0	3				
36*	8	25	16	Ch	CG[2]		9	4	2	0	7	13	W		3–2	2–0
37n*	9	29	22	C	PH		4	3	3	3	4	7		L	1–8	2–1
38	10	32	26	NY	KO		6⅓	8	2	2	2	3	W		5–3	3–1
39*	11	37	30	P	KO		4⅔	6	2	2	1	2		L	1–2	3–2
40n	12	42	6/ 4	Ch	KO		7⅔	4	5	5	5	12	W		7–5	4–2
41*	13	66	27	M		F	⅔	0	0	0	0	2				
42	14	72	7/ 4	P		F	2	1	0	0	1	2				
43t	15	85	19	Ch	PH		7	2	2	2	2	11				
44	16	88	21	Ch		PH	⅔	0	0	0	0	1				
45n	17	91	24	SL		F	1	1	1	1	0	1				
46n*	18	93	26	C	KO		4⅓	7	5	5	0	5				
47*	19	97	30	Ch		F	2	1	1	1	1	2				
48*	20	100	8/ 1	Ch	CG		9	4	3	3	4	11	W		12-3	5–2
49*	21	103	4	M		PH	1	0	0	0	0	0				
50n*	22	108	9	P		REM	⅓	0	0	0	0	0				
51*	23	111	11	P		F	2	2	1	1	4	0				
52	24	116	17	P	KO		4⅔	6	6	6	4	5		L	3–7	5–3
53n	25	123	23	M	KO		7+	4	2	2	2	8				
54	26	125	25	SL		KO	0	0	0	0	2	0				
55n	27	127	28	Ch	PH		5	8	3	2	1	5				
56	28	129	31	NY		KO	0	1	0	0	0	0				
57	29	130	9/ 1	NY		F	2⅓	1	0	0	0	3				
58*	30	139	10	Ch	PH(KO)		1	3	3	3	2	0		L	2–9	5–4
59*	31	144	15	C		F	2	3	3	3	2	4				
60n	32	148	20	Ph		F	⅓	0	0	0	0	0				
61n*	33	152	27	Ph		F	1	0	0	0	0	2				
62*	34	154	29	Ph		F	1	0	0	0	2	1				

1. First relief win.
2. First road complete game (10th road start).

Koufax: lifetime game no.	Koufax: season game no.	Dodgers: season game no.	Date	Opposition	As starter	In relief	IP	H	R	ER	BB	SO	W L	Score	Season W–L
63	1	9	4/24	Ch		F	1	1	0	0	0	0			
64n	2	21	5/ 6	Ph	KO		5+	4	4	4	4	4			
65	3	26	13	SF		PH	2	4	2	2	2	1			
66*	4	30	17	SL		PH	1	4	1	1	0	0			
67n*	5	33	20	M	CG		11	2	3	2	4	6	W	6–3	1–0
68*	6	36	24	C	KO		0	0	0	0	2	0			
69n*	7	39	28	P	CG		9	6	1	0	4	4	W	7–1	2–0
70*	8	41	30	Ch		F	0	2	2	2	0	0	L	8–10	2–1
71n	9	44	6/ 3	C	KO		2⅔	0	5	5	6	3	L	3–8	2–2
72n	10	48	7	M	KO		7+	6	2	2	2	8	W	5–2	3–2
73n	11	53	13	P	KO		4+	5	4	3	3	4			
74	12	55	15	P		PH	2	3	1	1	0	2			
75n*	13	59	20	P	PH		4	3	2	2	1	3	L	1–2	3–3
76*	14	60	21	P		F	1	1	0	0	0	1			
77*	15	62	22	P		F	3	1	0	0	1	4	W	3–2 10-inn	4–3
78t*	16	64	24	C		F	4⅔	4	2	2	4	5	W	13–10	5–3
79n*	17	65	24	C		F	⅔	0	0	0	0	1	SV		
80n*	18	67	27	M	CG		9	7	1	1	2	8	W	3–1	6–3
81n*	19	71	7/ 1	SL	KO		7⅔	7	3	3	2	3	W	9–3	7–3
82n	20	74	5	Ch	INJ[1]		1⅔	0	0	0	0	2			
83n	21	86	18	Ph	KO		⅔	0	1	1	4	2			
84n	22	87	19	Ph	KO		7⅓	5	4	3	6	3	L	2–6	7–4
85n*	23	90	23	P	STIFF		0	1	2	2	1	0			
86n*	24	93	26	Ph	CG		9	7	4	4	4	7	W	10–4	8–4
87n*	25	97	30	M	KO		7⅓	6	4	4	5	4	L	3–4	8–5
88*	26	101	8/ 3	C	KO		4⅔	4	3	3	3	5			
89*	27	106	7	Ch	KO		8⅓	4	1	1	3	10	W	3–1	9–5
90	28	109	10	SF		KO	⅓	3	3	3	1	0			
91n	29	111	13	Ch	KO		6⅓	5	5	5	5	4			
92	30	115	17	SL	KO		1⅓	4	4	4	2	1	L	8–12	9–6
93n	31	120	21	M	KO		4⅓	6	4	1	1	3	L	0–4	9–7
94n	32	124	26	C	KO		1+	2	3	3	4	0	L	4–6	9–8
95*	33	129	31	SF	KO		⅔	3	5	5	4	1	L	2–14	9–9
96n	34	133	9/ 3	SF		F	7	2	1	1	2	7	W	5–3	10–9
97*	35	137	7	SL		KO	0	0	0	0	1	0			
98n*	36	138	9	Ph	KO		5⅓	5	4	4	4	8	L	3–4	10–10
99*	37	142	13	P		PH	1	1	2	0	1	0			
100n*	38	146	16	C	KO		1⅔	3	4	4	5	2			
101*	39	149	21	Ch	KO		7+	6	0	0	5	6	W	2–1	11–10
102n	40	153	26	Ch	CG[2]		9	5	2	1	7	9	L	1–2	11–11

1. Injured ankle in collision at first base.
2. First complete game at Coliseum.

Koufax: lifetime game no.	Koufax: season game no.	Dodgers: season game no.	Date	Opposition	As starter	In relief	IP	H	R	ER	BB	SO	W	L	Score	Season W-L
103*	1	2	4/12	Ch	PH		3	5	3	3	2	2				
104n	2	5	16	SL	KO		1⅓	3	1	1	1	0				
105*	3	14	26	SL	KO		2⅓	4	3	3	3	1				
106n*	4	17	30	Ph	KO		3⅔	3	3	3	7	5				
107*	5	19	5/2	C		KO	9⅔	4	5	5	4	1				
108n	6	33	16	M		F	1	1	1	1	0	0				
109n	7	38	20	C		F	2	1	0	0	1	2				
110n*	8	43	26	SF	KO		8⅓	5	5	4	4	11		L	4-6	0-1
111	9	48	31	SL	KO		6+	5	3	3	5	9	W		5-3	1-1
112*	10	53	6/6	M	PH		7	8	2	0	3	4	W		3-2	2-1
113n*	11	55	9	Ph		F	⅔	0	0	0	0	0	SV			
114*	12	59	13	P	PH		5	7	3	3	2	3				
115*	13	61	14	P		F	2	0	0	0	1	3				
116t	14	64	17	M	CG		9	5	2	2	6	7	W		10-2	3-1
117n	15	70	22	Ph	CG		9	10	2	1	3	16[1]	W		6-2	4-1
118n	16	75	27	P	CG[2]		9	6	0	0	2	8	W		3-0	5-1
119n	17	77	29	SF		PH	3	0	0	0	0	5				
120*	18	80	7/3	SL	PH		7	2	1	1	2	7		L	2-3	5-2
121*	19	84	5	Ch		KO	3⅔	4	1	1	3	6				
122*	20	86	11	M	PH		3	4	3	3	2	3				
123n	21	106	8/1	Ph	PH		4	1	2	2	4	7				
124	22	111	9	M		F	1	0	0	0	0	3				
125*	23	112	11	Ch		KO	⅔	2	1	1	1	1				
126n*	24	114	13	SL	KO		8+	7	5	5	4	6	W		7-6	6-2
127t*	25	118	17	M	KO		1⅓	4	4	3	4	2		L	1-8	6-3
128n*	26	121	19	C	KO		7+	9	4	4	2	7		L	4-9	6-4
129n*	27	123	21	P		F	⅓	0	0	0	0	0	SV			
130*	28	127	24	Ph	CG		9	4	2	2	4	13	W		8-2	7-4
131n	29	131	31	SF	CG		9	7	2	2	2	18[3]	W		5-2 (10-inn)	8-4
132	30	135	9/6	Ch	CG		10	5	3	3	7	10[4]		L	0-3	8-5
133t	31	140	11	P	KO		7⅓	7	4	4	4	6				
134n	32	145	16	C	KO		7⅓	11	5	5	1	6		L	4-7	8-6
135*	33	149	20	SF	KO		⅓	0	0	0	3	0				
136n	34	150	22	SL	KO		⅔	2	4	4	2	0				
137	35	156	29	M		KO	⅔	0	0	0	3	1				

1. Set major-league strikeout record for night game—which lasted only until August 31.
2. First time three complete games in row.
3. Tied strikeout record, set major-league record for two games.
4. Set major-league record for strike-outs, three games (41).

Koufax: lifetime game no.	Koufax: season game no.	Dodgers: season game no.	Date	Op-position	As starter	In relief	IP	H	R	ER	BB	SO	W L	Score	Season W–L
138	1	5	4/17	SL		F	3	1	0	0	3	3	SV		
139n*	2	8	22	SL	KO		0	4	5	5	1	0	L	7–11	0–1
140n	3	15	30	SF		KO	⅔	0	0	0	3	0		10-inn	
141n	4	20	5/ 6	Ph	KO		9⅔	9	5	5	7	15	L	1–6	0–2
142n	5	25	11	P	KO		7⅔	6	4	4	5	5	L	3–6	0–3
143n*	6	31	19	C	CG		8⅔	9	5	3	3	10	L	4–5	0–4
144n*	7	34	23	P	CG		9	1[1]	0	0	6	10	W	1–0	1–4
145*	8	38	28	Ch	KO		13+	3	4	3	9	15	L	14-inn 3–4	1–5
146n	9	42	6/ 1	SL	KO		4⅓	8	4	4	2	4	L	2–5	1–6
147	10	46	5	Ch	KO		5⅔	3	5	5	5	9	L	8–12	1–7
148n	11	47	7	M		F	1	0	0	0	1	0			
149n	12	50	10	C	KO		1⅓	1	4	4	4	3	L	3–4	1–8
150n	13	54	15	Ph	CG		9	5	2	2	2	5	W	14–2	2–8
151	14	58	19	P	KO		4⅓	4	5	4	6	4			
152n*	15	62	24	M	KO		1+	3	3	3	3	2			
153n*	16	67	29	Ph	KO		7+	3	2	2	4	10	W	5–2	3–8
154*	17	72	7/ 4	SL	KO		⅓	3	2	2	2	1			
155	18	79	10	SL		KO	0	0	1	0	1	0			
156*	19	82	17	SF		PH	2	1	0	0	1	3			
157n	20	85	21	P		F	2	1	0	0	0	2			
158n	21	89	26	C		F	1	1	0	0	0	0			
159n	22	93	30	M	PH		4	5	4	2	1	6			
160*	23	100	8/ 7	Ph	CG		9	4	1	1	3	11	W	2–1	4–8
161n*	24	104	11	C	CG		9	2	0	0	1	13	W	3–0	5–8
162*	25	109	16	Ch	KO		4+	7	5	5	3	4			
163*	26	111	18	Ch		F	2⅓	0	0	0	1	4	W	4–3	6–8
164*	27	114	21	SL	PH		7	6	1	1	1	8	L	0–2	6–9
165n	28	118	25	M	KO		2+	4	4	4	3	4	L	2–4	6–10
166n	29	123	30	P	KO		4⅓	8	4	4	2	1	L	2–5	6–11
167*	30	127	9/ 3	SF	PH		7	7	1	1	2	6	L	0–1	6–12
168n*	31	133	8	C	CG		9	8	4	4	3	10	W	7–4	7–12
169n*	32	138	13	Ph	CG		9	5	1	1	2	11	W	4–1	8–12
170*	33	142	17	Ch	KO		7⅓	3	4	4	5	8	L	3–7	8–13
171n*	34	145	20	SL		F	⅓	1	0	0	1	0			
172n	35	148	26	SF		F	1	1	0	0	0	1			
173n	36	151	29	SL	KO		7+	6	3	3	3	7			
174n	37	153	10/ 1	Ch		PH	2	0	0	0	1	2			

1. Only hit was 2nd-inning single by pitcher Benny Daniels.

Koufax: lifetime game no.	Koufax: season game no.	Dodgers: season game no.	Date	Op-posi-tion	As starter	In relief	IP	H	R	ER	BB	SO	W	L	Score	Season W–L
175n	1	4	4/14	P	PH		5	5	4	3	1	3		L	3–6	0–1
176n	2	11	21	C	CG		9	6	3	3	3	11	W¹		5–3	1–1
177*	3	18	30	Ch		PH	1	1	1	1	1	1				
178n*	4	19	5/ 2	M	KO		3⅓	6	5	2	2	6				
179*	5	21	4	M		KO	0	1	1	1	1	0				
180*	6	24	7	P	KO		6⅓	8	2	2	0	3	W		4–2	2–1
181n	7	28	12	Ch	KO		8⅔	4	2	2	5	11	W		4–2	3–1
182n	8	32	16	M	KO		4+	7	5	5	3	3		L	3–5	3–2
183*	9	36	21	SF	CG		9	4	2	2	2	6	W		3–2	4–2
184n*	10	40	25	SL	CG		9	3	0	0	3	8	W		1–0	5–2
185n	11	44	29	SL	CG		9	3	1	1	5	13	W		2–1	6–2
186n	12	48	6/ 3	SF	CG		9	7	3	3	5	7	W		4–3	7–2
187n	13	52	7	P	CG		9	7	3	3	2	7	W		7–3	8–2
188	14	56	11	Ph	CG²		9	5	3	3	2	10	W		6–3	9–2
189n	15	61	16	M	KO		6⅓	8	2	2	4	8		L	1–2	9–3
190*	16	64	20	Ch	CG		9	2	0	0	2	14	W		3–0	10–3
191*	17	69	24	C	PH		3	5	5	5	1	3				
192*	18	70	25	C		PH	2	1	0	0	0	3				
193n*	19	73	29	P	KO		7⅔	7	3	3	1	11		L	2–4	10–4
194n*	20	77	7/ 3	M	PH		8	3	2	2	6	7	W		3–2	11–4
195t	21	81	7	C	KO		3⅔	7	8	4	3	4		L	7–11	11–5
196	22	84	9	C		KO	2	3	2	2	1	2				
197	23	87	15	Ph	KO		7⅓	8	5	5	1	7		L	2–7	11–6
198n	24	89	17	P		F	2	0	0	0	0	2	SV			
199n*	25	91	20	C	CG		9	7	1	1	1	7	W		10–1	12–6
200n*	26	95	25	Ph	CG		9	6	2	2	1	10	W		7–2	13–6
201*	27	99	29	P	PH		6	8	2	2	4	7				
202n	28	103	8/ 4	Ch	PH		7	4	4	4	3	7		L	2–4	13–7
203n	29	106	8	M	KO		5⅓	8	3	3	1	4				
204n	30	111	15	C	KO		6+	8	5	4	3	6		L	2–5	13–8
205*	31	116	20	SF	KO		3+	8	6	6	2	3		L	8–11	13–9
206n*	32	120	25	C	CG		9	5	2	2	5	6	W		7–2	14–9
207*	33	124	29	Ch	CG		9	2	1	0	5	12	W		2–1	15–9
208*	34	128	9/ 2	M	PH		7	7	4	2	1	2		L	0–4	15–10
209n	35	132	6	SF	KO		4⅔	8	5	5	2	10				
210*	36	135	10	SF		PH	2	2	3	3	1	5				
211n	37	137	12	Ph	KO		1⅓	5	6	6	1	4		L	10–19	15–11
212n	38	140	15	M	CG		9	5	2	1	3	10	W		11–2	16–11
213	39	142	9/17	M		F	2	4	1	1	0	1	W		4–3	17–11
214n	40	145	20	Ch	CG		13³	7	2	2	3	15	W		3–2	18–11
215*	41	148	24	SL	PH		3	4	4	2	3	3		L	7–8	18–12
216n*	42	151	27	Ph	CG		8	3	2	0	3	7⁴		L	1–2	18–13

1. First April win of career.
2. Sixth consecutive complete game win.
3. Made 205 pitches in 13 innings.
4. 269 strikeouts set National League record, breaking Mathewson's 267 set in 1903.

Koufax: lifetime game no.	Koufax: season game no.	Dodgers: season game no.	Date	Op-posi-tion	As starter	In relief	IP	H	R	ER	BB	SO	W L	Score	Season W–L
217	1	2	4/11	C	CG		9	4	2	2	3	7	W	6–2	1–0
218	2	6	15	M	KO		6⅓	8	5	4	3	7	L	3–6	1–1
219n*	3	10	19	C	KO		7⅔	7	3	3	3	9	W	4–3	2–1
220*	4	14	24	Ch	CG		9	6	2	2	4	18[1]	W	10–2	3–1
221	5	18	28	P	CG		9[2]	6	1	1	1	6	W	2–1	4–1
222n	6	23	5/ 2	Ch	KO		6⅓	8	3	1	1	8	L	1–3	4–2
223n*	7	27	8	H	KO		5⅔	7	4	2	2	8			
224n*	8	31	12	SL	PH		6	9	4	3	0	7			
225n	9	35	17	H	PH		6	8	4	4	1	4			
226n	10	39	21	SF	CG		9	5	1	1	1	10	W	8–1	5–2
227	11	44	26	Ph	CG		9	5	3	2	2	16	W	6–3	6–2
228*	12	47	30	NY	CG		9	13	6	6	3	10	W	13–6	7–2
229n*	13	54	6/ 4	Ph	CG		9	3	3	3	2	13	W	6–3	8–2
230n*	14	56	6	P		F	1	0	0	0	0	2	SV		
231n*	15	59	8	H	KO		5⅓	2	2	2	3	6			
232n*	16	64	13	M	CG		9	3	1	1	2	6	W[3]	2–1	9–2
233n	17	69	18	SL	CG		9	5	0	0	0[4]	9	W	1–0	10–2
234n	18	72	22	C	PH		8	5	2	1	3	11	L	3–4	10–3
235n	19	76	26	M	PH		8	6	2	1	1	13	L	1–2	10–4
236n	20	80	30	NY	CG		9	0[5]	0	0	5	13	W	5–0	11–4
237	21	84	7/ 4	Ph	CG		9	5	1	1	3	10	W	16–1	12–4
238*	22	89	8	SF	KO		8⅓	3	0	0	3	9	W	2–0	13–4
239n*	23	90	12	NY	INJ[6]		7	3	0[7]	0	3	6	W	3–0	14–4
240n*	24	95	17	C	INJ[8]		1		2	2	0	1	L	5–7	14–5
241n*	25	154	9/21	SL	KO		⅔	1	4	4	4	1	L	2–11	14–6
242*	26	156	23	SL		F	2	2	1	1	3	2			
243n	27	159	27	H	REM		5	3	2	2	1	4			
244*	28	163	10/ 1	SF	KO		1+	4	3	3	0	0	L	0–8	14–7

1. Tied strikeout record (Feller, Koufax).
2. Jammed finger.
3. Hit first home run of career, vs. Spahn, winning run, in fifth.
4. First no-bases-on-balls complete game of career (154th start, 46th complete game).
5. No-hitter.
6. Finger injury.
7. Allowed 4 earned runs in 67⅓ IP from 6/13 to 7/12 for 0.53 ERA.
8. Finger injury.

Koufax: lifetime game no.	Koufax: season game no.	Dodgers: season game no.	Date	Op-position	As starter	In relief	IP	H	R	ER	BB	SO	W	L	Score	Season W-L
245*	1	2	4/10	Ch	CG		9	5	1	1	2	10	W		2-1	1-0
246*	2	6	14	H	KO		5⅓	6	5	4	2	4		L	4-5	1-1
247n	3	10	19	H	CG		9	2	0	0	2	14	W		2-0	2-1
248n	4	15	23	M	INJ		6⅔	2	0	0	2	5				
249n*	5	27	5/ 7	SL	REM		8	5	1	1	1	5	W		11-1	3-1
250n	6	31	11	SF	CG		9	0[1]	0	0	2	4	W		8-0 (12-inn)	4-1
251n	7	34	15	Ph	CG		12	11	2	2	0	12	W		3-2	5-1
252	8	38	19	NY	CG		9	2	0	0	1	5	W		1-0	6-1
253n*	9	42	24	SF	KO		⅓	5	5	5	2	1		L	1-7	6-2
254n*	10	45	28	M	CG		9	6	0	0	2	8	W		7-0	7-2
255n*	11	49	6/ 1	C	PH		7	3	1	1	1	10		L	0-1	7-3
256n*	12	53	5	H	CG		9	8	1	1	2	8	W		5-1	8-3
257*	13	56	9	Ch	KO		4⅔	8	6	6	1	6				
258n	14	60	13	H	CG		9	3	0	0	2	10	W		3-0	9-3
259n*	15	65	17	SF	CG		9	4	0	0	4	9	W		2-0	10-3
260n*	16	68	21	SL	KO		8⅔	6	3	3	3	9	W		5-3	11-3
261n*	17	72	25	C	CG		9	6	1	1	3	9	W		4-1	12-3
262n	18	75	29	M	KO		4⅔	8	5	5	1	8				
263n	19	79	7/ 3	SL	CG		9	3	0	0	0	9	W		5-0	13-3
264	20	83	7	C	CG		9	3	0[2]	0	1	4	W		4-0	14-3
265n*	21	87	12	NY	CG		9	3	0[3]	0	1	13	W		6-0	15-3
266t*	22	91	16	Ph	CG		9	6	2[4]	2	0	7	W[5]		5-2	16-3
267*[6]	23	96	20	M	KO		5⅓	8	3	3	2	6				
268n	24	101	25	P	PH		6	8	4	4	1	12		L	2-6	16-4
269n	25	105	29	Ph	CG		9	5	2	2	4	7	W		6-2	17-4
270n*	26	109	8/ 3	H	CG		9	3	0	0	0	4	W		2-0	18-4
271*	27	112	7	Ch	KO		9⅓	7	1	1	3	11				
272*	28	116	11	C	KO		5⅓	9	5	5	1	4		L	4-9	18-5
273*	29	119	15	M	KO[7]		⅓	4	4	4	0	0				
274*	30	121	17	NY	KO		8+	6	2	1	2	9	W		3-2	19-5
275n	31	125	21	SL	PH		12	9	1	1	2	10				
276	32	129	25	M	KO		8⅔	5	1	1	2	6				
277n	33	133	29	SF	CG		9	3	1	1	1	7	W		11-1	20-5
278	34	137	9/ 2	H	CG		9	7	3	3	0	13	W		7-3	21-5
279n*	35	142	6	SF	REM		8	9	2	2	2	8	W		5-2	22-5
280n*	36	145	10	P	CG		9	6	2	1	0	9[8]	W		4-2	[9]23-5
281t*	37	148	13	Ph	PH		7	4	1	1	1	8				
282n*	38	153	17	SL	CG		9	4	0[10]	0	0[11]	4	W		4-0	24-5
283n	39	156	21	P	KO		7⅔	8	3	3	2	10				
284n	40	159	25	NY	REM		5	4	0	0	0	8	W		1-0	25-5

1. Second no-hitter.
2. His eighth shutout, new Dodger club record, 99 pitches.
3. Third consecutive shutout.
4. Extended scoreless streak to 33rd inning.
5. Ninth win in row.
6. His second National League home run (2 on, vs. Lemaster).
7. Sore elbow.
8. Broke own National League strike-out record, bringing total to 276.
9. Twenty-third win, new club record for left-hander.
10. His eleventh shutout, major-league record for left-hander.
11. Made only 87 pitches (19 balls).

Koufax: lifetime game no.	Koufax: season game no.	Dodgers: season game no.	Date	Op-position	As starter	In relief	IP	H	R	ER	BB	SO	W	L	Score	Season W-L
285n¹	1	1	4/14	SL	CG		9	6	0	0	0	5	W		4–0	1–0
286t	2	5	18	C	PH		8	3	3	3	3	6		L	0–3	1–1
287n*	3	8	22	SL	INJ		1	2	3	3	1	1		L	6–7 10-inn	1–2
288n	4	20	5/ 4	Ch	CG		10	3	1	1	3	13	W		2–1	2–2
289*	5	24	9	SF	PH		6	4	3	3	3	4		L	2–3	2–3
290*	6	27	14	Ch	PH		4	6	4	4	2	4				
291	7	31	17	P	KO		7⅔	10	2	2	0	8	W		3–2	3–3
292n	8	36	21	NY	CG		9	7	1	1	2	11	W		6–1	4–3
293	9	39	24	Ph		F	3	1	0	0	0	2	SV		(3–0)	
294n*	10	41	27	C	PH		7	3	1	1	5	7		L	0–1	4–4
295*	11	45	31	P	KO		7+	8	4	3	4	8	W		6–4	5–4
296n*	12	48	6/ 4	Ph	CG		9	0²	0	0	1	12	W		3–0	6–4
297n	13	53	8	C	CG		9	4	1	1	0	5	W³		2–1	7–4
298n	14	57	12	SL	CG		9	4	0	0	3	6	W		3–0	8–4
299n	15	62	17	M	CG		9	3	0	0	1	8	W		5–0	9–4
300*	16	65	21	C	REM⁴		6	7	2	2	1	6	W		4–2	10–4
301n*	17	70	25	SF	PH		9	6	1	1	5	10⁵				
302n	18	75	7/ 1	Ph	CG		9	5	2	2	1	10	W		3–2	11–4
303	19	79	5	NY	CG		9	6	0	0	1	5	W		5–0	12–4
304n*	20	81	10	H	KO		5⅓	5	2	2	3	8	W		4–3	13–4
305n*	21	86	14	SL	KO		7⅔	8	4	4	2	7				
306	22	90	18	Ch	CG		9	8	1	1	1	10	W		3–1	14–4
307n	23	95	22	H	CG		9	4	0	0	0	12	W⁶		1–0	15–4
308	24	99	26	SF	CG		9	11	5	1	2	10		L⁷	2–5	15–5
309n*	25	101	30	NY	PH		7	5	3	3	1	7				
310t*	26	105	8/ 4	P	KO		8⅓	6	1	1	5	6	W		5–1	16–5
311*	27	110	8	M	CG		9	7	4	3	1	9	W		5–4	17–5
312n*	28	114	12	C	CG		9	5	1	1	1	10	W		4–1	18–5
313	29	117	16	SL	CG		9	7	0	0	1	13	W		3–0	19–5

1. First opening-day start of career.
2. His third no-hitter.
3. Hundredth National League win.
4. Because of heat.
5. His 55th 10-strikeout game. New major-league record.
6. Eleventh win in row.
7. Winning streak broken on 4 unearned runs in ninth.

Koufax: lifetime game no.	Koufax: season game no.	Dodgers: season game no.	Date	Opposition	As starter	In relief	IP	H	R	ER	BB	SO	W	L	Score	Season W-L
314*	1	4	4/18	Ph	CG		9	6	2	2	5	7	W		6-2	1-0
315n	2	7	22	NY	CG		9	9	1	0	1	9	W		2-1	2-0
316n	3	11	26	Ph	PH		6	6	3	3	1	6		L	3-4	2-1
317n	4	15	30	SF	INJ[1]		5+	7	3	2	0	7				
318n*	5	19	5/5	C	CG		9	9	2	1	1	8	W		4-2	3-1
319*	6	23	9	SF	KO		7+	6	5	5	4	11		L	3-6	3-2
320n	7	27	13	H	CG		9	3	0	0	0	13	W		3-0	4-2
321n*	8	32	17	H	KO		10⅓	5	3	3	3	13	W		11-inn 5-3	5-2
322*	9	36	22	Ch	CG		9	6	1	1	1	12	W		3-1	6-2
323n	10	40	26	SL	PH		8	7	2	2	1	6		L	1-2	6-3
324	11	44	30	C	CG		9	5	5	2	2	13	W		12-5	7-3
325n*	12	48	6/3	SL	KO		2+	6	7	2	1	1				
326n*	13	53	7	Ph	CG		9	9	3	3	2	13	W		14-3	8-3
327*	14	58	12	NY	CG		9	5	0	0	1	8	W		5-0	9-3
328n	15	62	16	SF	CG		9	6	1	1	1	8	W		2-1	10-3
329	16	66	20	NY	CG		9	1[2]	1	1	2	12	W		2-1	11-3
330n	17	71	25	P	CG		9	6	1	1	1	12	W		4-1	12-3
331*	18	75	29	SF	CG		9	8	3	3	1	10	W		9-3	13-3
332n*	19	80	7/3	H	CG[3]		9	5	1	1	1	10	W		3-1	14-3
333n*	20	84	7	C	KO		4⅔	9	5	5	3	6				
334*	21	88	11	P	CG		9	5	2	2	2	10	W		4-2	15-3
335n	22	91	16	Ch	CG		9	4	0	0	2	9	W		3-0	16-3
336n	23	95	20	H	CG		9	3	2	2	2	10	W[4]		3-2	17-3
337n	24	99	24	SL	PH		9	4	2	2	3	8				
338n	25	103	28	C	PH		8	5	4	3	1	8		L	1-4	17-4
339*	26	106	8/1	SL	CG		9	5	2	2	0	11	W		3-2	18-4
340n*	27	110	5	M	CG		9	7	3	3	2	12	W		6-3	19-4
341n	28	114	10	NY	CG		9	7	3	3	2	14	W		4-3	20-4
342n	29	117	14	P	CG		10	5	0	0	0	12	W		10-inn 1-0	21-4
343n	30	121	18	Ph	KO		7+	5	3	3	4	9				
344*	31	125	22	SF	CG		8	4	4	4	4	8		L	3-4	21-5
345n*	32	129	26	NY	PH		7	4	3	2	2	5		L	2-5	21-6
346n*	33	131	28	Ph		F	1	1	0	0	0	2				
347t*	34	133	9/1	P	CG		10⅔	8	3	3	3	10[5]		L	11-inn 2-3	21-7
348*	35	138	5	H	PH		7	4	2	2	3	5				
349n	36	141	9	Ch	CG		9	0	0[6]	0	0	14	W		1-0	22-7
350*	37	145	14	Ch	PH		6	5	2	1	0	3		L	1-2	22-8
351*	38	147	16	Ch		F	1	0	0	0	0	0		SV	(2-0)	
352n*	39	149	18	SL	CG		9	4	0	0	1	6	W		1-0[7]	23-8
353n*	40	152	22	M	KO		2+	6	5	5	0	3				
354n	41	154	25	SL	CG		9	5	0	0	3	12[8]	W		2-0	24-8
355t	42	158	29	C	CG		9	2	0[9]	0	1	13	W		5-0	25-8
356	43	161	10/2	M	CG		9	4	1	1	4	13	W[10]		3-1	26-8[11]

1. Pulled leg muscle.
2. Only hit was fifth-inning home run by Jim Hickman.
3. Seventh consecutive complete game win.
4. Eleventh win in row.
5. Strikeout total—313—new National League record.
6. Perfect game, his fourth no-hitter.
7. Third 1-0 win in row.
8. Strikeout total 356, new major-league record.
9. Fifth straight shutout win.
10. Clinched pennant.
11. Tied major-league record for wins by left-hander.

	Innings Pitched	Strikeouts	SO average per 9 IP	Games started	10-SO games
Season totals	335⅔	382[1]	10.25	41	21[1]
At home	170	208	11.01	20	11
On road	165⅔	174	9.45	21	10
Vs. Chicago	34	38	10.06	4	2
Cincinnati	39⅔	48	10.89	5	2
Houston	44⅓	51	10.35	5	4
Milwaukee	20	28	12.60	3	2
New York	43	48	10.05	5	2
Philadelphia	32	37	10.41	4	1
Pittsburgh	38⅔	44	10.24	4	4
St. Louis	46	44	8.61	6	2
San Francisco	38	44	10.42	5	2
In April	29	29	9.00	4	0
May	61⅓	76	11.15	7	5
June	56	64	10.29	7	4
July	57⅔	61	9.52	7	3
August	60	73	10.95	7	4
Sept.-Oct.	71⅔	79	9.92	9	5
Before All-Star Game	169	195	10.38	21	11
After All-Star Game	166⅔	187	10.10	20	10

1. Major-league record.

	First seven seasons 1955–1961	Last four seasons 1962–1965			First seven seasons 1955–1961	Last four seasons 1962–1965
Games	216	140		Won	54	84
Games started	138	135		Lost	53	25
Complete games	37	73		Percentage	.505	.771
Innings pitched	948	1054		Shutouts	7	28
Hits	795	718		Earned Run Average	3.94	2.02
Runs	464	268				
Earned runs	415	236		CG percentage	.268	.541
Bases on balls	501	239		Hits per 9-IP	7.55	6.13
Strikeouts	952	1127		BB per 9-IP	4.76	2.04
				SO per 9-IP	9.04	9.62

Toughest Batters for Koufax among Active N.L. Players, Based on Batting Average

(among players with at least 20 AB against Koufax)

Right-handed hitters	AB	H	2B	3B	HR	Average
Gene Oliver	42	19	1	0	4	.452
Jesus Alou	23	10	1	0	1	.435
Henry Aaron	106	38	6	3	6	.358
Dick Stuart	59	20	2	0	5	.339
Deron Johnson	32	10	2	0	3	.313
Roberto Clemente	98	30	6	1	5	.306
Eddie Kasko	62	19	1	0	0	.306
Willie Mays	83	25	7	1	5	.301
Left-handed hitters						
Eddie Mathews	83	24	3	0	2	.289
Vada Pinson	104	29	7	1	2	.279
Billy Williams	53	14	2	1	2	.264

Koufax—Tough to Hit

Year	IP	AB	Hits	Opponents' batting average	Hits per 9 IP	Hits-per-9-IP ranking in N.L.
1955	42	153	33	.216	7.07	**
1956	59	231	66	.286	10.07	**
1957	104	385	83	.216	7.18	**
1958	159	599	132	.220	7.47	2nd
1959	153	579	136	.235	8.00	**
1960	175	641	133	.207	6.84	1st
1961	256	954	212	.222	7.45	1st
1962	184	680	134	.197	6.55	1st
1963	311	1135	214	.189	6.19	1st
1964	223	806	154	.191	6.22	1st
1965	336	1205	216	.179	5.79	1st
Lifetime	2002	7368	1513	.205	6.80	1st

** Not enough IP to qualify.

Koufax—Hits Allowed in Complete Games

	Number of hits allowed												
Year	0	1	2	3	4	5	6	7	8	9	10	11	13
1955	—	—	1	—	—	1	—	—	—	—	—	—	—
1957	—	—	—	—	2	—	—	—	—	—	—	—	—
1958	—	—	1	—	—	1	1	2	—	—	—	—	—
1959	—	—	—	—	1	2	1	1	—	—	1	—	—
1960	—	1	1	—	1	2	—	—	1	1	—	—	—
1961	—	—	2	3	1	3	2	4	—	—	—	—	—
1962	1	—	—	2	1	4	2	—	—	—	—	—	1
1963	1	—	2	6	2	2	4	1	1	—	—	1	—
1964	1	—	—	2	3	2	2	3	1	—	—	1	—
1965	1	1	1	2	5	7	4	2	2	2	—	—	—
Lifetime	4	2	8	15	16	24	16	13	5	3	1	2	1

Koufax—Complete Games

Year	Games started	Complete games	CG percentage	Rank in N.L.[1]
1955	5	2	.400	—
1956	10	0	.000	—
1957	13	2	.154	—
1958	26	5	.192	26th(Td.)
1959	23	6	.261	20th
1960	26	7	.269	19th(Td.)
1961	35	15	.429	2nd(Td.)
1962	26	11	.423	9th
1963	40	20	.500	3rd
1964	28	15	.536	2nd
1965	41	27	.659	1st
Lifetime	273	110	.403	
1955–1960	103	22	.214	
1961–1965	170	88	.518	

1. Among 20-game starters.

Koufax—Shutouts

Year	Games started	Shutouts	At home	On road	Starts per shutout
1955	5	2	2	0	2.50
1956	10	0	0	0	—
1957	13	0	0	0	—
1958	26	0	0	0	—
1959	23	1	1	0	23.00
1960	26	2	0	2	13.00
1961	35	2	0	2	17.50
1962	26	2	2	0	13.00
1963	40	11[1][2]	6	5	3.64
1964	28	7[1]	6	1	4.00
1965	41	8	6	2	5.13
Lifetime	273	35	23	12	7.51
1955–1962	164	9	5	4	18.22
1963–1965	109	26	18	8	4.19

1. Led league. 2. Major-league record for left-handers.

	Nine-Inning Averages			
	Earned Runs	Hits	Bases on Balls	Strikeouts
Sandy Koufax	2.93	6.80	3.33	9.35
Grover Alexander	2.56[1]	8.44	1.65	3.81
Bob Feller	3.25	7.69	4.14	6.07
Lefty Grove	3.09	8.79	2.71	5.19
Carl Hubbell	2.98	8.67	1.82	4.20
Walter Johnson[2]	—	7.48	2.13	5.31
Christy Mathewson[2]	—	7.90	1.56	4.72
Warren Spahn	3.08	8.29	2.46	4.43
Dazzy Vance	3.54	8.52	2.55	6.20

1. Not including his first season, 1911, whean earned runs were not compiled.
2. Lifetime earned runs are not available.

Koufax—Control

Year	IP	BB	9-inning average	N.L. 9-inning average	CG	No. of BB per complete game							
						0	1	2	3	4	5	6	7
1955	42	28	6.00	3.47	2	—	—	—	—	—	1	—	1
1956	59	29	4.42	3.24	0	—	—	—	—	—	—	—	—
1957	104	51	4.41	3.10	2	—	—	—	—	1	—	—	1
1958	159	105	5.94	3.32	5	—	—	1	—	3	—	—	1
1959	153	92	5.41	3.24	6	—	—	3	1	1	—	1	—
1960	175	100	5.14	3.19	7	—	1	2	3	—	—	1	—
1961	256	96	3.38	3.26	15	—	2	4	5	—	4	—	—
1962	184	57	2.79	3.27	11	1	2	3	3	1	1	—	—
1963	311	58	1.68	2.82	20	7	4	6	1	2	—	—	—
1964	223	53	2.14	2.72	15	3	8	2	2	—	—	—	—
1965	336	71	1.90	2.91	27	4	10	8	2	2	1	—	—
Lifetime	2002	740	3.33	3.12	110	15	27	29	17	10	7	2	3
1955–1960	692	405	5.27	3.26	22	—	1	6	4	5	1	2	3
1961–1962	440	153	3.13	3.27	26	1	6	7	4	1	5	2	3
1963–1965	870	182	1.88	2.82	62	14	22	16	5	4	1	—	—

Koufax—Lifetime Strikeouts

Year	Total 10-SO games	10-strikeout games Number of strikeouts per game								IP	SO	Average SO per 9 IP
		10	11	12	13	14	15	16	18			
1955	1	—	—	—	—	1	—	—	—	42	30	6.43
1956	0	—	—	—	—	—	—	—	—	59	30	4.58
1957	4	—	2	1	1	—	—	—	—	104	122	10.56
1958	1	1	—	—	—	—	—	—	—	159	131	7.42
1959	5	1	1	—	1	—	—	1	1[2]	153	173	10.18
1960	9	4	2	—	1	—	2	—	—	175	197	10.13
1961	11	4	3	1	1	1	1	—	—	256	269[1]	9.46
1962	9	3	1	2	3	—	—	1	1[2]	184	216	10.57
1963	11	5	1	2	2	1	—	—	—	311	306[1]	8.86
1964	10	5	1	2	2	—	—	—	—	223	223	9.00
1965	21[2]	5	2	6	6	2	—	—	—	336	382[2]	10.23
Lifetime	82[2]	28	13	12	17	5	3	2	2[2]	2002	2079	9.35[3]

1. Led league, establishing N.L. record.
2. Major-league record.
3. Major-league record for a 1000-inning pitcher.

Koufax—Lifetime against Opposing Clubs

	G	GS	CG	IP	H	ER	BB	SO	SHO	Won	Lost	Pct	ERA
vs. Mets	15	15	10	124	70	17	27	135	5	13	1	.929	1.23
Astros	17	17	9	131	78	28	27	146	5	11	1	.917	1.92
Cubs	47	36	14	281⅓	177	82	124	335	3	18	11	.621	2.62
Phillies	39	32	19	253⅓	166	77	94	293	1	19	7	.731	2.74
Pirates	46	31	11	236⅔	202	77	90	221	4	15	10	.600	2.93
Cardinals	49	40	11	245⅓	204	82	88	217	9	17	10	.630	3.01
Giants	41	27	11	207⅔	172	77	80	217	2	13	11	.542	3.34
Braves	49	34	10	230⅓	202	87	94	224	2	15	9	.625	3.40
Reds	53	41	15	291⅓	242	124	116	291	4	17	18	.486	3.84

Koufax—Big Strikeout Games

Date	Opponent	Location	IP	Score	Strikeouts	SO right-handed hitters	SO left-handed hitters
Aug. 31, 1959	San Francisco	Los Angeles	9	5–2	18	16	2
Apr. 24, 1962	Chicago	Chicago	9	10–2	18	12	6
June 22, 1959	Philadelphia	Los Angeles	9	6–2	16	15	1
May 26, 1962	Philadelphia	Los Angeles	9	6–3	16	11	5
May 6, 1960	Philadelphia	Los Angeles	9⅔	1–6	15	15	0
May 28, 1960	Chicago	Chicago	13	3–4	15	7	8
Sept. 20, 1961	Chicago	Los Angeles	13	3–2	15	7	8
Oct. 2, 1963	N.Y. Yankees	New York	9	5–2	15	11	4